Architecturally Speaking

ſY C
TF

Architecturally Speaking is an international collection of essays by leading architects, artists and theorists of locality and space. New work by celebrated contributors including Mark Augé, Krzysztof Wodiczko, Anthony Vidler, Lebbeus Woods and Zaha Hadid is juxtaposed with seminal essays by Bernard Tschumi, Doreen Massey and Kenneth Frampton. Brand new work on city space and architecture by radical young companies such as *muf* and performance artist Graeme Miller are joined by challenging new visions of orientation in the city by anthropologist Franco le Cecla and the technologist William J. Mitchell. Together these essays build to reflect not only what it might mean to "speak architecturally" but also the innate relations between the artist's and architect's work, how they are distinct and in inspiring ways, how they might relate through questions of built form. The interdisciplinary is often evoked but in this collection the specificity of practices and their relation with everyday contexts announces innovative grounds for collaboration. This book will appeal to urbanists, geographers, artists, architects, theatre practitioners, cultural historians and theorists.

Alan Read is Professor and Chair of Drama and Theatre Studies at the University of Surrey Roehampton. Previously he was Director of Talks at the Institute of Contemporary Arts, London. A series of talks he arranged there, *Spaced Out*, was the genesis of this collection. He is an affiliated professor of Boston University and founding associate editor of the journal *Performance Research*.

D0243122

Architecturally Speaking

Practices of Art, Architecture

and the Everyday

edited by Alan Read

London and New York

First published 2000 by Routledge 11 New Fetter Lane, London EC4P 4EE

Simultaneously published in the USA and Canada
by Routledge
29 West 35th Street, New York, NY 10001

Routledge is an imprint of the Taylor & Francis Group

© 2000 selection and editorial matter: Alan Read;
individual chapters: the contributors

Typeset in Akzidenz Grotesk Regular by Wearset, Boldon, Tyne and Wear
Printed and bound in Great Britain by St Edmundsbury Press, Bury St Edmunds, Suffolk

British Library Cataloguing in Publication Data
A catalogue record for this book is available from the British Library

Library of Congress Cataloguing in Publication Data
Architecturally speaking: practices of art, architecture, and the everyday / edited by
Alan Read.
    p. cm
  Includes bibliographical references and index.
    1. Architecture–Philosophy. 2. Architecture and society. 3. Artists and architects. 4.
City planning–Philosophy. I. Read, Alan, 1956–

NA2500.A712 2000
720'.1–dc21
                                                                            00-032186
ISBN 0-415-23543-X (Hbk)
ISBN 0-415-23544-8 (Pbk)

For my mother
Veronica Mary Read
and in memory of my father
Alan Read (1916–1956)

Contents

Contributors

Marc Augé

Marc Augé is Director of Studies at the École des Hautes Études en Sciences Sociales in Paris. His books include *La traversée du Luxembourg*, *Un ethnologie dans le métro* and *Domaines et Chateaux*. His work *Non-Places: Introduction to an Anthropology of Supermodernity*, translated by John Howe, is published in the UK by Verso.

Marc Augé spoke with Alan Read at the Institute of Contemporary Arts, London as part of *Spaced Out II* on 15th November 1995. The text published here is an edited version of that talk.

Franco La Cecla

Franco La Cecla is currently Senior Research Assistant at the Department of Communication Studies, University of Bologna. His work is concerned with urban anthropology, indigenous dwelling, resettlements and migrations, multi-ethnic cities and environmental psychology. His books, published in Italian, include, *Mente Locale: An Anthropology of Dwelling*, *Misunderstandings: An Anthropology of Encounters* and *Getting Lost: Man Without Environment*. The text published here is the first English language translation from this work.

Franco la Cecla spoke at the Royal Society of Arts, London on Monday 16th November, 1998 on "The Space of Play" with Lucy Bullivant and Alan Read.

Beatriz Colomina

Beatriz Colomina teaches in the School of Architecture at the University of Princeton. She is the author of *Privacy and Publicity: Modern Architecture as Mass Media* and editor of *Sexuality and Space*. Her work considers the developing systems of communication within which architecture emerges, and architectural discourse as the intersection of a number of systems of representation.

Beatriz Colomina spoke with Robert Harbison at the Institute of Contemporary Arts, London, as part of *Spaced Out I* on 13th March 1995. The following essay is an edited version of that talk which has subsequently been published in different form in: Francesca Hughes (ed.) *The Architect: Reconstructing Her Practice* (MIT Press 1996).

Kenneth Frampton

Kenneth Frampton is Ware Professor of Architecture at Columbia University and author of many books including, *A Critical History of Modern Architecture* and *Studies in Tectonic Culture: The Poetics of Construction in Nineteenth and Twentieth Century Architecture*. In the latter work Frampton focuses on architecture as a constructional craft, redressing the postmodern preference for abstract space and form.

Kenneth Frampton spoke at the Institute of Contemporary Arts, London, as part of *Spaced Out II* on 19th February 1996. The contribution included here was adapted from an essay first published in the journal *Architectural Design*, 1990, vol. 60 no. 3–4.

Zaha Hadid

Zaha Hadid's architectural practice is based in London, and she is well known for her plans for The Peak in Hong Kong, the building of the Vitra Fire Station in Weil am Rhein and her winning of the design competition for the ill-fated Lottery-supported project of the Cardiff Opera House. Her work has appeared in numerous group and one-woman shows including *Deconstructionist Architecture* at the Museum of Modern Art, New York.

Zaha Hadid spoke at the Institute of Contemporary Arts, London as part of *Spaced Out II* on 22nd February 1996. The contribution included here is a new overview of her work since the Cardiff project.

Oliver Kruse

Oliver Kruse was born in Nürnberg and became an apprentice to a joiner in Cologne. He studied and worked with Professor Erwin Heerich at Düsseldorf, Insel Hombroich, before taking his Masters Degree in Fine Art, Sculpture at Chelsea College of Art, London. He has lived and worked in London, contributing to several group shows before setting up a studio in the former NATO rocket station near the Insel Hombroich, Neuss. Oliver Kruse is a board member of the Hombroich foundation.

Oliver Kruse spoke at the Institute of Contemporary Arts, London with the architect Claudio Silvestrin as part of *Spaced Out III* on 3rd June 1997. The text included here is an edited version of that talk.

Doreen Massey

Doreen Massey is Professor of Geography in the Faculty of Social Sciences at the Open University. She is the author of numerous articles and books including, *Spatial Divisions of Labour*, *Geography Matters*, *High Tech Fantasies* and *Space Place and Gender* published in the UK by Polity Press.

Doreen Massey spoke with Richard Sennett at the Institute of Contemporary Arts, London as part of *Spaced Out I* on 10th March 1995, and again in the same year as part of a panel discussion on conceptions of the "uncanny" in Rachel Whiteread's sculpture "House". This essay was subsequently published by Phaidon in association with Artangel as part of their volume *House,* edited by James Lingwood (1996).

Graeme Miller

Graeme Miller is a musician and performance maker. He has produced numerous performances including "Dungeness", "A Girl Skipping", "The Desire Paths" and the installation "The Sound Observatory" at the Ikon Gallery in Birmingham.

Graeme Miller spoke at the Institute of Contemporary Arts, London, in a panel discussion: "Between Here and There: The Artist as Walker" chaired by Andrea Phillips as part of *Spaced Out II* on 17th November 1995. The contribution here was given as a paper at the conference "Urban Hymns" curated by Lois Keidan and Catherine Ugwu in Nottingham as part of the NOW '98 festival on 8th November 1998.

William J. Mitchell

William J. Mitchell is Professor of Architecture and Media Arts and Sciences, and Dean of the School of Architecture and Planning at MIT. He is the author of *City of Bits: Space, Place, and the Infobahn*. His recent book, *E-Topia: Urban Life, Jim – But Not As We Know It*, was published by the MIT Press in 1999.

William Mitchell spoke with Philip Tabor and John Lansdown at the Institute of Contemporary Arts, London, in the first event of *Spaced Out I* on 2nd February 1995. His contribution here is an edited and revised version of his talk.

muf

muf architects is a practice based in London led by architects and artists Juliet Bidgood, Katherine Clarke and Liza Fior. They have been carrying out a commission for Southwark Council London for the environmental and urban regeneration of a thoroughfare in the area of the Tate Modern at Bankside.

muf spoke with Katherine Shonfield, of the South Bank University at the Institute of Contemporary Arts, London, as part of *Spaced Out III* on 10th April 1997. They discuss their working methods on recent projects in London, Stoke and Manchester and the nature of public territory.

Ann M. Pendleton-Jullian

Ann M. Pendleton-Jullian is Associate Professor of Architecture at Massachusetts Institute of Technology and Principal Architect with Atelier Jullian and Pendleton in

Boston. She is the author of *The Road that is not a Road: The Open City Ritoque, Chile* published by MIT Press.

Ann M. Pendleton-Jullian spoke at the Institute of Contemporary Arts, London, as part of *Spaced Out III* on 18th February 1997. Her contribution here is an edited version of that talk.

Alan Read

Alan Read is Professor and Chair of Drama and Theatre Studies at the University of Surrey Roehampton. He was Director of the Rotherhithe Theatre Workshop in South East London in the 1980s, worked as a freelance writer in Barcelona in the early 1990s and was Director of Talks at the Institute of Contemporary Arts, London from 1994–7. He is the author of *Theatre and Everyday Life: An Ethics of Performance*, published by Routledge and editor of *The Fact of Blackness: Frantz Fanon and Visual Representation* (Bay Press) and "On Animals", an edition of *Performance Research* journal (Routledge).

Alan Read curated *Spaced Out* series I, II and IV and co-curated *Spaced Out III* with Lucy Bullivant. He is currently working on a collection of essays exploring the architectural and performance histories of London's "speech sites". The text included here is a new piece of writing which arose from his curation of *Spaced Out IV*, which took place at the Institute of Contemporary Arts, London in November 1997.

François Roche

The organic, oppositional architectural projects of François Roche and Stéphanie Lavaux of Roche DSV were prominent in the French pavilion at the 11th Venice Architecture Biennale. Based in Paris and the island of La Réunion in the West Indies, their practice is concerned with the bonds between building, context and human relations. Now working within the expanded practice R. DSV & Sie. P., Roche and Lavaux with Gilles Desèvedavy and François Perrin have exhibited their work in Paris, Berlin and Venice and have major projects in development in Johannesburg and La Réunion.

François Roche spoke with Alan Read at the Institute of Contemporary Arts London as part of *Spaced Out III* on 3rd June 1997. The contribution included here is a new piece of writing, *@morphous mutations,* which accompanied the exhibition of R, DSV & Sie. P. at the Fonds Régional d'Art Contemporain du Centre, Orléans, France in 1998.

Edward W. Soja

Edward W. Soja was born in the Bronx, received his doctorate from Syracuse

University and for two decades specialised in the political geography of modern-isation and nation-building in Africa, holding appointments at the Universities of Ibadan, and Nairobi. Following a period at Northwestern University, he joined the Graduate School of Architecture and Urban Planning, UCLA where he has spe-cialised in writing about the postmodernisation of Los Angeles where he lives with his family. His books include *Postmodern Geographies: The Reassertion of Space in Critical Social Theory* and more recently *Thirdspace: Journeys to Los Angeles and other Real-and-Imagined Places*, and *Post Metropolis* published by Blackwell.

Edward W. Soja spoke at the Institute of Contemporary Arts, London, as part of *Spaced Out II* on 29th January 1996. This work has subsequently been pub-lished in Doreen Massey et al (eds) *Human Geography Today* (Polity Press 1998).

Bernard Tschumi

Bernard Tschumi is equally well known for his architecture and his work as a theo-rist. His books include *Architecture and Disjunction* and *Event Cities*, both pub-lished by MIT Press. He is Dean of the Graduate School of Architecture, Planning and Preservation, Columbia University.

Bernard Tschumi spoke with Nigel Coates at the Institute of Contemporary Arts, London, as part of *Spaced Out I* on 6th June 1995. The contribution included here was first published as the final part of *Architecture and Disjunction* (MIT Press) in 1994.

Krzysztof Wodiczko

Krzysztof Wodiczko is an artist, theorist of public art and Head of Research, Inter-rogative Design Group, Massachusetts Institute of Technology, USA. He is the author of numerous publications and his work has been seen internationally in many one-man and group shows including retrospectives at the Fundació Antoni Tàpies, Barcelona and the Walker Arts Center Minneapolis. His work ranging across vehicles, public projections and the "alien staff" project discussed here are aspects of a critical public art which engages in strategic challenges to city struc-tures and mediums. He is represented in New York by Galerie Lelong.

Krzysztof Wodiczko spoke at the conference "Smart Practices in a Complex World" at the Institute of Contemporary Arts, London, as part of *Spaced Out III* on 22nd March 1997. A different version of this talk was previously published by *Performance Research*, Vol: 2 No. 1, "On Refuge", Routledge, London.

Lebbeus Woods

Lebbeus Woods co-founded the New York based Research Institute for Experi-mental Architecture. He has been a visiting professor at Harvard and Columbia

Universities and visiting professor at the Cooper Union in New York. He has been the subject of numerous one-person exhibitions and his books include: *The New City*, *Centricity* and *OneFiveFour*. He is the subject of an Academy Editions Architectural Monograph: No. 22, *Lebbeus Woods, Anarchitecture: Architecture is a Political Act*. His work in the former Yugoslavia, the Zagreb Free Zone Project, was conceived as an architecture of liberation, to initiate a dialogue and a means of social and political transformation.

Lebbeus Woods spoke at the Institute of Contemporary Arts, London, as part of *Spaced Out II* on 26th January 1996. The text included here is an edited and revised version of that talk.

Anthony Vidler

Anthony Vidler is author of *Claude-Nicolas Ledoux: Architecture and Social Reform at the end of the Ancien Régime* and *The Architectural Uncanny: Essays in the Modern Unhomely*, published by MIT Press.

Anthony Vidler spoke at the ICA as part of the "Uncanny Conversations" series giving a paper on "The Window of Anxiety" in 1994. The contribution here is a new essay published for the first time.

Richard Wentworth

Richard Wentworth is an artist who has shown internationally in numerous one-person and group shows at venues including the Tate Gallery, Camden Arts Centre, the Hayward Gallery and the Serpentine Gallery, London.

Richard Wentworth spoke at the Institute of Contemporary Arts, London with Adam Caruso, of Caruso St John, whose practice was responsible for the Walsall Art Gallery in the UK. The discussion was part of *Spaced Out III* and occurred on 6th March 1997. The contribution here is a version of an installation made by Richard Wentworth for the Walsall Art Gallery and exhibited there in 1998.

Introduction

Addressing architecture, art and the everyday
Alan Read

The discourses of architecture, space, built form and urban context have, at the turn of the millennium, become the pre-eminent critical idioms for cultural practitioners from a surprising diversity of fields. Sensitive to questions of community in new and radical languages, artists, performance makers, theoreticians, social scientists and interdisciplinary thinkers within, and beyond, the architectural profession, reach for the strategies and structures of the populated street to articulate the sense of their work.

Seeking theoretical paradigms that are sufficiently flexible for their work, practitioners seem increasingly unsettled by the disciplinary corrals of sociology and anthropology and troubled by the interior logics of the psychoanalytic turn and the hermeticism of literary poetics. For them the possibilities of spatial critique are beguiling, promising the opportunity to shift between private and public domains, interior and exterior landscapes, local and geo-political contexts, demographic and situationist analyses, theoretical design and structural fantasy. As the critic Terry Eagleton recently said in *The London Review of Books*, "To be spaced-out was no longer to be depleted." All now seems possible where space is at issue.

For some time, the publishing of late modernism has been underpinned by geographical inquiry, while history has been superseded. Space, not time, has become the privileged domain. This volume recognises this shift towards the spatial yet is critical of the valorisation of space at the expense of the critical relations between temporality, built form and the performative dynamics of architecture within everyday life. It will situate the relations between spatial and architectural debate and parallel debates in the performing, visual and digital arts and engage throughout with an agenda for constructive rapprochement between the diversity of languages that constitute these already well-acquainted fields.

The book combines contributions from celebrated names from the worlds of architecture, urban theory and art and introduces a generation of younger innovative practitioners and thinkers. It brings together, in one place, and in an unusual way, the innate collaborative nature of all architecture and cultural practice, and places that practice within a fully-rounded theoretical frame.

Addressing architecture, art and the everyday combines a sense of both speaking to these interrelated categories and sending them somewhere. The move here is away from polarised caricatures of contemporary architecture, from hapless visions of artists at sea in public contexts, from preordained conceptions of the city, towards more complex understandings of the involutionary nature of the contemporary, the presence of the artist within any architect's fashioning of form (and vice versa the architectonic in all artists' work) and the consequent grasp of *specificities*, distinctive cities, rather than amorphous urban backdrop settings to the works of the mystically-unhinged individual talent.

Addressing here means to write something towards a certain direction, and purpose, the purpose here being more *just* arrangements of social organisation within more *imaginative* spaces of social life. This process of address converts a previously spoken form (the following texts originated in a public forum of presentation and debate) to script. This conversion still bears the traces of the original where the uniformity of scale one might expect of a set of essays is sacrificed for individual and eclectic lengths and depths. For some, the editing of a transcript was an opportunity to limit and concentrate; for others, a chance to expand and develop. For all, it was an opportunity to say something now about long-held concerns and questions.

The book opens with a new intervention by the theorist Marc Augé to position the reader both within some of the recent debates about the nature of space and then to problematise this field with regard to the "non-places" of super-modernity. Edward Soja deepens this discussion, drawing on a range of theoretical positions from gender and post-colonial studies to advance an interpretive category of "thirdspace". Getting lost within this landscape, as the Italian anthropologist Franco la Cecla shows, becomes one delinquent means by which the pedestrian interrupts the apparently prescriptive terms of endearment between individual and environment. Drawing out the manifestation of these concerns in the physical form of public sculpture and interactive architectural practice, the geographer and theoretician Doreen Massey explores the work of artist Rachel Whiteread while the architectural practice *muf* discuss their radical approaches to built form and public context. Here the subjectivities of the city, its "soft" centre and mutating boundaries of the everyday are evoked as a possibility of movement and articulation within an apparently oppressive and threatening terrain. Both the artist Krzysztof Wodiczko and the theatre maker and musician Graeme Miller extend the interrogation of the creative, performative possibilities of everyday politics within the urban sphere. Responses to specific sites continue as I return the reader to nineteenth-century London, as a metropolis in the making, to question how the speech of the city might be echoed, amplified and recorded in the interests of social justice now, while Beatriz Colomina conducts a forensic examination of an Eileen Gray house, exploring its hidden histories and concealed politics.

In this first part of the volume a number of contributions are concerned with the site of a metropolitan "capital". The density of intracultural texture evoked for London suggests that closer attention to the "here" of where one is working from, rather than the "everywhere" one likes to imagine in the interests of representation, might serve some purpose in opening out the possibility of artistic and architectural practices within a complex urban context, beyond any one particular realm.

Having oriented within, located practices for, and moved beyond, the city, the possibility of building becomes the fulcrum of the book. Here, in the work of four leading figures of the architectural firmament, Bernard Tschumi, Kenneth Frampton, Lebbeus Woods, and Zaha Hadid, the question of what might constitute the conception and construction of architecture and its relationship with event and movement becomes the issue. The relations between artistic practice and architectural forms that grow from these questions of construction are reconsidered in the work of artists Oliver Kruse and Richard Wentworth, in settings where cultural exhibition is wedded neither to genre of work nor historical lineage. Architects Ann M. Pendleton-Jullian and François Roche move out towards radically dissimulating projects where the entity and validity of the city itself is brought into question within the context of questions of ecology, globalisation and poetic deconstruction. By this point the penultimate section of the book implies a perhaps building-free, but not architecture-free electronic landscape in the digitally-inspired work of William Mitchell and Anthony Vidler.

The final section of the book is a brief epilogue returning to the original site of the discussions from which this book arose and the nature of speech from which interdisciplinary work arises. I will return there to the response of speech to architecture, art and the everyday, but here, I simply wish to briefly characterise this project within its wider cultural context, alerting the reader to the emergence of what follows within dialogue and hopefully addressing the reader of this collection towards the same responsive direction and dimension.

Spaced Out was the title of four series of talks that I curated at the Institute of Contemporary Arts in London during the 1990s. Each series took as its focus the relationship between architecture, the urban environment and their relations with interdisciplinary arts practices. These talks and conferences, numbering more than 50 events in all, tapped into the current fascination for space-debate and drove it towards a deeper sense of itself. Drawing on the world's leading theoreticians of space, on anthropologists and architects, geographers and artists, the ascendancy of space was simultaneously articulated and addressed.

Each series simply brought together a number of key theorists and practitioners whose work opened up debates about the nature of space and built form. In this sense, the discussions were following the emphasis of precedents set over a long period by pedagogic institutions such as the Architectural Association in London, Cooper Union in New York, and radical geography journals such as *Antipode* where the social construction of space and the endeavour to more fully understand what took place there took primacy over the urge to design and build for abstracted, decontextualised settings.

From my own specialism of performance and its relations to the everyday I was drawn towards this spatial turn in architectural discourses and sought to reacquaint them with their border disciplines: with the new geographical thinking of figures such as Doreen Massey and Edward Soja, with the post colonial anthropology of figures such as Charles Rutheiser and James Clifford, with the artistic interventions of Krzysztof Wodiczko and Richard Wentworth, with the historical geneaologies of Beatriz Colomina and Richard Sennett, with the new technological thinking of William Mitchell and Marco Susani, with the geo-political revisionism of François Roche and Dolores Hayden, and the theoretical audacity of Kenneth Frampton and Joseph Rykwert.

Thus working broadly under the title of architectural discourse but continually disrupting its traditional hermeticism with the Trojan horse of companion fields of enquiry, the purpose of the talks was threefold:

- to reinvigorate discussion of arts practice by framing them within architectural and urban contexts;
- to address the built environment with the expectation that it might reveal new possibilities for social interaction, communication and creative expression;
- to situate previously disconnected fields of enquiry within an overarching concern for the future of the everyday life of the city and its inhabitants.

Architecturally Speaking is a collection that draws from this complex agenda, yet one with a simple beginning in a regular public forum that popularised the framing of architectural debate within wider discourses of artist practice and everyday politics of the city. While the range of writing is broad, the collective intention is focused towards articulating the specificity of fields of practice and the inevitable relations that proceed from these practices within the everyday realm. In this sense, to speak architecturally is to reconvene a complex of associated undertakings through the sign of the interdisciplinary without giving up on the particular contexts from which these practices arose.

ACKNOWLEDGEMENTS

An edited collection owes many debts and a volume drawn from a series of live events even more. The two contexts are quite different but each is a reminder of the collaborative nature of dissemination and debate. My first debt of gratitude is to the contributors to this collection who found time to readdress their work for this publication and to Caroline Mallinder, Senior Editor at Routledge, who has brought our work to publication. I am grateful to Claire Pollock and the Architecture Unit of the Visual Arts Department of the Arts Council of England for working rapidly to secure support for the visual infrastructure of the book, to Andrea Phillips and Tristan Palmer who, from an early stage, encouraged me to work on the volume, to Ian Farr who, while working at the ICA, initiated work on the collection and returned later while at Phaidon to assist with the Doreen Massey text, to James Lingwood and Artangel for agreeing to the inclusion of the same piece, to Lois Keidan and Catherine Ugwu, curators of the *Urban Hymns* conference as part of NOW '98, for permission to include the conference paper presented by Graeme Miller there, to Deborah Robinson, Senior Exhibitions Officer at the Walsall Museum and Art Gallery, for assistance in producing the Richard Wentworth essay, to Cecile Panzieri of Galerie Lelong, New York, for her assistance with the work of Krzysztof Wodiczko, to Claude Gibou-Coste, Cynthia Wilkes, Andrea Day and Aliki Hasiotis in the respective offices of Marc Augé, William Mitchell, Bernard Tschumi and Kenneth Frampton for communicating the demands and deadlines of the project so persuasively, to Joseph Rykwert, Marco Susani, Diana Fuss, Richard Sennett and Barbara Engh who for different reasons are not able to be included here but who showed the project great good will, to the Hammersmith History Archive, David Rodgers of the William Morris Society, and the William Morris Gallery, Walthamstow for sharing their insights and images of William Morris in Hammersmith, to Ingrid Swenson and Athlone for undertaking and supporting the original transcriptions from the *Spaced Out* series, to Rebecca Casey, Lesley Daughton and Carl Gillingham who took the book through production, to Nico Macdonald at Spy, to Ivor Tillier in Roehampton, and the team at the Boston University, London Programme, for their technical support, and to colleagues at the University of Surrey Roehampton, School of Arts, for recognising, and participating, in interdisciplinary research of this kind in the name of performance.

I am also grateful to those contributors to the *Spaced Out* series of talks for providing the context and spur for the partiality of the practices and thoughts represented here. I am indebted to Helena Reckitt, my former colleague at the ICA, for supporting work on the *Spaced Out* series throughout (and for coining the title of the series), I am grateful to Ann Twiselton of MIT Press in London for single-handedly encouraging me to develop a field that I had little experience in and supporting the series from beginning to end, and to Roger Conover as editor of many of the MIT books around which the early series revolved, for supporting the series, to Lucy Bullivant for her co-curation of the third series and for inviting me to chair an event at the Royal Society of Arts with Franco la Cecla which led to his inclusion in this collection, to Sholto Ramsay and David Pinder for encouraging me to widen the terrain of the field, to Steve Tompkins and Mark Cousins for guiding the perplexed at an early stage, to Iain Borden, Malcolm Miles, Peter Buchanan and Naomi Stungo for advice, to Shelley Malcolm, Deva Palmier and Mark Mason who at different times but with equal accuracy recorded, amplified and disseminated the proceedings, to Alicia Pivarro, then of the Architecture Unit of the Arts Council of England, for financially securing the second, third and fourth series of discussions, to the London Arts Board for financially assisting the "Racing Space" series of carnival talks, to Mik Flood and Katy Sender who, as Director and Deputy Director of the ICA, were responsible for fashioning an environment where work of this ambition might be undertaken, to my curatorial colleagues at the ICA: Lois Keidan and Catherine Ugwu in Live Art, Simon Field and John Mount in Cinema, Emma Dexter and Kate Bush in Exhibitions, Lisa Haskell, curator of "Towards the Aesthetics of the Future", and to my co-ordinators on the *Spaced Out* series, particularly Hilary Clarke, Gabriel Pinhero, Grace Brockington and Emma Holmes. While I was working at the ICA as Director of Talks in the mid-1990s, this group of people and the audiences they attracted through their work with artists made the ICA a vivid environment in which to discuss the shape of cities, cultural practices and politics.

Above all, I am indebted to Beryl Robinson who discussed this work at every stage and took time from her own work for this to be completed, to our daughter Florence who, having become the recipient of a dedicated library of first editions from each of the *Spaced Out* participants, agreed to lend them to me to prepare for this book, and to Hermione who was born into this.

Orienting

Chapter 1

Non-places
Marc Augé

In the last few years there has been continuous debate about the crisis of meaning. We have celebrated the demise of meta-narratives and of coherent explanation. The collapse of the Communist regime appeared as a symbol of the useless and dangerous pretensions of systems which claimed to speak and act in the name of totality, of definitive answers, of meanings. The horrors of this century – genocide, the death camps – have brought a rude jolt to the idea of progress on the moral level and, by a sort of contamination, on an intellectual level as well. In contrast with these factors of scepticism, if not pessimism, it should be acknowledged of course that there has been a certain progression in the world of the idea of democracy, and of a recognition of human rights. As for progress in science, it is not only incontestable but spectacular.

Even in these areas, however, a certain anxiety can surface, either in denouncing the characteristics of representative democracy, or in suspecting that the democratic ideal is simply a tool of the major powers whose interests are promoted by the idea of a New World Order. In the domain of science one can highlight the uselessness of new discoveries, or their threatening nature from moral or ethical points of view.

All of these factors have cast doubt on the concept of modernity. This idea, as it was defined in the nineteenth century, proceeded from history and developing events. It brought heritage and newness together in one movement which reconciled the two. Modernity is linked to the idea of an accumulation and progress, to the idea of synthesis.

Today the concept of postmodernity, at least in the way it is used by some of its exegetists, challenges the idea of movement which is linked to the idea of modernity. So far as it describes a world in which differences may co-exist in an arbitrary fashion, a patchwork world, the concept of postmodernity can be aptly applied to a society defined as multicultural. It can also, however, contribute to a fixing and rigidifying of difference, to a concretisation of the national culture and a break in the process of distinction and identification which is essential to all integration.

This cumulative vision of time, aligned with the idea of a progress, does not proceed by abrupt ruptures but by successive devolutions and combinations of various heritages. In the contrasting, but nonetheless united, spaces which correspond to this definition, to this conception of time, the feature of the "other" always finds its place and remains both necessary and relative.

The idea of postmodernism disrupts this progressive scheme in affirming the brutal and sudden eruption of all others, of all otherness, at the very moment when the events of history seem to demonstrate the inanity of meta-narratives or explanations which illustrate and succour the idea of progress.

Based on this view we have proclaimed in art, as elsewhere, the possibility and legitimacy of "patchwork", not simply the mixing of genres but the end of genres. And the end of "others" as well, if it is true that in the arbitrary synthesis of postmodernity "the other" has no more consistency than the concept of "the same".

But the contemporary situation seems to me better explained by the word "supermodernity", or perhaps I would prefer to say "over-modernity". I think in English one says "over-determination", in the language of Freud or Lacan – and what I want to say echoing these constructions is "over-modernity". The current situation is better explained by these terms than by postmodernity. If I choose to employ the term "super-" or "over-modernity", it is because other words appear more marked by an acceleration of the cumulative process to which we have given the name modernity than by their disappearance.

I would characterise the super-modern by three types of excess:

1   An excess of time. We all have the impression that time is accelerating. The overloading of events in the world, which is obviously linked to the increased rule of the media and of the proliferation of information, results in our immersion in history. However history itself catches up with us and becomes the news of the day.

2   An excess of space. The planet is shrinking, and while on the one hand we are becoming more and more conscious of our planetary identity, and the influence of the ecology movements is certainly linked to this new consciousness, on the other hand we are constantly projected to the four corners of the world through images and through the imagination.

3   An excess of individualisation, which is linked to the first two concepts. Under the weight of information and images, each one of us has a feeling of being not only a witness to the events of the world but somehow to western civilisation itself. This reaction produces a feeling of discomfort, of crisis, which is linked to the consciousness that each one of us can see everything and do nothing. And this is just as true in the case of the many individuals who have the conviction that it is up to them to give a meaning to life and to the world.

The cosmologies that ethnologists have organised in groups around powerful symbolic images become individual even when there are variations on a common theme. The important aspect from this point of view is not whether any particular individual has illusions about the originality of their own interpretation of life, their manner of believing in God, or of understanding politics, but the fact that they invent or implicitly adopt this reality of interpretation.

It should be clear that the outline of what I choose to call super-modernity includes a paradox and a contradiction. In one sense it opens each individual to the presence of others. It corresponds to a freer circulation of people, things and images. In another sense, however, it turns individuals back on themselves, making them more like witnesses than actors in contemporary life.

Today we have the illusion of being near everything and a feeling of increased individuality or loneliness. It is at this point perhaps that the notion of "non-place" can help us to characterise the situation of over- or super-modernity.

I first developed the notion of non-space as a negation of the notion of place. Place, at least in the view of the anthropologist, is a space long taken over by human beings and where something is said about relationships which human beings have with their own history, their natural environment and with one another.

Anthropology has taught us that spatial organisation of the greatest refinement can be achieved in certain societies. For example, a single person is bound by the rules of residency to live with so and so, and so it goes from the cradle to the grave. Throughout each one of these social and biological periods of life – birth, marriage, procreation, old age – a change in status often brings about a change in the place of residence so that even the choice of a permanent place is given over to chance. From this point of view, non-places begin with unrootedness, nineteenth-century countrymen drawn from their land and thrown into human life, migrants, refugees – all of these people have direct experience of non-place, and the act of establishing colonies and of settling in new areas is related to the growth of turning space into place.

At this point, it is possible to see that the notion of non-places has an objective as well as a subjective dimension. A non-place comes into existence, even negatively, when human beings don't recognise themselves in it, or cease to recognise themselves in it, or have not yet recognised themselves in it. Deserts, islands, virgin forests, cannot be called non-places, for they were in fact spaces – and even tourist spaces – to be conquered, that is to say potential places.

The criteria for recognition is here essential, in which we recognise ourselves and in which others can recognise us as easily as we recognise them. Therefore it is possible to think that the same place can be looked upon as a place by some people and as a non-place by others, on a long-term or a short-term basis. For example, an airport space does not carry the same meaning for the passenger boarding the plane and for the employee who is working there.

In the full sense of the word, a place is a space where relationships are self evident and inter-recognition is at a maximum, and where each person knows where they and others belong. Therefore place is also interested in time. A village people, or indeed a village clock, has symbolic value in language, for we call home any place where we are understood by others, and in turn understand them, without having to spell things out. Anything that takes us away from a system of social relations takes us away from the place attached to it as well.

Today all of our circulation, information and communication spaces could be considered non-places. As a rule they don't serve as meeting places. They make very little use of language. Television screens carry all the information you need.

Through virtue of this temporal paradox one can be alone and, at the same time, in contact with everybody else around the world. This is a point of the greatest importance because of the inter-relatedness of the place/non-place opposition depending on our usage or subject. A place can become a non-place and vice versa.

Three major events may be called to our attention. First, that of the planet's urbanisation, certainly more dramatic in developing countries than in the most highly-developed countries, and its corollary, the unsymbolised characteristics of the new spaces thus occupied. These, of course, are of great interest to the urbanists and architects, being relatively indescribable, unqualifiable and uncontrolled intellectually. These are being designed as urban filaments.

We suppose that a strictly political question in global terms can be added to the aesthetic and sociological questions raised by this state of affairs. Traditional state borders are perhaps getting even more artificial as telecommunication's unprecedented development establishes the prerogative of instantaneity through which interconnected cities gain a rapidly-growing influence.

In fact, the conquest of space seems today more dedicated to the planet's technological and economical management than to exploring the unknown. The "spectacular display of the world" is the expression I would suggest to give a sense of this second major event and its numerous aspects, in relation to the evolution of images and its consequences on the way we relate to reality. Everyday images are sent to us from around the world, to people living in the middle of nowhere, thousands of miles away from the nearest town, yet nevertheless belonging to the same planet, sometimes at their own expense, and caught in the same history.

This over-abundance of images has perverse consequences in so far as the more we get a chance to see everything, the less we can be sure we are still able to really look at them. The world becomes, one might say, abstractly familiar to us, so that, socially speaking, there are literally no more relations between the world and us, in so far as we are content with the images imparted to us, as is the case today for a lot of people. Other facts appear more enigmatic though they also promote, and participate, in the spectacular display of the world.

There has been such a growth in video technology that to view an event without its visual, or sometimes audiovisual, prolongations has almost become unthinkable. Video recorders, as cameras, as images converted to processes, are processors of reality derivable only from this reality of images. World news is delivered to us fragmentarily with only a vague and faint familiarity. The television newscasters, the politicians, the heroes of TV series are indistinguishable from the actors and vice versa, and in the end, they turn out to share the reality and unreality factor to the same extent. Television reports on the Gulf War showed us images identical in source to video war games. The elimination of the real experience in tourism is particularly remarkable in France, though France is not exceptional; this form of theatricalisation being applicable, for example, to natural sites like the Niagara Falls and so on. It seems as if everything has to be done to turn the landscape into postcards so as to hold peoples' attention. A lot of tourists seem more eager to buy reproductions than to really look at the paintings they can only briefly glance at during their all-too-short visits to the museums.

In the so-called amusement park, the quintessential environment of this kind, the spectacle of display of the world is at its height, as what people come to see is mostly the spectacle of spectacle: for example Disney characters walking through a fake American street in a non-American region of the world, and filmed by real tourists hence restoring them to "real" nature and making them again into movie characters. Through a process that is a reversal of Woody Allen in his film *The Purple Rose of Cairo* they inflict the same treatment on their families who, in turn, step into the screen to join their heroes.

This is a sad development, that one has every good reason to wish had never happened. Psychological and sociological factors might give us hope that its appearance will be postponed, or its manifestation negated. It is, however, already gaining ground on the street. I am speaking of the constitution of a totally fictional ego evolving through exposure to virtual reality networks, with the ego cast naked by images of images. The object of this fascination would be even less real than dreams and figments of imagination, obscuring how all traditional cultures have been made meaningful because they were the product of a given place and cosmology. We would then have gone from the edge of non-place to the edge of non-ego.

Chapter 2

Thirdspace: expanding the scope of the geographical imagination
Edward W. Soja

My purpose here, and in the writing of *Thirdspace: Journeys to Los Angeles and Other Real-and-Imagined Places* (1996), is to encourage the development of a different way of thinking about space and the many associated concepts that compose, comprise, and infuse the inherent spatiality of human geography. In encouraging geographers and others to "think differently" about such familiar notions as space, place, territory, city, region, location, and environment, I am not suggesting that you discard your old and familiar ways of thinking, but rather that you question them in new ways that are aimed at opening up and expanding the scope and critical sensibility of one's already established spatial or geographical imaginations.

In this essay, I compress what I have written in *Thirdspace* into five summative arguments or theses. Each is rather boldly stated, and expansive and open in its implications for human geography today. The brief commentaries following each statement amplify and, I hope, help to clarify the fundamental points being made, while at the same time providing cumulative and fugue-like variations on the many ways of defining Thirdspace. There is no singular definition presented for this different way of thinking about space and spatiality, but rather an open-ended set of defining moments, every one of which adds potential new insights to the geographical imagination and helps to stretch the outer boundaries of what is encompassed in the intellectual domain of critical human geography.

Thesis I: Contemporary critical studies in the humanities and social sciences have been experiencing an unprecedented spatial turn.

In what may in retrospect be seen as one of the most important intellectual developments of the late twentieth century, scholars have begun to interpret space and the spatiality of human life with the same critical insight and interpretive power that has traditionally been given to time and history (the historicality of human life) on the one hand, and to social relations and society (the sociality of human life) on the other.

Few would deny that understanding the world is, in the most basic sense, a simultaneously historical and social project. Whether in writing the biography of a particular individual or interpreting a momentous event or simply dealing with the intimate routines of our everyday lives, the closely-associated historical and social (or sociological) imaginations have always been at the forefront in the effort to gain practical and informative knowledge of the subject at hand. This has been especially true in the development of critical thinking within the broadly-defined human sciences, where the express purpose is to gain knowledge that is useful and beneficial, if not emancipatory, in its cumulative effect.

Without reducing the significance of life's inherent historicality and sociality, or dimming the creative and critical imaginations that have developed around their practical and theoretical understanding, a third critical perspective, associated with an explicitly spatial imagination, has in recent years begun to infuse the study of history and society with new modes of thinking and interpretation. As we emerge from the *fin de siècle*, there is a growing awareness of the simultaneity and interwoven complexity of the social, the historical, *and the spatial*, their inseparability and often problematic interdependence. It is this important "spatial turn," as it is now being described, that I associate with the emergence of a Thirdspace perspective and an expansion in the scope and critical sensibility of the geographical imagination.

These new developments revolve, in large part, around what can be described as an *ontological shift*, a fundamental change in the way we understand what the world must be like in order for us to obtain reliable knowledge of it. For the past two centuries, ontological discussion has focused primarily on the temporal and social characteristics of human existence, on what can be described as the existential relations between the historicality and sociality of being or, more concretely, of being-in-the-world. There were earlier attempts, by such critical philosophers as Martin Heidegger and Jean-Paul Sartre, to give to this existential being and to its dynamic expansion in the notion of "becoming" a pertinent spatiality, but until very recently this spatiality remained fundamentally subordinated to the dominant dialectic of historicality–sociality, the interplay between what might more collectively be called the making of histories and the constitution of societies. Today, however, the inherent and encompassing spatiality of being and becoming is beginning to be more forcefully recognized than ever before, injecting an assertive third term into the ontology of human existence. This momentous development is creating what I have described, reflecting this assertive "thirding," as an ontological *trialectic* of spatiality–sociality–historicality, or more simply, a three-sided rather than two-sided way of conceptualizing and understanding the world. Stated somewhat differently, the social production of human spatiality or the "making of geographies" is becoming as fundamental to understanding our lives and our lifeworlds as the social production of our histories and societies.

Figure 2.01 is an attempt to capture this now three-sided relation in visual form. A different rendering appears in primary colors on the cover of *Thirdspace*.

Within this configuration are three interactive relationships that apply not only to ontology, but also equally well to all other levels of knowledge formation: epistemology, theory building, empirical analysis, and praxis, the transformation of knowledge into action. There is not only the long-standing historicality–sociality relation that has been the dominant focus of Western critical thought for at least the past 200 years, but also the relation between sociality and spatiality that I described some years ago as the "socio-spatial dialectic;" and the relation between historicality and spatiality, time and space, that gives rise to a substantive spatio-temporal or geohistorical dialectic that I explored in some detail in *Postmodern Geographies* (1989) and again in *Thirdspace*, most directly in Chapter 6, "Re-Presenting the Critique of Historicism."

The key to understanding the "trialectics of being" and a major reason why the reassertion of critical spatial thinking is of transdisciplinary importance and not just confined in its impact to geographers, architects, urbanists, and others for whom spatial thinking is a primary professional preoccupation, lies in the absence of any *a priori* privileging of the three terms. Studying the historicality of a particular event, person, place, or social group is not intrinsically any more insightful than studying its sociality or spatiality. The three terms and the complex interactions between them should be studied together as fundamental and intertwined knowledge sources, for this is what being-in-the world is all about. Making theoretical

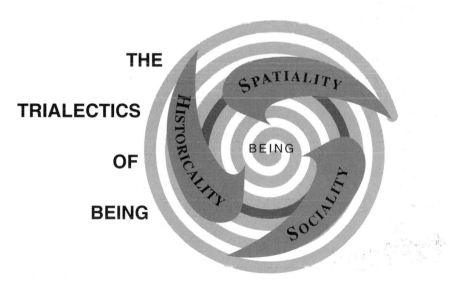

2.01 The trialectics of being.

and practical sense of the world is best accomplished by combining historical, social, and spatial perspectives. Specialists (historians, geographers, sociologists) may focus more deeply on one of these modes of thinking, but when this is done in ways that exclude significant attention to the other two existential dimensions there is the danger of silencing too much of what matters in human life, of falling into narrow-minded historical, social, or spatial-geographical determinisms. Practicality and inclination may dictate that we emphasize one of the three fields over the others, but we must always try to maintain a critical consciousness that is aware of and open to the potentially equivalent powers of all three working interdependently together.

The very nature and social timing of this ontological "restructuring," however, involve at least a temporary highlighting, if not a cautious privileging, of spatiality. This is not because spatiality is intrinsically more important but because it has until recently been relatively peripheralized in the humanities and social sciences and especially in the construction of critical social theory. In *Postmodern Geographies* and in *Thirdspace*, I pointed specifically to a deep tradition of historicism as a primary reason for the diminishment of critical spatial thinking. Unfortunately, this has been frequently interpreted, most often by geographers I might add, as either an attempt to reduce the importance of historical analysis, a kind of anti-history that verges on spatialism; or else as a failure to recognize that good historians have always been sensitive to space and geographical analysis. I cannot emphasize enough that my spatial critique of historicism is not an anti-history, an intemperate rejection of critical historiography or the emancipatory powers emanating from the creative historical imagination. Historians have always produced some of the best human geographies and they continue to do so today. My critique of historicism can be best described as an attempt to *rebalance* the fundamental trialectic of historicality–sociality–spatiality, to make all three modes of thinking operate together at "full throttle" at every level of knowledge formation, without any one being inherently privileged, or diminished for that matter, with respect to the others.

If the current transdisciplinary spatial turn continues with the same intensity as it has in the 1990s, a point may be reached when there may no longer be a need to accentuate the importance of the critical spatial imagination or to emphasize the space-blinkering effects of a persistent historicism or sociologism. In the same way that we have come to accept that everything in the world and every mode of thinking about the world has a significant social and historical dimension, to the point that we have historians and sociologists of science, of philosophy, of geography, even of sports and sexuality, so too may we eventually recognize the inherent and encompassing spatiality of everything and every mode of thought, with human geographers accepted on equal terms with social scientists and historians as critical analysts of the human condition. But this moment has not yet arrived. The project of rebalancing the trialectic still has a long way to go, and the persistent powers of historicism and sociologism (or should we describe it as "socialism"?) in constraining the development and expanding scope of the geographical imagination continue to be worth fighting against. But is the geographical imagination and human geography today up to this challenge? This brings me to my second argument.

Thesis II: The geographical imagination, especially as it has developed within the spatial disciplines, continues to be confined by an encompassing dualism, or binary logic, that has tended to polarize spatial thinking around such fundamental oppositions as objectivity versus subjectivity, material versus mental, real versus imagined, things in space versus thoughts about space.

Expanding the scope of the geographical imagination to the breadth and depth that has been achieved for historicality and sociality, and hence rebalancing their critical empowerment, requires a creative deconstruction and rethinking of this bifurcation into two modes of spatial thinking and analysis.

Figure 2.02 summarizes visually a central argument in *Thirdspace* that pertains to what I call, following the ontological triad mentioned earlier, the "trialectics of spatiality." It identifies in Thirdspace, here defined by Henri Lefebvre's notion of *espace vécu*, or "lived space," an alternative mode of spatial inquiry that extends the scope of the geographical imagination beyond the confining dualism of what I describe as Firstspace and Secondspace epistemologies – or what Lefebvre refers to as spatial practices or "perceived space" on the one hand, and the representations of space or "conceived space" on the other. A few simple definitions help to explain the diagramed relations, which mirror closely those of Figure 2.01.

Firstspace (Perceived Space) refers to the directly-experienced world of empirically measurable and mappable phenomena. This materialized spatiality, which presents human geographies primarily as *outcomes*, has been the dominant and familiar focus for geographical analysis, often to the exclusion of other ways of thinking about space and geography. For many, especially those who see geography as a formal science, this has been the only objective or "real" space worth studying. It forms the geographer's primary "text" or subject matter, and can be "read" or explained in two broad ways. Endogenous approaches explain Firstspace geographies through accurate descriptions of patternings and distributions (as in the study of areal differentiation), the search for recurrent empirical regularities (the foundation of specifically spatial science), and the correlation or spatial covariation of one geographical configuration with another (the basic method of both idiographic and nomothetic geographies). The key point here is that empirical analysis,

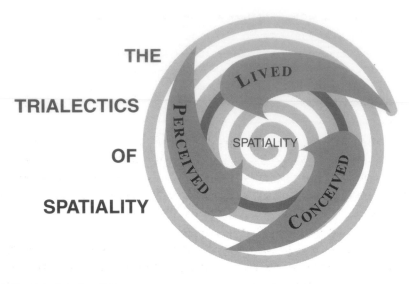

2.02 The trialectics of spatiality.

theory building, and explanation remain internal to geography; that is, geographies are used to explain other geographies. Exogenous approaches explain material geographies by focusing on the underlying social or physical processes that produce them. Human geographies are seen here as the product or outcome of forces which are not in themselves geographical or spatial, but are derived from the inherent sociality and historicality that lies behind the empirical patternings, distributions, regularities, and covariations. These approaches are particularly well developed in most critical forms of geographical thinking and interpretation, such as in the application of class analysis in Marxist geography or the analysis by feminist geographers of the space-shaping impact of patriarchy and masculinism. But various kinds of exogenous analysis, including those that use the physical environment as an explanatory variable, infuse all fields of human geographical inquiry.

Secondspace (Conceived Space), in contrast, is more subjective and "imagined," more concerned with images and representations of spatiality, with the thought processes that are presumed to shape both material human geographies and the development of a geographical imagination. Rather than being entirely fixed on materially perceivable spaces and geographies, it concentrates on and explores more cognitive, conceptual, and symbolic worlds. It thus tends to be more idealist than materialist, at least in its explanatory emphasis. If Firstspace is seen as providing the geographer's primary empirical text, then Secondspace represents the geographer's major ideational and ideological "discourses," the ways we think and write about this text and about geography (literally "earth-writing") in general.

Although there is an epistemology to the study of Firstspace, it is in Secondspace that epistemological discourse receives the greatest attention. In the long history of geographic thought, Secondspace approaches have been turned to most often when mainstream Firstspace approaches have become too rigidly materialist and "scientistic," as with the various critiques that emerged in response to the epistemological closures of positivist human geography. For Henri Lefebvre, however, Secondspace is not so secondary. He argues in *The Production of Space* (1991) that "conceived space" is the dominant space in that it powerfully controls the way we think about, analyse, explain, experience, and act upon or "practice" human spatiality (or the "making" of geographies). I cannot dwell on his argument here, but I suggest that it provides a very different way of approaching the subject matter that conventionally comprises what is called the history of geographic thought.

The Firstspace–Secondspace Dualism: most human geographers do not work at the extremes of these two approaches, but somewhere in between, conceiving of "pure" materialism/objectivity and idealism/subjectivity as opposite poles of a continuum of approaches. There has been a persistent tendency, however, to see Firstspace and Secondspace as together defining the whole of the geographical imagination, as encompassing in their varying admixtures all possible ways of conceptualizing and studying human geography and the spatiality of human life. This "bicameral" confinement of the geographical imagination, I argue, has been primarily responsible for the difficulty most geographers and other spatial thinkers have had in understanding and accepting the deeper meaning of the ontological restructuring discussed earlier, and hence in comprehending Thirdspace (Lived Space) as a *different* way of thinking. Instead of responding to the growing spatial turn as a profound challenge to develop a new mode of understanding the spatiality of human life (human geography in its broadest sense) that is commensurate in scope and critical insight with life's instrinsic historicality and sociality, many geographers, pleased with the growing attention being given to their discipline, simply pour the new wine into the same old double-barreled containers, thus reinforcing the constraints and illusions of the Firstspace–Secondspace dualism. It is not surprising then that many of the primary sources for the reconceptualization of spatiality and the expansion in scope of the geographical imagination have been coming from outside the traditionally spatial disciplines.

Thesis III: A radical break from this confining dualism was initiated in France in the late 1960s, largely through the works of Michel Foucault and Henri Lefebvre.

I describe their method of criticizing the Firstspace–Secondspace dualism as a "critical thirding-as-Othering" and attribute to their challenging geographical imaginations the origins of Thirdspace as a radically different way of looking at, interpreting, and acting to change the embracing spatiality of human life.

Drawing primarily from Lefebvre's major work, *The Production of Space* (for a discussion of Foucault's "heterotopologies," see Chapter 5 in *Thirdspace*), we can see a very different picture of the scope and substance of the geographical imagination. For Lefebvre, the persistent dualism between mental and materialist approaches to space, or between what he called Spatial Practice and the Representation of Space, was a form of reductionism that was akin to that produced by many other "Big Dichotomies" that run through the history of Western philosophy and social theory: subject–object, abstract–concrete, agency–structure, real–imagined, local–global, micro–macro, natural–cultural, center–periphery, man–woman, black–white, bourgeoisie–proletariat, capitalism–socialism. Confined in such a way, the geographical imagination could never capture the experiential complexity, fullness, and perhaps unknowable mystery of actually *lived space*, or what he described somewhat cryptically (by intent?) as the Spaces of Representation (translated from the French as Representational Spaces).

Whenever faced with such Big Dichotomies, Lefebvre sought to break them open to new and different possibilities. As he would repeatedly say, two terms are never enough to deal with the real and imagined world. *Il y a toujours l'Autre*: there is always an-Other term, a third possibility that works to break down the categorically closed logic of the "either–or" in favor of a different, more flexible and expansive logic of the "both-and-also." Note that this approach differs from seeking an "in-between" position along the presumed continuum that connects the opposite extremes of the dichotomy, for such a positioning still remains within the totalizing dualism. Lefebvre seeks instead to break out from the constraining Big Dichotomy by introducing an-Other, a different alternative that both reconstitutes and expands upon the original opposition.

Such thinking was not unique to Lefebvre. It has been a feature of dialectical thinking from the Ancient Greeks to Hegel and Marx, and has featured prominently in the more recent development of postmodern, poststructuralist, postcolonial, and feminist critiques of modernism and the persistent constraints and closures of modernist epistemologies and such "closed" binariziations as those between agency and structure, man and woman, colonizer and colonized, etc. But Lefebvre was the first to apply this critical method comprehensively to the ways we think about, and practice, what he described as the production of space, or, in other words, the making of human geographies. In doing so, he also engaged in another philosophical (and political) project: the spatialization of dialectical thinking itself. Lefebvre called his approach *une dialectique de triplicité*. I have chosen to describe it as a *critical thirding-as-Othering*, retaining the capitalized emphasis on the Other.

Critical thirding-as-Othering creatively expands upon the dialectics of Hegel and Marx, moving beyond the presumed completeness and strict temporal sequencing of its classical framing in the form of thesis–antithesis–synthesis. Rather than a culminatory synthesis or a conclusive statement that can itself trigger another dialectical round of thesis–antithesis–synthesis, thirding introduces a disruptive "other-than" choice. This Othering does not derive simply and sequentially from the original binary opposition and/or contradiction, but seeks instead to disorder, deconstruct, and tentatively reconstitute in a different form the entire dialectical sequence and logic. It shifts the "rhythm" of dialectical thinking from a temporal to a more spatial mode, from a linear or diachronic sequencing to the configurative simultaneities, the synchronies, I have attempted visually to capture in the diagrams of Figures 02.01 and 02.02. As Lefebvre described it, "the dialectic today no longer clings to historicity and historical time, or to a temporal mechanism such as "thesis–antithesis–synthesis". . . . To recognise space, to recognise what "takes place" there and what it is used for, is to resume the dialectic." To underline his point and to avoid reducing the "contradictions of space" only to the Firstspace–Secondspace dualism, he adds, "*We are not speaking of a science of space but of a knowledge (a theory) of the production of space* . . . this most general of products" (Lefebvre 1976: 18; emphasis in the original).

Lefebvre saw this thirding as the beginning of a heuristic chain of "approximations" that builds cumulatively in an ever-expanding process of knowledge formation. There are no closures, no permanent structures of knowledge, no intrinsically privileged epistemologies. One must always be moving on, nomadically searching for new sources of practical knowledge, better approximations, carrying along only what was most usefully learned from earlier voyages. To avoid the dangers of hyper-relativism and a freewheeling "anything goes" philosophy that is often attached to such radical epistemological openness, one must be guided by and committed to a challenging intellectual and political project. Thirding thus does not end with the assertion of a third term or with the construction of what some might describe as a holy trinity. Making practical and theoretical sense of the world requires a continuous expansion of knowledge formation, a radical openness that enables us to see beyond what is presently known, to explore "other spaces" (see Foucault's *des espaces Autres* and "heterotopologies") that are both similar to and significantly different from the real-and-imagined spaces we already recognize.

In this sense, Thirdspace (as Lived Space) is simultaneously:

1   a distinctive way of looking at, interpreting, and acting to change the spatiality of human life (or, if you will, human geography today);

2   an integral, if often neglected, part of the trialectics of spatiality, inherently no

better or worse than Firstspace or Secondspace approaches to geographical knowledge;

3   the most encompassing spatial perspective, comparable in scope to the richest forms of the historical and sociological imaginations;

4   a strategic meeting place for fostering collective political action against all forms of human oppression;

5   a starting point for new and different explorations that can move beyond the "third term" in a constant search for other spaces; and still more to come.

Thesis IV: Over the past decade, the most creative explorations of Thirdspace, and hence the most accomplished expansions in the scope of the geographical imagination, have come from the broadly defined field of critical cultural studies.

Particularly prominent here has been the work of feminist and postcolonial critics who approach the new cultural politics of class–race–gender from a radical postmodernist perspective. One of the accomplishments of these scholars and activists has been to make human geography today more transdisciplinary than it ever has been before.

The African–American writer and social critic bell hooks occupies a special place in widening the scope of the spatial imagination. Drawing inspiration and insight from the works of both Lefebvre and Foucault, she creatively enriches our understanding of lived space by infusing it with a radical cultural politics and new political strategies to deal with the multiple axes of oppression built around race, class, and gender. Although she speaks specifically as a radical woman of color, her words resonate with much broader implications for contemporary politics as well as for the practice of human geography. She does this in part by empowering lived space with new communicative meaning and strategic significance. For hooks, lived space and what I would describe as a Thirdspace consciousness provide a new political grounding for collective struggles against all forms of oppression, whatever their sources and at whatever geographical scale they are expressed, from the intimacies of the human body (what the poet Adrienne Rich once called the "geography closest in") to the entrapments built in to the global political economy. What follows is a series of passages from hooks' most spatial work, *Yearning: Race, Gender and Cultural Politics* (1990), and especially from a chapter evocatively titled, "Choosing the Margin as a Space of Radical Openness."

> As a radical standpoint, perspective, position, "the politics of location" necessarily calls those of us who would participate in the formation of counter-hegemonic cultural prac-tice to identify the spaces where we begin the process of re-vision ... For many of us,

that movement requires pushing against oppressive boundaries set by race, sex, and class domination. Initially, then, it is a defiant political gesture. (145)

For me this space of radical openness is a margin — a profound edge. Locating oneself there is difficult yet necessary. It is not a "safe" place. One is always at risk. One needs a community of resistance. (149)

I am located in the margin. I make a definite distinction between that marginality which is imposed by oppressive structures and that marginality one chooses as site of resistance — as a location of radical openness and possibility. This site of resistance is continually formed in that segregated culture of opposition that is our critical response to domination. We come to this space through suffering and pain, through struggle.... We are transformed, individually, collectively, as we make radical creative space which affirms and sustains our subjectivity, which gives us a new location from which to articulate our sense of the world. (153)

It was this marginality that I was naming as a central location for the production of a counter-hegemonic discourse that is not just found in words but in habits of being and the way one lives. As such, I was not speaking of a marginality one wishes to lose, to give up, but rather as a site one stays in, clings to even, because it nourishes one's capacity to resist. It offers the possibility of radical perspectives from which to see and create, to imagine alternatives, new worlds. (152)

Postmodern culture with its decentered subject can be the space where ties are severed or it can provide the occasion for new and varied forms of bonding. To some extent, ruptures, surfaces, contextuality, and a host of other happenings create gaps that make space for oppositional practices which no longer require intellectuals to be confined to narrow separate spheres with no meaningful connection to the world of the everyday ... [A] space is there for critical exchange ... [and] this may very well be "the" central future location of resistance struggle, a meeting place where new and radical happenings can occur. (31)

Radical postmodernism calls attention to those shared sensibilities which cross the boundaries of class, race, gender, etc., that could be fertile ground for the construction of empathy — ties that would promote recognition of common commitments, and serve as a base for solidarity and coalition.... To change the exclusionary practice of postmodern critical discourse is to enact a postmodernism of resistance. (27, 30)

Spaces can be real and imagined. Spaces can tell stories and unfold histories. Spaces

> can be interrupted, appropriated, and transformed through artistic and literary practice. As Pratibha Parmar notes, "The appropriation and use of space are political acts." (152)

> This is an intervention. A message from that space in the margin that is a site of creativity and power, that inclusive space where we recover ourselves, where we move in solidarity to erase the category colonizer/colonized. Marginality is the space of resistance. Enter that space. Let us meet there. Enter that space. We greet you as liberators. (152)

In these eye-opening passages, there are many glimpses of a different kind of human geography, one that combines the grounded and politically-conscious materialism of Firstspace analyses and the rich, often metaphorical representations of space and spatiality characteristic of Secondspace geographies; and at the same time stretches beyond their mere additive combination to create "Other" spaces that are radically open and openly radicalized, that are simultaneously material-and-metaphorical, real-and-imagined, concretely grounded in spatial practices yet also represented in literary and aesthetic imagery, imaginative recombinations, epistemological insight, and so much more. It can be said that hooks literally cracks open lived space to new insights and new expectations that extend well beyond the long established boundaries of the traditional geographical imagination.

But it is to the specifically political implications of hooks' emphasis on "choosing the margin as a space of radical openness" and her explicit but cautious adoption of a radical postmodernism that I wish to draw your attention to, for it is this combination of an expansive Thirdspatial imagination, a strategic attachment to a new cultural politics of difference and identity, and a radical postmodernist critical positioning that has become the source of some of the best new writings emanating not just from radical women of color such as bell hooks but from the wider fields of feminist and postcolonial criticism. Here is a brief sampling from Chapter 4 of Soja (1996), "Increasing the Openness of Thirdspace." Page numbers refer to this chapter, not the original sources.

The following comes from the artist and urban critic Rosalyn Deutsche on the significance of geographically uneven development within the city and "spatial design" as a tool for the social control of class, race, and gender.

> Lefebvre's analysis of the spatial exercise of power as a construction and conquest of difference, although it is thoroughly grounded in Marxist thought, rejects economism and predictability, opening up possibilities for advancing analysis of spatial politics into realms of feminist and anti-colonialist discourse and into the theorization of radical democracy. More successfully than anyone of whom I am aware, Lefebvre has speci-

fied the operations of space as ideology and built the foundations for cultural critiques of spatial design as a tool of social control. (1996: 106)

From Teresa de Lauretis, *Technologies of Gender*, on moving the "subject of feminism" beyond a simple man/woman dichotomy into a wider frame of cultural representations related to class, race, and sexuality. Note how de Lauretis, like hooks, intertwines the material and metaphorical to define the importance of spaces on the margin.

> [We are looking at] the elsewhere of discourse here and now, the blind spots or space-off, of its representations. I think of it as spaces in the margins of hegemonic discourses, social spaces carved in the interstices of institutions and in the chinks and cracks of the power-knowledge apparati.... It is a movement between the (represented) and what the representation leaves out or, more pointedly, makes unrepresentable. It is a movement between the (represented) discursive space of the positions made available by hegemonic discourses and the space-off, the elsewhere of these discourses.... These two spaces are neither in opposition to one another or strung along a chain of signification, but they exist concurrently and in contradiction. (111–12)

Another newcomer to the spatial disciplines, Barbara Hooper, focuses her work on the disruptive interplay of bodies, cities, and texts in an unpublished manuscript that focuses on "The Case of Citizen Rodney King."

> [T]he space of the human body is perhaps the most critical site to watch the production and reproduction of power.... It is a concrete physical space of flesh and bone, of chemistries and electricities; it is a highly mediated space, a space transformed by cultural interpretations and representations; it is a lived space, a volatile space of conscious and unconscious desires and motivations – a body/self, a subject, an identity: it is, in sum, a social space, a complexity involving the workings of power and knowledge *and* the workings of the body's lived unpredictabilities.... Body and body politic, body and social body, body and city, body and citizen-body, are intimately linked productions.... These acts of differentiation, separation, and enclosure involve material, symbolic, and lived spaces ... and are practiced as a politics of difference. (114)

The geographer Gillian Rose brings home the critical power of the spatial feminist critique to break down the masculinist hegemony that continues to dominate the discipline. From *Feminism and Geography* (1993):

> Social space can no longer be imagined simply in terms of a territory of gender. The

geography of the master subject and the feminism complicit with him has been rup-
tured by the diverse spatialities of different women. So, a geographical imagination is
emerging within feminism which, in order to indicate the complexity of the subject of
feminism, articulates a "plurilocality." In this recognition of difference, two-dimensional
social maps are inadequate. Instead, spaces structured over many dimensions are
necessary. (124)

Rose adds her own expansions of hooks' space of radical openness and what I
have been describing as Thirdspace.

The subject of feminism, then, depends on a paradoxical geography in order to
acknowledge both the power of hegemonic discourses and to insist on the possibility
of resistance. This geography describes that subjectivity as that of both prisoner and
exile; it allows the subject of feminism to occupy both the centre and the margin, the
inside and the outside. It is a geography structured by the dynamic tension between
such poles, and it is also a multidimensional geography structured by the simultaneous
contradictory diversity of social relations. It is a geography which is as multiple and
contradictory and different as the subjectivity imagining it ... a different kind of space
through which difference is tolerated rather than erased. (124–5)

Gloria Anzaldúa, a poet and cultural critic of the lived spaces found along the
US–Mexico borderlands, creates another form of "plurilocality" around what she
calls the consciousness of the *mestiza*, or *mestizaje*, another way of being outside
and inside at the same time.

As a *mestiza*, I have no country, my homeland casts me out; yet all countries are mine
because I am every woman's sister or potential lover. (As a lesbian I have no race, my
own people disclaim me: but I am all races because there is the queer of me in all
races.) ... I am an act of kneading, of uniting and joining that not only has produced
both a creature of darkness and a creature of light, but also a creature that questions
the definitions of light and dark and gives them new meanings. (128–9)

Anzaldúa's poetics also journey into theorizing space:

We need theories that will rewrite history using race, class, gender and ethnicity as categories of analysis, theories that cross borders, that blur boundaries.... Because we
are not allowed to enter discourse, because we are often disqualified or excluded from
it, because what passes for theory these days is forbidden territory for us, it is *vital* that
we occupy theorizing space, that we not allow white men and women solely to occupy

it. By bringing in our own approaches and methodologies, we transform that theorizing space. (129)

Of all the cultural critics of Eurocentrism and postcolonialism, Edward Said has probably received the greatest attention from human geographers. Derek Gregory's excellent expansion upon Said's "Imaginative Geographies" (1995) provides us with the following observations from Said.

> Just as none of us is outside or beyond geography, none of us is completely free from the struggle over geography. That struggle is complex and interesting because it is not only about soldiers and cannons but also about ideas, about forms, about images and imaginings.... What I find myself doing is rethinking geography.... charting the changing constellations of power, knowledge, and geography. (137–8)

Finally, some passages from Homi Bhabha, whose fascinating work on the "location of culture" and the notion of "hybridity" are framed by his own conceptualization of a "Third Space," similar to, yet different from, what is being defined as Thirdspace in this essay.

> All forms of culture are continually in a process of hybridity. But for me the importance of hybridity is not to be able to trace two original moments from which the third emerges, rather hybridity to me is the "third space" which enables other positions to emerge. This third space displaces the histories that constitute it and sets up new structures of authority, new political initiatives, which are inadequately understood through received wisdom.... The process of cultural hybridity gives rise to something different, something new and unrecognisable, a new area of negotiation of meaning and representation. (140)

Bhabha grounds his Third Space in the perspectives of postmodernism, postcolonialism, and postfeminism, but urges us to be ready to go "beyond," to cross boundaries, "to live somehow beyond the border of our times." From *The Location of Culture* (1994):

> It is significant that the productive capacities of the Third Space have a colonial or post-colonial provenance. For a willingness to descend into that alien territory – where I have led you – may reveal that the theoretical recognition of the split-space of enunciation may open the way to conceptualizing an *inter*national culture, based not on the exoticism of multiculturalism or the *diversity* of cultures, but on the inscription and articulation of culture's *hybridity*. To that end we should remember that it is the "inter" – the cutting

edge of translation and negotiation, the *in-between* space – that carries the burden of the meaning of culture.... And by exploring this Third Space, we may elude the politics of polarity and emerge as others of ourselves. (141)

Thesis V: Continuing the project initiated by Lefebvre and expanding it in new directions that resound with more contemporary relevance, the new human geographers emerging from critical cultural studies are explicitly spatializing radical subjectivity and political practice, imbuing both with a critical spatial consciousness that extends far beyond what has existed in the past. Reflecting what was earlier described as an ontological shift and a critical thirding-as-Othering, these scholars are opening up a new and still relatively unexplored realm of radical political action centered and sited in the *social production of lived space*, a strategic choice that is aimed at constituting a community of resistance which can be as empowering and potentially emancipatory as those formed around the making of history and the constitution of human societies.

Never before have human geographies been given such transdisciplinary attention. But these are human geographies of a different sort, more comprehensive in scope, more empowered and potentially empowering, more explicitly politicized at many different levels of knowledge formation, from ontology to praxis, from the materially concrete to the imaginatively abstract, from the body to the planet. They are made more "real" by being simultaneously "imagined." The metaphorical use of space, territory, geography, place, and region rarely floats very far from a material grounding, a "real and imagined" that signals its intentional Otherness from more conventional geographies. Thirdspace as Lived Space is portrayed as multi-sided and contradictory, oppressive and liberating, passionate and routine, knowable and unknowable. It is a space of radical openness, a site of resistance and struggle, a space of multiplicitous representations, investigatable through its binarized oppositions but also where *il y a toujours l'Autre*, where there are always "other" spaces, heterotopologies, paradoxical geographies to be explored. It is a meeting ground, a site of hybridity and *mestizaje* and moving beyond entrenched boundaries, a margin or edge where ties can be severed and also where new ties can be forged. It can be mapped but never captured in conventional cartographies; it can be creatively imagined but obtains meaning only when practiced and fully *lived*.

For the past two centuries, radical subjectivity and progressive political action with regard to the unequal power relations associated with class, race, and gender have revolved primarily around conscious interventions into the historicality and sociality of human life, around how societies make histories and organize their social relations and modes of production. For the most part, these struggles have tended to remain relatively confined to separate channels of collective identity and consciousness, with either class or race or gender (codified in such Big Dichotomies as Capital versus Labor, White versus Black, Man versus Woman), occupying entrenched and essentialized positions so politically and theoretically privileged that forming effective coalitions between these often chauvinistic and exclusive channels was extremely difficult. Even when linkages were formed, they tended to remain unstable as each radical movement retained a distinctive and exclusive prioritization of its own particular binarized axis of oppression.

Inspired by the breakdown of these totalizing modernist political epistemologies (i.e. the orthodoxies of Marxism, radical feminism, and black nationalism) and the possibility of a radical postmodernism (a possibility which many on the left still refuse to recognize), a new socio-spatial movement or "community of resistance" is beginning to develop around what I am describing as a Thirdspace consciousness and a progressive cultural politics that seeks to break down and erase the specifically spatial power differentials arising from class, race, gender, and many other forms of marginalizing or peripheralizing (both pre-eminently spatial processes) particular groups of people. Rather than operating in separate and exclusive channels, this new movement/community is insistently inclusive (radically open) and recombinative, searching for new ways of building bridges and effective political coalitions across all modes of radical subjectivity and collective resistence. In this coalition-building, it is a *shared spatial consciousness* and a collective determination to take greater control over the *production of our lived spaces*, that provides the primary foundation – the long-missing "glue" – for solidarity and political praxis.

Coalition-building is a long established political strategy, but these progressive coalitions have formerly been mobilized in the largest sense primarily around taking collective control over the making of history and the way social relations of power and status are constituted and maintained; that is, to redress the inequalities and oppression produced in the historical course of societal development. The new coalitions retain these empowering sources of mobilization and political identity, but add to them a reinvigorated spatial consciousness and subjectivity, an awareness that the spatiality of human life, the making of human geographies, the nexus of space–knowledge–power also contain the sources of continued oppression, exploitation, and domination.

This newly-spatialized form of individual and collective struggle is still in its earliest stages and not yet a formidable force in contemporary politics. And it must be recognized that the new spatial politics is not exclusively confined to progressive forces. Indeed, conservative and neoliberal approaches to spatial politics in the new information age of globalization and economic restructuring have been significantly empowered all over the world over the past 30 years. This makes it all the more important for progressive thinkers and activists to set aside their internal conflicts over postmodernism and to find new ways to contend strategically with the postmodern right in the struggle to shape our contemporary human geographies. We must recognize and participate in the expanding sites and communities of resistance and assertion that bell hooks and others invite us to enter, to move in consciously spatial solidarity and begin a process of re-visioning the future. This opportunity to reassert the expanded theoretical and strategically political importance of the critical spatial imagination may be what is most new and different – and most challenging – about human geography today.

References

Anzaldúa, Gloria, *Borderlands/La Frontera* (San Francisco: Spinsters/Aunt Lute Press, 1987).

— (ed.) *Making Face/Making Soul* (San Francisco: Spinsters/Aunt Lute Press, 1990).

Bhabha, Homi K., *The Location of Culture* (New York and London: Routledge, 1994).

— "The Third Space: Interview with Homi Bhabha," in Rutherford (ed.), *Identity, Community, Culture, Difference* (London: Lawrence and Wishart, 1990).

Deutsche, Rosalyn, "Uneven Development," *October* 47: 3–52, 1988.

Gregory, Derek, "Imaginative Geographies," *Progress in Human Geography* 19: 447–85, 1995.

hooks, bell, *Yearning: Race, Gender, and Cultural Politics* (Boston: South End Press, 1990).

Hooper, Barbara, "Bodies, Cities, Texts: The Case of Citizen Rodney King," 80pp unpublished mss, 1994.

Lefebvre, Henri, *The Survival of Capitalism* (London: Allison and Busby, 1976).

— *The Production of Space* (Oxford UK and Cambridge US: Blackwell, 1991) (translation by D. Nicholson of Lefebvre, *La production de l'espace*, Paris: Anthropos, 1972).

Rose, Gillian, *Feminism and Geography* (Cambridge: Polity Press, 1993).

Soja, Edward W., *Postmodern Geographies: The Reassertion of Space in Critical Social Theory* (London: Verso, 1989).

— *Thirdspace: Journeys to Los Angeles and Other Real-and-Imagined Places* (Oxford UK and Cambridge US: Blackwell, 1996).

Chapter 3

Getting lost and the localized mind
Franco La Cecla

translation by Stuart Wylen

"There is a spot of mud on your seaward cheek"
Raymond Firth, "We the Tikopia" (London 1936)

It can happen on the freeway, in a city that we don't know, or even on the way home. It is a frustrating, embarrassing and at the same time ridiculous experience. We are put in a position of being displaced, misplaced. It shows an ambiguous, vaguely defined, confused relationship with the environment in which we get lost. We suddenly find ourselves without sense of direction, without reference points. We are "here", but "here" doesn't correspond to a "where" we would like to be.

An old Hungarian joke tells of two Alpine climbers that get lost in the mountains. One of them has a map, takes it out from his bag and consults it. After a while he says to the other climber, "I found it, we're on that mountain over there." The story shows that it is generally impossible for us to lose our cognition of being "here". But knowing that we are here is not all it takes to get oriented.

Getting oriented, like getting lost, is a cultural experience. It is the acquisition, the building, the discovery or the lack of a network of references. It is an activity that we usually share with other people. Or it can put us into a pre-existent social and cultural context. There are various ways and degrees of getting lost.

AS IMMERSION INTO THE UNKNOWN

We can get lost in the woods, like the Temne children in Guinea who are sent by their parents into the bush by the edge of the village to collect leaves for wrappings. They know that sometimes "as you walk through the trees you begin to feel queer, your head becomes dizzy, you don't know where you are. You shout for your parents, then they come and find you. This spell, the Temne say, is Aronshon's work and nearly all seem to succumb to it at least once in childhood, and some in adulthood too; adults are said to receive a whipping from Aronshon so that they return cut and bruised."[1] This type of getting lost is an immersion in the unknown. The unknown offers apparitions, ambiguities, fright, confusion, danger.

In Brahmanic India, the Sanskrit word "aranya", which is commonly translated as "forest", is derived from "arana", "strange", which is in turn related to the Indo-European root "al/ol", itself the source of the Latin words "alius", "alter", and "ille". The aranya, before defining a territory distinguished from the village space by certain material traits (a zone without agriculture, covered with trees), "designates the other of the village" in these societies.[2]

For the Gourmantche' of Gobinangou in Upper Volta, the idea of "fuali" cannot be translated in terms of physical or geographical reality. "It is over there, far away, always far away." But far away doesn't necessarily mean situated at a great geographical distance. What is far away can be right next to you. Fuali is not a surveyable territory but a space with shifting boundaries, which vary notably as a function of time.

> At night the Fuali advances into the village up to the point marked by the habitation's enclosures, sometimes even penetrating its interstices. When the sun is at its zenith, the village territory seems to be dotted with little islands of bush into which it is danger-ous to penetrate. Fuali implies indistinction, the absence of differentiated contours, the elimination of boundaries. Thus at night any space outside of the house tends to turn into "bush"; the way the landscape looks in the raw light of the moon, when things seem to return to a state of indifferentiation is, equally, the bush.
>
> The root "fua", from which "fuali" is derived, is opposed in certain contexts to the root "do", which provides the basis for the word village, "dogu". These two roots serve to form a long series of pairs of contrasting terms. The semantic field covered by the root "fua" includes the notion of a space affecting the human body in a specific way: if you stay "fuali-ni" (in the bush) for too long, or find yourself in a certain situation, it is as if you were "emptied", "pumped out", "pressed", "flattened", "to the point of evapora-tion".[3]

Getting lost could mean being outside the limits, off track, cheated by the ambigui-ties of a place. We are attracted to these limits by the similarities they have with other places that we know, but these suddenly reveal themselves to be unknown when taken outside of the context which is familiar to us:

> A knight in a Praguese tale gets lost in a wood. The maze of branches and the dark-ness of the night confuse him. He wanders for a long time, to no avail. Finally he sees a breach in the forest and a light in the distance. He reaches the light; it is an inn. The innkeeper opens the door and asks him where he is coming from. The knight tells his story. The innkeeper reveals to him that he has been in the Black Forest. The knight dies of fright.

The fear of getting lost is sometimes stronger than the act itself, because it means to be adrift, with none of the security associated with the familiar, with one's orientation in places that are ours, our culture and world. In her famous essay about the "Balinese Character", Margaret Mead describes how important it is for a Balinese to always know where he is located:

> The words for the cardinal points are among the first that a child learns and are used even for the geography of the body. A Balinese will tell you that there is a fly on the West side of your face.... .Orientation in time, space and status are the essentials of social existence, and the Balinese, although they make very strong spirits for ceremonial occasions, with a few exceptions resist alcohol, because if one drinks one loses one's orientation. Orientation is felt as a protection rather than a straight jacket and its loss provokes extreme anxiety. If one takes a Balinese quickly in a motor car away from his native village so that he loses his bearings, the result may be several hours of illness and a tendency to sleep.[4]

AS A BEGINNING

Then there is getting lost as a condition of beginning. There are many fairy tales about children that get lost in the forest and learn to find their way, utilizing a unique sense in the threatening confusion of the place that surrounds them.

To grow up means, in fact, to become free of the dramatic consequences of getting lost like children in the crowd at a fair, or in the human river of the street. This means learning how to get oriented by oneself, and to need no guide to leave behind the meanders and the pitfalls of the surrounding environment. To get out of trouble is to overcome the fear of being terminated by the indifference and dispersion of the place where we are, and find in it our point of reference.

For Andrea, the protagonist of Hugo Von Hoffmansthal's novel, *Andrea or the Reunited Ones*, the "forest" is eighteenth-century Venice. The disorientation that Andrea experiences at the passage between adolescence and a new world is made up of "sottoporteghi" and ambiguous "campielli", the physical features of his everyday environment.

Has he been there before or is he mistaking it for some other place? There are characters that appear and disappear among the "call", "pergole" and enclosed gardens. Andrea must get to know the illusion, the chameleon-like nature of the place, its everlasting deception.

Andrea gets lost in the city and in himself, in his mistaking of dream for reality, but he learns to deal with the slippery, ungraspable density of reality and to give it some order without underestimating its complexity. The maps that he makes of Venice and of reality represent getting oriented in the unknown without denying its power of seduction.

AS ADJUSTMENT TO NEW SURROUNDINGS

Nonetheless, getting lost is a continually latent experience. We spend most of our time conquering, defining and affirming the buoys around which we move and orient ourselves, the landmarks which enable us to keep from despair in the incognito journey between known scattered places. The reciprocal side of this experience, the use of this feeling of a possible and imminent danger, is the sense of adventure, "the conquest of space", that gives us new space for our movements, new friends, new places and extends our mental map. Getting lost in these cases is a condition of beginning, the need and the ground on which to start or to resume getting oriented.

Between getting lost and getting oriented there is a cultural process, the use of external, arbitrary occasions to make them propitious, to make the unknown hospitable, and to become able to settle in it.

Getting oriented could mean, for an individual or a group of people that have recently immigrated to a new city, all the frustrations, failed attempts, acquaintances, long waits, senses of new reality, life preservers made up of people and places. Day by day, it starts as an elementary network – those two or three friends, those street corners, the grocery store, maybe a bar, the first informal approaches of the workplace, and then becomes a more complex net to recognize and include the remaining unknown sites, parting from and returning to more familiar places.

> Never before our time have so many people been uprooted. Emigration, forced or chosen, across national frontiers or from village to metropolis is the quintessential experience of our time. That industrialization and capitalism would require such a transport of men on an unprecedented scale and with a new kind of violence was already prophesied by the opening of the slave trade in the sixteenth century. The Western Front in the First World War with its conscripted massed armies was a later confirmation of the same practice of tearing up, assembling, transporting and concentrating in a "no-man's land". Later concentration camps, across the world, followed the logic of the same continuous practice.[5]

To this day these practices can take the name of resettlements and relocations. They are the heavy burden of the survivors, of people that have lost their land. Is it possible for them to find another one to belong to? Or does the process of incorporation mean the loss of their culture? How they will leave their mark on the new land depends on the strength and the degree of freedom of the immigrants. In this sense the immigrant's daily life in a new, unknown city could be compared to an activity of foundation.

AS FOUNDATION

At the end of the nineteenth century, the Lobi emigrated from the Ivory Coast towards the Upper Yolta, escaping the arrival of the Portuguese, the slave trade, the Anglo-French colonial occupations and looking for more fertile lands. In this migratory movement they left behind a thick trail of physical marks and landmarks.

> Every seven years during the ceremony of "dyoro" (an initiation rigorously kept secret to every foreigner) the young of both sexes are led by initiated adults to retrace the ancestors' paths. Every agnatic group visits the sites lived by its own lineage, learning how to recognize even the smallest tracks. In this way every Lobi recovers his own story and at the same time gives life and identity to the entire territory.[6]

What does it mean to look for a place in which to settle? What gestures are to be made to settle? The word settlement in its original meaning stands for an action, a process and a dynamic. To land on a Sicilian shore as did the Megarese settlers, to start a village in the Brazilian veredas at the beginning of this century, to move our own village to a new region, to rebuild our own town destroyed by a natural disaster or by war; all of these are situations of founding. The founders have to tame a place that is uninhabited or has been previously inhabited by other people. For the newcomers, the territory is a chaos, an "adama" land, a wild place.

One fairy tale about founders is the myth of Thesaeus and the Labyrinth. After having escaped the danger of being swallowed by the confusion and chaos of the maze, Thesaeus becomes the heroic founder of Athens.

But it is very important to negotiate with the chaos, to ingratiate oneself with it, trying to guess its intentions and not to overlook its power. This is the challenge of the augur's science, the ability to predict the future of a settlement. This recognition of the good or bad omens of a site is a knowledge that takes different forms in every traditional culture. It is always a science of placement, a strong local knowledge combined with the decipherment of the sacrificed animals' viscera, the number of passing birds at a certain hour, the direction of the clouds, the movement of a sacred spider and so on.

The mark of Romulus or Costantino's plough stands for the choosing, encircling and cutting out of a specific place. The mark of the furrow is a distinction, a barrier between this space and the untamed rest of the land. It describes a square, a circle, a fenced area, and gives it orientation. It is a gesture full of consequences, some of them dangerous. The stories of foundations are often stories in which the founder goes insane or kills his own brother. The founder is often attacked by the same power he tries to tame. He is punished because he goes too far with his "hubris", his pride or haughtiness. To found is allowed only to whoever is able to maintain the awareness that beyond his provisional order and orientation the possibility of getting lost is always there.[7]

The "lares", domestic gods of the early Roman tradition, protected houses, inhabited places and trivia, and often enforced the boundaries that separated the inhabited land from the sylvan and rocky kingdom.[8]

Inhabited is the opposite of uninhabited, but every inhabited place runs the risk of returning to the category of the uninhabited, to the indifference of infinite possibilities, to the unknown powers of the deserted land.

IN THE DESERT

A famous story by Jorge Louis Borges tells of a king "of the islands in Babylonia" who asked his magicians and architects to build for him a labyrinth "tan perplejo y sutil" that the most prudent men wouldn't dare to enter, and those who did would get lost.

One of the kings of Arabia came to visit the King of Babylonia, and was invited to enter his labyrinth. The Arabian king wandered lost and confused until sunset, then finally implored Allah to come to his aid and the divine succor helped him to find the exit. He didn't complain to the other king, he just told him that he had a better labyrinth in Arabia.

When he got back to Arabia, he assembled his army and attacked the King of Babylonia, and managed to overcome and imprison him. Then he brought him on his camel to the desert and left him there, saying: "Oh, king of the time and substance and sum of the century, in Babylonia you tried to make me lost in a bronze maze with many stairs, doors and walls; now The Omnipotent has willed that I show to you my own maze, in which there are no stairs to climb, no doors to force, no tiring tunnels to cross, nor walls that block the way."[9] The King of Babylonia, the story goes, died in the desert. His labyrinth was a man-made artifact. Nobody could live in it, except perhaps some sort of Minotaur. The desert, however, although it is the prototype of the uninhabited places, can be lived in, but only by its indigenous inhabitants, such as the King of Arabia.

In order to avoid getting lost in the labyrinth one needs a map or a thread, or divine help. Not to get lost in the desert, one has to have lived in it. To live in the desert means to mark it with the points of reference of a knowledge available only with a long acquaintance that is not available to a transient visitor.

There is no nomadic people that doesn't know the details of the various threads of their movements. They have learned through inherited knowledge that the desert, the wasteland, the prairie, the snow and the tundra are full of lines and points that are invisible to a foreign eye.

The "Mauris" that live in the wide spaces of the Western Sahara give different names to the different movements of the land. This naming relates to the belief that the ground is a living being. For this reason it is always oriented in the four directions that divide the horizon: "geble" and "tell", "sahel" and "sarg". The different parts of a hill, a dune or an inselberg have names which refer to the four directions. Simply saying the name of that part is enough to indicate its direction.[10]

> For an Eskimo or an inhabitant of the Sahara constant directions may be recognized, not by heavenly objects, but by prevailing winds, or by sand or snow formations which are the products of such winds.[11]

Edward Sapir gives an example of this differential focus of attention in the language of Southern Paiute. They have single terms in their vocabulary for such precise topographical features as a "spot of level ground in mountains surrounded by ridges" or "canyon wall receiving sunlight" or "rolling country intersected by several small hill-ridges". Such accurate reference to topography is necessary for definite locations in a demi-arid region.[12]

> Way-finding is the original function of the environmental imago and the basis on which its emotional associations may have been founded. But the image is valuable not only in this immediate sense in which it acts as a map for the direction of movement; in a broader sense it can serve as a general frame of reference within which the individual can act, or to which he can attach his knowledge. In this way it is like a body of belief, or a set of social customs: it is an organizer of facts and possibilities.[13]

In this sense, the labyrinth of the King of Babylonia could correspond to the maze of the modern built environment, to which it is difficult to give any frame of meaning, because its function, as for the labyrinth, is alien to our interest. It follows the caprice of some foreign king whose aim is to make his subjects lost.

AS A JOURNEY

The nomads' journey is the continuous repetition of a gesture of foundation. It represents the turning over of the carpet of correspondence between their mind, symbolic cultural maps and the places of their movements. As John Berger masterfully states:

> Originally home meant the center of the world not in a geographical, but in an ontological sense. Mircea Eliade demonstrated how home was the place from which the world could be "founded". A home was established, as he says, "at the heart of the real". In traditional societies everything that made sense of the world was real: but the surrounding chaos existed and was threatening, but it was threatening because it was "unreal". Without a home at the center of the real, one was not only shelterless, but also lost in non-being, in unreality. Without a home everything was fragmentation. Home was the center of the world because it was the place where a vertical line crossed with a horizontal one. The vertical line was a path leading upwards to the sky and downwards in the underworld. The horizontal line represented the traffic of the world, all the possible roads that led across the earth to other places. Thus, at home, one was nearest to the gods in the sky and to the dead in the underworld. This nearness promised access to both. And at the same time, one was at the starting point and, hopefully, the returning point of all terrestrial journeys. The crossing of the two lines, the reassurance their intersection promises, was probably already there, in embryo, in the thinking and belief of nomadic people, but they carried the vertical line with them as they might carry a tent pole."[14]

The Australian Aborigines don't even have a tent pole. But in their journeys they structure their territory mythically, mentally, and symbolically, without displaying any visible mark.

One of the best descriptions of the dreamroads that lead the Aborigines in their journey is a report by the poet Gary Snyder:

> I was traveling by truck over dirt track west from Alice Springs in the company of a Pintubi elder named Jimmy Tjungurray. As we rolled along the dusty road, sitting in the bed of a pickup, he began to speak very rapidly to me. He was talking about a mountain over there, telling me a story about some wallabies that came to that mountain in the dreamtime and got into some kind of mischief there with some lizard girls. He had hardly finished that and he started in on another story about another hill over here and another story over there. I couldn't keep up. I realized after about half an hour of this that these were tales to be told while "walking", and that I was experiencing a speeded-up version of what might be leisurely told over several days of foot travel.... We made camp at a waterhole called Ilpili and rendezvoused with a number of Pintubi people from the surrounding desert country. The Ilpili waterhole is about a year across, six inches deep, in a little swale of bush full of finch. The people camp a quarter mile away.

It's the only waterhole that stays full through drought years in several thousand square miles. A place kept by custom, I am told, welcome and open to all. Through the night, until one or two in the morning, Jimmy Tjungurray and the other old men sat and sang a cycle of journey songs, walking through a space of desert in imagination and song. They stopped between songs and would hum a phrase or two and then argue a bit about the words and then start again, and someone would defer to another person and would let him start. Jimmy explained to me that they have so many cycles of journey songs they can't quite remember them all, and that they have to be constantly rehearsing them. Night after night they say, "What will we sing tonight?" "Let's sing the walk up to Darwin." They'll start out and argue their way along through it, and stop when it gets too late to go any farther. I asked Jimmy, "Well, how far did you get last night?" He said, "Well, we got two thirds of the way to Darwin."[15]

AS IF IT WERE POSSIBLE

Getting lost intentionally today becomes more difficult. In a world in which the natural environment is being invaded and substituted by the built, the unknown moves itself farther and farther away, towards the ungraspable. Traveling and its modern mythology can be seen today in the overwhelming amounts of travel agencies, reports and literature available as a cheap and hopeless attempt at getting lost. The promise of traveling to exotic places has turned getting lost into a commodity affected by the market laws, that is, a scarce commodity to be bought at an increasingly high price.

This started with the Western colonization of Asia and Africa. It is the journey as imagination, discovery and exploration of "virgin lands", "far away cultures and peoples". It is Africa, Asia or the Americas seen through the eyes of Western civilization anxious to lose its own tracks. It continues today in the last frontier of Rondonia, the "virgin part of Amazonia" where a new generation of colonists are chasing after their new world.

This kind of travel, in the history of mentalities, the history of the last 50 years and in personal histories, heads toward an extinction. Anything new is left out of reach. Everything has been channelled in known directions by explorers, missionaries, anthropologists, travelers, tourists and photographers. One can always track down the way home.

As Socrates once said about someone that was unable to enjoy his traveling: "Of course; he is always taking himself with him."[16] To "take ourselves with us" means colonizing with our presence every step of our journey. To know new places corresponds in this century with denying their difference. This is not the same as the gesture of the founder, who was asking for a conciliation with the pre-existent.

He was negotiating with the "powers" of the place that was new to him. Getting lost has become impossible because we overwhelm the place where we stop or settle with our order; it is not the result of a long, prudent, sometimes cautious interaction. Today's traveller, as full of amazement he might be, can usually only fake his getting lost. He doesn't fit into any of the roles that could make it possible. He is becoming less and less a "stranger", that is, someone who understands that he must be accepted by the hospitality of the inhabitants and is aware of the risks of his or her anomalous identity. Those who don't play the role of the stranger are "tourists", destroyers. But "travelling" still owes its hidden fascination to the meaning of the journey for the *homo viator* of the Middle Ages,[17] for the pilgrim in every traditional culture, for the "enchanted traveler".

For them the journey is in itself a "sense", because it is oriented, has a destination, and is an introduction to the terrestrial condition of provisionality, the ultimate impossibility of imposing our own settlement order onto the general order of things and of the cosmos.

> The mere fact of spatial separation from the familiar and habitual is an example of this. It may, in various cultures have punitive, purificatory, expiatory, cognitive, instructional, therapeutic, transformative, and many other facets, aspects and functions. But basically the process and state of liminality represents at once a negation of many, though not all, of the features of preliminal social structure and an affirmation of another order of things and relations.

As Victor Turner suggests, about the traveling of the pilgrim:

> My point is that there is a "rite de passage", even an initiatory ritual character about pilgrimage. I tend to see pilgrimage as that form of institutionalized or symbolic anti-structure (or perhaps meta-structure) which succeeds the major initiation rites of puberty in tribal societies as the dominant historical form. It is the ordered anti-structure of patrimonial feudal systems. It is infused with voluntariness though by no means independent of structural obligatoriness. Its limen is much longer than that of initiation rites (in the sense that a long journey to a most sacred place used to take many months or years) and it breeds new types of secular liminality and communitas.
>
> As the pilgrim moves away from his structural involvements at home his route becomes increasingly sacralized at one level and increasingly secularized at another. He meets with more shrines and sacred objects as he advances, but he also encounters more real dangers such as bandits and robbers, he has to pay attention to the need to survive and often to earn money for transportation, and he comes across markets and fairs, especially at the end of his quest, where the shrine is flanked by the

bazaar and by the fun fair. But all these things are more contractual, more associational, more volitional, more replete with the novel and the unexpected, fuller of possibilities of *communitas*, as secular fellowship and comradeship and sacred communion, than anything he has known at home. And the world becomes a bigger place. He completes the paradox of the Middle Ages that it was at once more cosmopolitan and more localized than either tribal or capitalistic society.

To embark on a journey to a far away place which is the goal of a pilgrimage, "from the standpoint of the believing actor", represents a threshold, a place and moment "in and out of time". Many times the peripherality of the sites of the shrines in regard to the villages or cities from where the journey begins is a confirmation of this "state of liminality".

Turner gives us the example of central Mexico:

This brings us to the very important point that, generally speaking, pilgrimage shrines in Central Mexico, though not in Yucatan, tend to be located not in the centers of towns and cities but on their peripheries or perimeters or even at some distance beyond them. Thus the hill of Teyepac, where the shrine complex of the virgin of Guadalupe is located, is on the northern rim of Mexico City; the Basilica of Our Lady of Zapopan, the great pilgrimage center of the city of Guadalajara which has the states of Michiacan, Nayarit, and Jalisco as its main pilgrim catchment area, is situated on the northwestern limits of the city; the Basilica of Our Lady of Ocotlan stands on a small hill outside the southwestern boundary of the city of Tlaxcala; while the extremely sacred image of Our Lady of the Remedies is kept in the Church of San Bartolo in Naucalpan, some nine miles northwest of the old Spanish colonial capital of Mexico, but now almost engulfed by spreading suburbia. . . . Of course the most popular contemporary European Catholic pilgrimages are also in peripheral places. One need only mention the shrines of the Virgin at Lourdes, Fatima, Czestochowa, La Salette, and Oostacker. This peripherality of the holiest shrines is by no means confined to Christian pilgrimage systems. For example, Deleury writes of the pilgrimages to Pandhapur that "Pandhapur is situated on the borderline of the region covered by the palkhis" (a palkhi is a literally a palancuin carrying a representation of a god's or saint's footprints, padukas, and here stands for a group of pilgrims following the same guru or spiritual teacher, living or dead). . . . Not only is Pandhapur not the center of the Marathi speaking countries, but is quite possible that in former times it was situated on the boundaries of Kannada speaking countries.

And again about Mexico:

It is interesting to note here that wherever a municipio contains or is near a major pilgrimage center, its inhabitants, though they may participate in festive and marketing activities associated with the pilgrimage saints' feast days, tend to go as pilgrims to distant shrines rather than to near ones.[18]

AS TAX COLLECTORS

The conflict between locality and its invasion by a new kind of traveler unable to get lost takes us to another category of getting lost. The municipal officials of Paris, before the drawing up of the "Plan of City Limits" in 1728, were often unable to find their way in the intrigue of the street life, of the "empasses", "cul de sacs", courts, stairs, rooms, barracks. Every "arrondissement" represented a Babel in itself, in which one who didn't belong to that specific neighborhood could easily get lost.[19]

"The Courts of Miracles" was a term used for the densely-inhabited parts of the city. The crowd was made up of inhabitants more than of residents. They were managing the inner life of the neighborhood with a mixture of crafts and local exchanges, of conflicts and solidarities, of local production and transformation of goods. This texture was subsistence oriented and brought with it a strong sense of its defensible boundaries. To enter them without the inhabitants or against their will could be difficult.

When the Plan was drawn up in 1728, the municipality attempted to clean out the intrigue of the arrondissement, to make the city easier for the public officials to manage, to wipe out all the obstructions in the streets, the provisional shelters, the blankets, baskets, tents. The tax collectors could enter the neighborhoods without fear only if its inner life was tamed. For this reason the municipal policies included the closing of all the doors after sunset, the numbering of every house, and the labeling of every street. Only after this operation could the map of the city be useful for their control.

These measures introduced a new kind of external orientation while denying the inner orientation of the inhabitants. Until then, in most European cities the orientation was not topographical but relativistic. In Dante's Florence[20] and in the pre-industrial Florentine territory until 1785, one could orient oneself according to the names of the "canti". These were focal points, as were "loggias", lamps, tabernacles, the houses of the important families, and the main shops, particularly the pharmacies. The names of the canti were to be used to designate the streets when they were labeled in 1785. The houses were not to be numbered until 1808. To find an address meant to find and ask some inhabitant of the "contrada" for directions. Asking was part of the role of the stranger, the foreigner. The same conception still exists today in Japan with the notion of "fudo",[21] which represents a range, a social and spatial domain with unitary characteristics.

Roland Barthes, in his book *The Empire of Signs*,[22] recounts his experience of getting oriented in Japan. In the absence of addresses as we know them, the inhabitants have an incredibly accurate ability to give directions with drawings and sketches. The predominance of an "areolar" conception of the city's space, as if it were constituted of different contiguous villages and the margins among them, corresponds to the Paris described by Rabelais.[23] It was a city full of many different activities performed in its open spaces as well as in unlocked rooms, markets, fairs, feasts; senses were confronted with animals, screams, odours, fights, games, bloody or healing activities, tricks, household goods, fruit and fishes and laundry drying. All the activity made rapid transit through the neighborhood impossible. This kind of city life clogged any attempt of crossing and kept in check any external intervention of the police or army. In Paris, after the decision of the municipality to label the streets, the inhabitants of the arrondissement resisted the measure, lynching and stoning the public officials for more than 20 years.[24] This kind of city presented a terror for the new state municipalities of Europe after the French Revolution, such as in London, where alleys and narrow streets, corners and sidewalks were to be the ground for the Victorian fantasies – in mystery stories of thieves and killers hiding themselves in caches and under trapdoors.[25] Or it could be San Francisco's Chinatown in the beginning of the last century, a mixture of real and fantasized inner-city life with the mythical underground galleries of three or more floors, opium dens and all sorts of illegal traffic.[26] It is against this terrible dominance of the "locality" that the first urban policies were meant. Their purpose was to wipe out the city of its inhabitants, allowing only disciplined residents to remain. This policy was applied through demolitions, evictions, destructions of courts, cul de sacs, winding streets, and unveiling the exclusive domains of the locality and its suspected danger for the hygiene, propriety and public morality.[27] Cities were forced to stop being an intricate, tangled forest in which foreigners get lost.

AS TOTAL DEMOLITION

Locality is a form of belonging to a place. The place which is ours belongs to us and we belong to it.[28] "If a man says he comes from Akenfield he knows he's telling someone from another part of the neighborhood a good deal more than this. Anything from his appearance to his politics could be involved."[29]

This belonging is ensured by the sharing of a mental map stretched over the territory, to which everyone makes their contribution, either maintaining or confirming it or modifying some part of it. This way of defining space contains in itself the process and the collective motivations of the settlement. If it is wiped out, the culture of the inhabitants of that locality cannot be recovered.

The denial of locality can be applied to the most recent category of getting lost. A classical example is that of the Bororo culture, a tribe in Brazilian Amazonia.

> In the circular village layout, clans of the Exerae moiety occupy specified positions in the northern crescent, and those of Tugarege moiety are placed opposite in the southern portion. But inside the men's house, which is "the axis of the categorical order which relates men to men, nature and deities", the relative positions of the moieties are reversed, thus expressing "the fundamental tenet of this order, that through ritual men become transformed into creatures antithetical to their usual social selves, into members of the other moiety.[30]

The whole symbolism is embedded and expressed in the spatial layout of the village. When the Salesian Missionaries arrived, they decided that in order to penetrate the Bororo culture and make the Christian message available to them, it was essential to unhinge their spatial system.[31] They reordered the Bororo huts into parallel lines. The effect was surprising. The Bororo lost their cultural orientation, they felt lost. They were no longer able to recall the complex symbolic system of inversions of their social organization. Their culture had been physically erased.

AS SWISS DISEASE

What Ernesto DeMartino calls "territorial anguish" are the consequences of a cultural system menaced being in its spatial configuration.[32] For the southern Italian peasant of the 1950s as well as for the "Balinese character", it could happen that "if one takes him in a motor car away from his native village" so that he loses sight of his "campanile", the result could be an extreme anxiety. This state of being "spaesato", spaced out, is mainly a result of the anguish created by the threatened loss of his own world. In 1678, a Swiss medical student named Johannes Hofer defined this kind of state as a disease and named it "Schweizerkrankheit", Swiss Disease, because it was affecting the Swiss emigrants and exiles. His symptoms were "insomnia, anorexia, palpitations and a persistent homesickness". Only since 1774 has this term been used for the disease, otherwise known as "nostalgia", to define these symptoms for people other than the Swiss.[33] Throughout the seventeenth and eighteenth centuries, physicians claimed that this disease could cause the death of a patient if he wasn't able to return home.[34]

AS LOSS OF DIRECTION

Today there exists a getting lost that is a sense of distraction as a broad attitude towards space. This is a totally new everyday psychopathology. The "lapsus" of getting lost is an attitude that creates a chronic alienation that affects us in our relationship with our environment. The less we handle our own environment, the less we are able to orient ourselves within it. Street life in the last two centuries has been forbidden, prosecuted, and deleted.[35] Place names given by people to their own environment have been replaced with numbers on every door and labels on the streets. The only place the dwellers are allowed to handle has become the interior of the apartment. Building codes, inspectors, bureaucracies and professional corporations have criminalized every creative intervention of citizens outside, and greatly reduced those inside their domiciles. We can walk through the streets of the city, cross its sidewalks, enter its buildings, stay in the rooms of various apartments yet leave no trace of our presence, no individual or collective mark. The activity of the modern citizen is not an activity of inhabiting, of creation of localities. He is only a consumer of space. This is a condition of chronic disorientation, of an effective tendency to get lost, to the extent of not being able to distinguish one place from another.

Modern literature about the suburbs, the peripheries and more recently about the gentrified centers of the cities is too crowded with examples of this malaise not to deal with it as the new urban condition. This condition could be described with the words used 30 years ago to describe the cases of men who, through brain injury, have lost the ability to organize their surroundings:

> They may be able to speak and think rationally, even to recognize objects without difficulty, but they cannot structure their images into a connected system. These men cannot find their own rooms again after leaving them, and must wander helplessly until conducted home, or until by chance they stumble upon some familiar detail. Purposeful movement is accomplished only by an elaborate memorization of sequences of distinctive detail, so closely spaced that the next detail is always within close range of the previous landmark.

A rule that became a law of following directions when driving:

> Locations normally identified by many objects in context may be recognizable only by virtue of some distinctive, separate symbol. One man recognizes a room by small sign, another knows a street by the tram car numbers. If the symbols are tampered with the man is lost. The whole situation parallels, in a curious fashion, the way in which we proceed in an unfamiliar city.[36]

AS ARCHITECTURE

An English social historian, Robin Evans, described our actual environmental situation like this:

> The cumulative effect of the architecture of the last two centuries resembles very much the effect of a general lobotomy operated on the whole society.... It is more and more employed as a prevention device, as a social pacification control and segregation factor. It is possible to say that in fact (in its own essence) it has impoverished the perceptible universe: reabsorbing noise transmission and the different kinds of movement and transportation, destroying any waste accumulation with the purpose of interdicting the propagation of diseases, banishing discomforts and confusion, locking out the indecent and abolishing useless gestures, has reduced daily life to a theatre of private shadows.[37]

Getting lost means having a spatial lapse. This omission is studded with the building and unbuilding of spaces that don't belong to us and that we don't belong to. It is supported by meaningless, indifferent architectures. Adolf Loos in a famous page written at the beginning of our century gave us for the first time a lucid description of our new condition.

> There are two houses next to the same lake. The first one is a peasant house, the second has been built by an architect. How does it happen that even though the architect's house has been designed with the most accurate attention, it looks strange in the landscape? It doesn't fit in. You can easily say that it wasn't there before. And why is it that the peasant's house, that is neither nice nor ugly, is already part of the landscape, *is* the landscape?

We could answer the question of Adolf Loos that the architect's house has been built based on an omission of orientation. It may be here, but its "here" has nothing to do with a cultural system of orientation that deals in direct co-operation with the landscape. The architect's house is not "here" near the house of Giovanni, behind the fig that was cut one year ago, facing the propitious winds and opportunities that are coming from the direction that is known by everyone that has lived here to be the right one. It is not on the site of a previous dwelling. It doesn't raise up from a process like the following, told about a peasant community in Bosnia:

> One day the owner of the neighboring garden brought a carpenter to the site and told him to build up a house. They stopped on a spot where the ground sloped gently down-

wards. The carpenter had a look at the trees of the garden, the ground, the environment and the town in the valley. Then he proceeded to extract from his cummerbund some pegs, paced off the distances and marked them with the pegs. Then he came to his main task. He asked the owner which tree might be sacrificed, moved his pegs for a few feet, nodded and seemed satisfied. He found that the new house would not obstruct the view from the neighboring structures . . ,[38]

Notes

1   James Littlejohn, "The Temne House", (ed.) J. Middleton, *Myth and Cosmos* (New York 1967).

2   Charles Malamoud, "Village and Foret dans l'Ideologie de l'Inde Brahmanique", *Archives Europeens de Sociologie*, 17: 3–20, 1976.

3   James Littlejohn, ibid.

4   Gregory Bateson and Margaret Mead, "Balinese Character, a Photographic Analysis" (New York Academy of Sciences 1947).

5   John Berger, "And Our Faces, My Heart, Brief as Photos" (New York 1984).

6   Giovanna Antongini and Tito Spini, "Presenze e Oggetti – la Costruzione dell'Ambiente Lobi (Alto Volta), in Storia della Citta" XIV, 7646, 1980.

7   Joseph Rykwert, *The Idea of a Town, the Anthropology of Urban Form in Rome, Italy and the Ancient World* (London 1976).

8   Joseph Rykwert, ibid.

9   Jorge Louis Borges, "Los dos Reyes y los dos Laberintos", *El Aleph* (Buenos Aires 1957).

10 Vincent Monteil, "La Topon
gie, l'Astronomie et l'Orientation chez le Maures", *Hesperia* I-2 Trim., 1949.

11 Kevin Lynch, "Some References to Orientation", in *The Image of the City* (MIT 1960).

12 Edward Sapir, "Language and Environment", *American Anthropologist*, Vol. 14, 1912.

13 Kevin Lynch, ibid.

14 John Berger, ibid.

15 Gary Snyder, "Good, Wild, Sacred", *Coevolution Quarterly*, 34, Fall 1983.

16 Pierre Clastres, *The Society Without State* (Paris 1974).

17 Gerhart Ladner, "Homo Viator, Medieval Ideas on Alienation and Order" Speculum, vol. VLII, no. 2, April 1964.

18 Victor Turner, *Drama, Fields, Metaphors, Symbolic Action in Human Society* (Cornell University 1974).

19 Bruno Fortier, "Il Piano dei Limiti di Parigi", *Le Macchine Imperfette* (Georges Teysoot ea., Rome 1980).

20 C. Casamorata, "I Canti di Firenze", *L'Universo*, 25, no. 3, 1944.

21 A. Berque, "Espace et Societe" en Japan: La Notion de Fudo", *Mondes Asiatique*, 16, Hiver 1978–9.

22   Roland Barthes, *The Empire of Signs.*

23   Mikhail Bakhtin, *Rabelais and His World* (MIT 1968).

24   Arlette Farge, *Vivre dans la rue a Paris au XVIII siecle* (Paris 1979).

25   Gareth Steadman Jones, *Class Sociali, Emarginazione e Sviluppo; uno Studio di Storia Urbana* (London 1976).

26   Dashiell Hammett, *The Maltese Falcon.*

27   F. Beguin, "Les Machineries Anglaises du Comfort", *Politique de l'Habitat (1800–1850), sous la direction de Michel Foucault* (Corda, Paris 1977).

28   Anthony Cohen (ed.) *Belonging, Identity and Social Organization in British Rural Cultures* (Manchester 1982).

29   Ronald Blithe, *Akenfield* (New York 1969).

30   Christopher Crocker, "Men's House Associates Among the Eastern Bororo", *Southwestern Journal of Anthropology*, 25: 236–60, 1969.

31   Robert Brain, *Into the Primitive Environment* (Englewood Cliffs, New Jersey 1972).

32   Ernesto DeMartino, "Angoscia Territoriale e Riscatto Culturale nel Mito Achilpa delle Origini", *Studi e Materiali di Storia delle Religioni*, XXIII: 52–6, 1952.

33   W.H. McCann, "Nostalgia, a Review of the Literature", *Psychological Bulletin*, 33: 165–82, 1941.

34   I. Relph, *Place and Placesness* (New York 1976).

35   Philippe Meyer, *L'enfant et le raison d'Etat* (Paris 1982).

36   Kevin Lynch, ibid.

37   Robin Evans, "Figures, Portes, Passages", *URBI 'V'* 1982.

38   D. Grabrijan and J. Neidhardt, *Architecture of Bosnia* (Ljubljana 1957).

Locating

Chapter 4

Space–time and the politics of location
Doreen Massey

The social spaces through which we live do not only consist of physical things: of bricks and mortar, streets and bridges, mountains and sea-shore, and of what we make of these things. They consist also of those less tangible spaces we construct out of social interaction. The intimate social relations of the kitchen and the interactions from there to the backyard and the living room. The relations with neighbours: talking across the back wall, the more formal hello in the street, the annoyance when they come home noisily and very late, yet again, on a Saturday night. These local spaces are set within, and actively link into, the wider networks of social relations which make up the neighbourhood, the borough, the city. Social space is not an empty arena within which we conduct our lives; rather it is something we construct and which others construct about us. It is this incredible complexity of social interactions and meanings which we constantly build, tear down and negotiate. And it is always mobile, always changing, always open to revision and potentially fragile. We are always creating, in other words, not just a space, a geography of our lives, but a time–space for our lives.[1]

Sitting there so solidly, so silently, so implacably, in Grove Road, so physically in just the place it always was, and yet so clearly out of place, Rachel Whiteread's sculpture *House* worked as a disruption of such social time–spaces. It jumped into and threw awry the "normal" time–spaces, and the ideas of time–spaces, which we construct in order to live our lives.

It worked this disruption, first and most obviously, in a predominantly temporal sense. It set a familiar past in the space–time of today; it made present something which was absent; it was the space of a house no longer there. Secondly, however, it worked spatially: it turned the space inside out. The private was opened to public view. The little intimacies were exposed: the print of the flex running down the wall to the light switch seeming so personal, so vulnerable now. By this means, the intimate was made monumental and yet retained its intimacy. And this effect of our prying into intimacies was reinforced by the tearing down of the rest of the terrace. Yet further exposure. For neighbouring houses provide protection, enable you to put on only your best face. With them gone we could see what lay behind that solid public

4.01 Rachel Whiteread, *House*, October 1993, Grove Road, London E3. Commissioned by Artangel and Beck's. Photo Susan Ormerod.

frontage. We could see the back-spaces as they fell away in size and somehow in significance, through back bedroom, back extension, scullery, lean-to shed. From public solidity and the front room to the more precarious, personal and informal spaces where most of daily life was lived. Now we could see all of this too.

And third, *House* disrupted our accustomed sense of time–space by apparently solidifying the volume that had once been the interior of the house: the living space, the space of life. Its openness had been filled in. All that was air was turned into solid. In *House*, social time–space was deadened, muted. The movement, the noise, the interchange; these things through which we create the time–spaces of our lives were gone. *House* was emptied of all that, and such a way of asserting what social time–space really is – precisely by so brilliantly emphasizing its absence, its current impossibility – is one of the most provocative things about this work. Through its very negation it brought home the true meaning of social space.

Given all of this, what is crucial to any assessment of *House* on these dimensions is the way in which the three aspects of space–time disruption work together. Much must turn on the way in which these disruptions functioned in the responses to, and interpretations of, *House*, perhaps especially by local people – people in the East End of London.

NOSTALGIA

Let us begin this enquiry with the fact of reference to the past – or, better, reference to "a past", since the point is precisely that there are many versions of this history. Much comment on *House* has focused on memory, on the first – temporal – disruption of space–time which it works. In articles, in interviews, in letters to newspapers, people talk of the sculpture "bringing back memories", of "making their [memories] real", of commemorating memory itself, of the evocation of emotional responses of absence/sadness/the transience of things. There is much reference to nostalgia and to nostalgia for a specific place and time.

Now, that kind of nostalgia has been interpreted by many as being a symptomatic, defining element of the postmodern condition. This, in turn, has been explained in various ways. On the one hand, commentators such as David Harvey see in a nostalgia for place merely a defensive response to the new burst of the globalization of capital, the new and accelerated phase of time–space compression.[2] For them, such a response is a negative evasion of "the real issues", and nostalgia for place is likely to end up in political "reaction". Yet there is another way of understanding this nostalgia which again would see it as a product of the present era but would not condemn it out of hand. Thus Angelika Bammer and Wendy Wheeler interpret it as a symptom emerging from the deprivations of modernity, a response to the too-long-maintained repression of affective desire by Modernism in its various forms. Postmodern nostalgia is the return of Modernism's repressed.[3]

How then is it to be interpreted? Wendy Wheeler, who links this aspect of affect precisely to notions of the uncanny, stresses the element of sharedness which it entails. Postmodern nostalgia she defines as "the desire for communal identifications". "Nostalgia . . . turns us towards the idea of the individual as non-alienated, as knowing and being known by others in the commonality of the community which is identified as 'home'."[4] It is not necessary to accept that this is the only form of postmodern nostalgia in order to agree that it is an important component. Angelika Bammer, too, addressing the specific issue of "home", writes of

> fictional constructs, mythic narratives, stories the telling of which have the power to create the "we" who are engaged in telling them. This power to create not only an identity for ourselves as members of a community. . ., but also the discursive right to a space (a country, a neighbourhood, a place to live) that is due us, is − we then claim, in the name of the we-ness we have just constructed − at the heart of what Anderson describes as "the profound emotional legitimacy" of such concepts as "nation" or "home".[5]

But if this interpretation, in contrast to that of Harvey, accepts − as it is surely correct to do − the "emotional legitimacy" of nostalgia for place and home (even if only on the grounds of recognizing its inevitability), it is nonetheless the case that such nostalgia can be problematical. For memory and the desire for communal identifications can cut both ways. They can be an aid to reactionary claims for a return (to something which of course never quite was, or which at least is open to dispute). They can erase other memories and other identifications. They can exclude some groups from membership in the commonality of the community which is identified as "home", or they can be a basis for the mobilization of emancipatory political change. Particular evocations of nostalgia must, for that reason, be evaluated individually, in their specificity. Jeffrey Peck, for instance, concludes that in certain times and places (he is writing of Germany at the end of the twentieth century), the particular concept of "home" is so unavoidably full of references to exclusion, blood and territory that it is virtually unusable for other, more disruptive emancipatory purposes.[6] Another approach, maybe in other contexts, might be to argue the pressing need for its reformulation. The question is how, in any particular circumstance, a specific form of evocation of memories functions? What effects does it produce? What solidarities (what weaknesses) does it conjure in the imagination? Are its workings those of exclusion or of openness?

House clearly aroused memories and provoked thoughts about nostalgia. Moreover it did so, and quite deliberately, at a specific moment in space–time: a late-nineteenth century house in a once-settled, now partly demolished residential street in the heart of London's East End. How, then, in relation to this question of nostalgia, did *House* work its effects?

The question can be posed at two spatial scales. First, it can be posed at the scale of house and home. Feminists, for instance, have long argued that the resonances once so usually associated with "home" must be disrupted: that home is not necessarily a place of rest or of respose, that it can be also a place of work, a place of conflict, a place of entrapment. Bammer suggests that "home, in a sense, has always been *unheimlich*, unhomely; not just the utopian place of safety and shelter for which we supposedly yearn, but also the place of dark secrets, of fear and danger, that we can sometimes only inhabit furtively."[7]

Second, the question of *House*'s affect/effect can be raised on a broader geographical scale: that of the local area in which it was made. Here what needs to be investigated is its relation to a politics of location. For the sculpture was set in the East End of London and, more specifically, in the borough of Tower Hamlets. And memory and nostalgia are difficult and dangerous things in that area these days. On the one hand is the enormous freight of meaning – and of different meanings – which the very words "the East End of London" bring with them. On the other hand is the wrenching disruption of this space in the recent past. The docks have closed, their use and meaning is being quite consciously re-worked; to the south, Canary Wharf rises on the obliteration of a past which is drawn on only to add a touch of local colour to the new, global developments. And in September 1993, at the very time when *House* was being constructed, the British National Party won a seat on the local borough council.

In this local area, memory and nostalgia are active forces precisely in the constitution of communal identifications and political subjectivities. They are crucial axes around which political constituencies are articulated and individuals interpellated into wider constellations of attitudes. So *House* is an irruption of a past time–space into a present where references to "the past", and interpretations of the nature of that past and of the relationship between past and present, are key political stakes.

The issue, therefore, is not to attempt to eradicate memory and nostalgia. It is, on the contrary, to ask: how do those other two aspects of the potentially uncanny spatiality of *House* work to subvert what could be, given its placing in this time and space, an all-too-comfortable nostalgia of home and locality?

HOUSE AND "HOME"

What effects, then, do the turning of the space inside out and the solidification of space have when considered at the level of the domestic: at the spatial scale of the home?

One thing to say first is that, of course, this sculpture was not called *Home*; it was called *House*. And this naming, it seems to me, reinforces mightily the impact of all the other challenges to sentimentalized notions of the domestic which it works so well. It immediately distances us, it uses a word somehow from the public sphere to designate a work which is so evidently redolent of what we customarily think of as private, and a word, too, which refers more to the physicality of the walls and roof, which have been removed, which now no longer are, than to the space of social interaction which, in contrast, has now so physically been both exposed and filled in. The very naming, then, gives clues to the spatial disruptions *House* effected.

The first of these two spatial reversions – the turning of the space "inside out" – works particularly powerfully at this scale of the individual house/home. It is immediately shocking and disruptive. It exposes the private sphere to public view and thereby to questioning. Most importantly, it defamiliarizes house and home. And in achieving that, it challenges us to put our own meanings on them. It exposes the normal, comfortable mythologizing of "home". Bammer, following up her argument for the intrinsic double nature of home, suggests that, "Perhaps, in this light, the best we can do about home at this point in time is to bring it, in all its complexity, out into the open."[8] This, surely, *House* achieves. It is not merely physical space which it turns inside out but the whole burden of meaning and metaphor which this space has so often had to carry (the actual bearing of the burden usually predominantly being done by the women who lived in those spaces). Potentially at least it exposes the complexity of the meaning of "home". *House* emphasizes – indeed it throws in our faces – the fact that its meaning always has to be interpreted; that there was never any simple "authenticity"; that the meaning(s) of home are always open to contestation.

Postmodern nostalgia, it has already been pointed out, has been argued to be the return of the repressed of Modernity. More specifically, it is the return of the repressed in the form of the "other" sides of all those dualisms which are made to provide the (ultimately oh-so-precarious) foundation for Modernity's assertion of the dominance of unsullied Reason.[9] Among the core set of this bastion of dualisms is that between the famous pair, the private and the public. For Hannah Arendt the distinction between the two is "between things that should be hidden and things that should be shown'.[10] In *House* the things which should be shown are removed, leaving only their defining shape; while the things which should be hidden are (almost, potentially, in outline) exposed to view. It is a reversal which, certainly, could bear "the name for everything that ought to have remained ... secret and hidden but has come to light". Moreover, to take a final step along this particular line of thought, Homi Bhabha, drawing on Carole Pateman's work in *The Disorder of Women*, argues that, "By making visible the forgetting of the 'unhomely' moment in civil society, feminism specifies the patriarchal, gendered nature of civil society and disturbs the symmetry of private and public which is now shadowed, or uncannily doubled, by the difference of genders which does not neatly map on to the private and the public, but becomes disturbingly supplementary to them."[11]

The second spatial reversal worked by *House*, the solidifying of the once-open space (even though it was only an apparent solidification) both further complicates this questioning of the public/private divide and produces other, different effects. For the "private" sphere (if we continue to use the now-problematized distinction) is of course not exposed to view. What used to be a space–time created out of living social relations is by this second reversal made mute and blind and inanimate. On the one hand this forces us, again, to interpret. By defamiliarizing, silencing, the private world now exposed to public view it compels us to do our own work. Mute it stood there, asking us to remember, to think, to question. On the other hand, by evoking so profoundly the absence of that previous life, those now-stilled social relations, by the fact that the house has gone and that the potential for the reconstruction of that social space has been so finally ended by both aspects of this spatial reversal, *House* insists on the impossibility of the recovery of that past. This is crucial; it is potentially, and productively, disturbing. It is a positive, dislocating, evocation of memories. It makes clear that, however you interpret the past, you can't have it back.

It may perhaps seem rather a prosaic comparison to make, but there does seem to be here a glaring – and fascinating – contrast with the way in which the classic "heritage site" performs its work. In many heritage sites not only are the buildings retained, but within them and around them a version of the social relations of the chosen moment of the past is acted out. A particular reading (sometimes more than one) of those social relations which constituted that particular space–time is preserved, and re-presented. There is frequently a commentary, maybe a written guide explaining things. Such sites, too, can be provocative of nostalgia. As Wheeler says, "That these are commodified images in no way lessens their effect."[12] But the effect of this nostalgia is likely to be different from that of *House*. While *House* is a prompt and a disturbance to the memory, the classic heritage site fills in those spaces and restricts the room for interpretation and imagination. Instead of questioning memory and pre-given understandings of the past, the classic heritage site will provide them ready-made. Instead of defamiliarizing the supposedly familiar, it is meant as an aid to further familiarization. It is, by design, an understandable rather than an unsettling space, a comfortable rapprochement with another space–time.

The use of such sites in particular localities can also sometimes have the effect of presenting history as continuity, as Tradition in its conventional sense. In this reading, "tradition" is something which we inevitably lose, as it fades into the past. Such notions of tradition can so easily be congealed into a static essence, as the real character of the place: what do we mean when we say "this is the real East End"? And what contexts would provoke us to say it?

It has recently been argued by many writers that white British culture and society are experiencing severe anxiety about the nature of Tradition and their relationship to it. Kevin Robins has argued that the burgeoning industry of "heritage culture" has been, in part, about attempts to construct, or to respond to the felt need for, "protective illusions" in the midst of all this anxiety.[13] In one way *House* clearly disallows such protective illusions; the very vulnerability of its inside-outness, for instance, prevents such easy recourse to Tradition in this sense. But there is another aspect to the critique of this concept of local Tradition which raises broader issues. In this critique, what is called for is a rejection of the all-too-frequently "internalist", inward-looking, character of Tradition and a recognition of the past – and the present – as always having been hybrid and open. Homi Bhabha, elaborating the notion of tradition to involve that of cultural translation, argues the need to take on board "the deep, the profoundly perturbed and perturbing question of our relationship to others – other cultures, other states, other histories, other experiences, traditions, peoples and destinies."[14] For some this is an issue which has taken on a particular urgency in a Britain which is both in decline and caught up in an accelerated globalization. Thus Robins argues that "older certainties and hierarchies of British identity have been called into question in a world of dissolving boundaries and disrupted continuities. In a country that is now a container of African and Asian cultures, the sense of what it is to be British can never again have the old confidence and surety."[15] And Hanif Kureishi insists, "It is the British, the white British, who have to learn that being British isn't what it was. Now it is a more complex thing, involving new elements."[16] (One might question, as I later shall, whether the issue of British identity was ever as simple as both these writers imply; but the complexities currently to be confronted are indisputable.) Robins, moreover, argues that many classic heritage sites (there are exceptions) do little or nothing to confront these responsibilities. Rather, they present a protective strategy of response to global forces "centred around the conservation, rather than reinterpretation, of identities".[17] Another question, then, must be: to what extent does *House* problematize these aspects of tradition and identity? It is here that we enter the wider spatial territory of the politics of location.

THE POLITICS OF LOCATION

House was conceived and made in the context of the East End of London. And the East End is an area which oozes meaning as a place, both locally and in the national psyche. The meanings are, however, varied and much contested. This is the home both of Alf Garnett and of a constantly-added-to ethnic mix; of the battle of Cable Street, Brick Lane and dockers marching against immigration. It is a locality in which notions of community and of constructing that "we" of which Angelika Bammer writes, and the communal identifications named by Wendy Wheeler, are at the very heart of politics and of daily life. A reference to "tradition" in the East End can bring to mind radicalism and ethnic diversity or racism and community closure. In such a context it becomes particularly important to ask how the evocation of memory is working and what effects – social and political – it is producing.

The debates which took place over *House* complicated these issues still further, sometimes productively, at other times troublingly. So-called "traditionalism" in art crossed swords at times with forms of traditionalism of the locality. The predictable debate as to whether or not this was "art", although a sterile confrontation in its own terms, threw into relief some other, less expected, alignments. On the one hand, as people from inside and outside the area, indeed from all over the

4.02 Rachel Whiteread, *House*, October 1993–January 1994. Photo Stephen White.

world, flocked to see it, there was an appreciation of the work which was at times undoubtedly elitist. Andrew Graham-Dixon wrote of *House*'s critics as "the myriad dullards . . . in all their unutterable boringness. . . . These people tend not to be actual art critics . . . they behave as if the entire history of twentieth-century art had either never happened or had been a terrible aberration."[18] In giving the 1993 Turner Prize, Lord Palumbo, then Chairman of the Arts Council, pleaded, "don't let the dunces have their day",[19] and so forth. And in reply came the equally dispiriting jibe from a local councillor that the whole business was "a little entertainment for the gallery-going classes of Hampstead".[20] Some highly dubious lines of counter-position were thereby drawn up, between experts and ordinary folk, between I-know-what-I-like traditionalists and an avant-garde which was actually now the establishment, between worthy locals (and local worthies) and elitist outsiders. Thus, one aspect of *House*'s provocation of constituencies looked at first sight pretty dismal.

Yet it was also interestingly contradictory. Thus in one, and only one sense, it was something of a relief that it was, in this public debate, the traditionalists and those who claimed to speak for "ordinary local people" who so often disliked the work. Had these defenders of all that was so great in those days really loved *House*, it might have been necessary to question the manner in which it was evoking memory. Had *House* stimulated a positive evocation of the East End for these groups, it would probably have fitted into images of good old England and cuddly (white and patriarchal) working-class communities. It says a lot for *House* that it does not seem to have been interpreted in this way directly; that it did not play to that kind of nostalgia, did not stimulate the reinforcement of a backward-looking, reactionary, communal identity. But neither was it rejected by these detractors because it problematized that kind of a nostalgia of place. The issue was simply not raised. What these commentators disliked was *House*'s nature as (not) Art, and not its representation of the East End.

Matters were equally confusing on the other side of these self-built fences. Although the work was proudly defended by some as modern in artistic terms, some of the evocations of its meaning by the self-consciously artistically adventurous were alarmingly traditional socially.

Take the issue of housing, and what it represents socially. John McEwen in The *Daily Telegraph* paraded the classic contrasts: "grim 1960s high-rises" and "tarted-up 1980s ones" and "the twenty-first century megastructure of Canary Wharf". And, having let us know what he doesn't like, he gives us the alternative: "the snug 1880s terraced family homes of which *House* is an example".[21] McEwen's response to *House* did not place him within a "traditionalist" camp. But when it comes to family-values, domestic bliss and housing, what he appreciates is snug families. Non-traditionalism in art combined with an utterly traditional nostalgia about home. Not only does such a response fail to take on board the potential critique of such forms of domestic organization, but it harks back uncritically to an age which itself has come to have many dubious and debatable political meanings – the Victorian era.

But housing in this area raises other issues too. The iconography of house and home performs a crucial role in the various imagined pasts of this part of London. The far-right election victory in September 1993 was largely orchestrated around battles over housing (of which there is a grotesque shortage), and over the right of "the locals" to local housing over the rights of others. Housing was at the centre of the battle over who was, and who was not, part of the local community. It was a crucial organizing issue for the increasingly vocal racisms. The British National Party in the East End uses a mythic version of the past of the place as white, as pure English. It refers to a non-existent past "before immigration". And Bow, where *House* stood, is, and is seen as, a relatively white enclave within that East End. It was one of the first places where the housing strategy "for locals" was tried. The fact of the work being a house, and in this precise location, was therefore potentially highly symbolic. What *House* did not do, maybe at the wider spatial scale it *could not* do, was challenge that kind of construction of home as once pure and now corrupted; that notion of tradition, of traditions of place now lost. While it said that no past is recoverable it didn't problematize, *at the level of the locality*, the memory of what that past was. Although its location was important, *House* did not say much about the East End as a wider area or about Bow within it: as a place of cohabitation of radicalism and racism, as a meeting-place of immigrants from all over the world and over centuries, as a repository of a bit of English identity, as a site of contradiction between a persistent localism and the context of having been, for two centuries and more, at the hub of a global Empire. It is often argued, as we have seen, that the current intensified phase of globalization has hybridized all our homes. In fact this is by no means a new phenomenon. Quintessential Englishness is utterly founded and dependent upon relations with elsewhere. And in few places is this clearer than the East End, with its constant flow of new communities and its centuries of contact with the trade routes of the world. The hybridity of a place called home is not new. Could *House* have set in motion forces towards the construction, the reinforcement or the subversion of communal identifications in this place? And what "discursive right to a space" (Bammer) does that allow such a community to claim? These issues are central to the politics of location in this area. Might the work provoke longings for an imagined past "pre-immigration"? Or could it help in the construction of a "we" which is inclusive, and neither defensive nor essentialist? To me, it seemed that *House* did not broach these issues substantively.

This is not to suggest that the work could have addressed these issues directly, and certainly not that it need have answered questions rather than merely raising them. For this is the point. At the level of the internal-domestic, *House* clearly problematized issues. One could not look at it without asking questions. At this level, *House* worked all three disruptions to time–space. It brought back a previous time–space, but it also inverted and apparently solidified it. It thoroughly de-familiarized it. It is less clear at the level of the locality, however, that *House* really posed questions, really *unsettled* in any way the terms of the accepted debate. Could it have de-familiarized the locality too? And while, certainly, it was mute, it was not without content. In its specific location and its evocation of house and home, it might have courted the danger of provoking a nostalgia for a white East End.

And yet it seems not to have had that effect, or not among the reactions which found a wider public. The alignments faced the other way. The British Nationalist Party, by all accounts, were utterly offended by the work. Maybe, ironically, what was active here was *House*'s glorious combination of the evocation of tradition precisely in a non-traditional form of "art". If this meant that the history of the locality was not problematized, at least it meant that the work did not become the focus for the celebration of a mythical white past. Indeed, the first graffiti sprayed on *House* read: "HOMES FOR ALL BLACK + WHITE".

Notes

1   For a more detailed discussion, see Doreen Massey, *Space, Place and Gender* (Cambridge: Polity 1994).

2   David Harvey, *The Condition of Postmodernity* (Oxford: Basil Blackwell 1989).

3   Wendy Wheeler, "Nostalgia Isn't Nasty – the Postmodernising of Parliamentary Democracy" in Mark Perryman (ed.) *Altered States: Postmodernism, Politics, Culture* (London: Lawrence and Wishart 1994).

4   ibid. 99.

5   Angelika Bammer, "Editorial: The Question of 'Home'," *New Formations* (London: Lawrence and Wishart no.17, xi, 1992).

6   Jeffrey M. Peck, "Rac(e)ing the Nation: Is There a German 'Home'," *New Formations*, no.17, 75–84, UK, 1992.

7   Bammer, op. cit., xi.

8   Bammer, op. cit.

9   Wheeler, op. cit.

10   Hannah Arendt, *The Human Condition* (Chicago: Chicago University Press, 1958) 72, in Homi Bhabha, *The Location of Culture* (London: Routledge p.10, 1994).

11   Bhabha, op. cit.

12   Wheeler, op. cit., 98

13   Kevin Robins, "Tradition and Translation: National Culture in its Global Context", in Corner, J. and Harvey, S. (eds), *Enterprise and Heritage*, 21–44, (London: Routledge 1991).

14   Homi Bhabha, "Beyond Fundamentalism and Liberalism", *New Statesman and Society*, London, 3 March 1989.

15   Robins, op. cit., 41.

16   Hanif Kureishi, "England, your England", *New Statesman and Society*, 21 July, London, 1989.

17   Robins, op. cit.

18   Andrew Graham-Dixon, "I don't know much about art, but I know what I hate ...", *The Independent*, London, 24 November, 1993.

19   Deyan Sudjic, "Art attack", *The Guardian*, London, November 25, 1993.

20   *The Independent*, London, January 14, 1994.

21   John McEwen, "The House that Rachel Unbuilt", *Sunday Telegraph*, London, 24 October, 1993

Chapter 5

Public territory
muf with Katherine Shonfield

The *muf* partners are Juliet Bidgood, architect, Katherine Clarke artist, and Liza Fior, architect. They aim for a positive, active role for the artist and architect in social change and to push all their projects to extend territory that can be called "public". This extended public territory includes both physical space and the space of the imaginary as well as the process of making the projects themselves.

Their method is to use practice as an active form of research. Further ideas emerge from joint practice, get tested and refined in practice and especially in the process of making which includes all the following: negotiation, agreement and relationships with institutions – planners, committees, highway engineers; the creative use of restrictive budgets; working in tandem, parallel or in response to people who live and work near by; turning obstacles, like dismissal, into opportunities for new avenues for practice.

In this conversation with Katherine Shonfield of the Faculty of the Built Environment, South Bank University, London, *muf* discuss their explorations of collaboration in Great Britain: with committees (the Millennium Dome, Greenwich), with people normally completely disempowered from changing anything (Can Do), with fabricators (Stoke Public Space) and children (Southwark Street, London).

> KC: Our design for the 1995 Royal Academy exhibition on the work of the architect Denys Lasdun acknowledged that to do an exhibition "about architecture" is impossible.
>
> To try to communicate a building is always an ersatz experience, less than really being there. The exhibition incorporated verbal narratives from the inhabitants of Lasdun's housing and schools. The visitor listened on headphones to these individual voices, looking at films of the buildings at the same time. Allowing people to tell of their own lived experience lets you get to know a building in a way that acknowledges this distance, the "less than really being there".

5.01 The Sir Denys Lasdun Retrospective Exhibition, The Royal Academy of Arts, London, 1997.

A fourteen-metre-long table, in the form of the plan of Halfield School, Lasdun's First project, holds 60 years of practice. Models, drawings and videos are laid out to allow readings between projects against a backdrop of large photographs. Lasdun's voice narrates the story of the making of the National Theatre. The voices of people who have lived and worked in his buildings tell of their experiences, speaking to you over models or videos. A slit is cut from the gallery to an adjacent exhibition of Braque's paintings, an acknowledged influence on his work.

In the Millennium Dome we knew we would not make a fabricated "local", but use the actuality of experience of people to allow a telling of what their own "locals" were like.

JB: The Dome proposal also gave back to the visitor the possibilities of their own environment, in the sense that the localities where they had come from were re-located and re-framed, as sites for potential transformation.

LF: We wanted the Dome to be an expansive catalytic site for what the public realm could be. Formally the act of pulling in the perimeter wall deep into body of the Dome itself, and fill the resulting gap with ice was our reaction to the Dome's hermetic enclosure and highly privatised face to the outside world. Our project proposed a space that was immersive, that was itself and had its own immediate physical reality, "local" to the Dome itself.

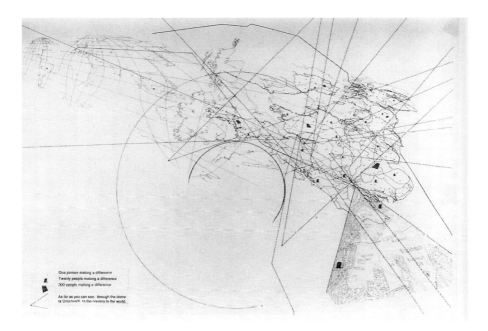

One person making a difference
Twenty people making a difference
300 people making a difference

As far as you can see: through the dome
to Greenwich, to the country, to the world.

5.02 Local Zone, The Dome, Greenwich, The New Millennium Experience Company, 1997/1998.

A pivotal and formative point in muf's practice came with their sacking from the London Millennium Dome project. Muf had been selected from a group of over 100 entrants to compete for the design role on one of the Dome's "zones".

The vast circular structure of the Dome is located on a contaminated site by the Thames in south-east London. The site is divided into segments corresponding to themes such as "work", "spirit" and "body". Muf were commissioned to design "local".

The commission to design the "local" segment was won through limited competition. The proposal was in a critique of the very idea of centralising debate. muf's "local" was a proposal for a jigsaw of projects borrowed from around the country (and connected to the world) that would explode the confines of the Dome; visiting Greenwich you could travel, for example, to Birmingham and beyond. The web of situations from different locales would explore the premise that "the everyday is amazing" and "that the everyday (can be) made amazing" through inflection. For example, freezing the Thames could connect north to south London. The jigsaw was to hover over an ice rink which penetrated the envelope of the Dome pushing the perimeter wall into the interior and disrupting the perfect circle of the Dome's envelope.

5.03 Purity and Tolerance, The Architecture Foundation, 1995.

An experimental environment which explored the perception of the gallery as a neutral environment. A highly reflective white latex ceiling was stretched across the ceiling and filled with water. The bulge distorted the appearance of the gallery and seemed to be about to burst and ruin the white space.

The diverse practices of art and architecture meant that when we first worked together, we argued about the difference between representing an absent experience – as in making drawings and models, and creating an immediate immersive experience, that was itself – as in much current art practice. This difference came to the fore during our first conversation about *Purity and Tolerance*, the title of an exhibition we were asked to make of our work at London's Architecture Foundation. What should we represent? What ideas should we represent?

Explicitly Katherine Clarke's influence led to us making a space that *was* the idea. The principle that the making of the thing (from start to finish) embodies an idea is now fundamental to our practice.

> *KC:*   In the Walsall Art Gallery competition proposal our intention was to keep
> as much of the budget in Walsall by having a "Made In ..." strategy where

everything was literally made in Walsall. The Stoke-on-Trent project, for a public space with ceramic patterned benches, could literally only have been made using the skills and talents of that city. We are now aware that making things entails diverse strategies: and also that making strategies requires, at the moment a physically *made* transformation, an exemplar. So rather than representation, the issue for us now is: what can things do?

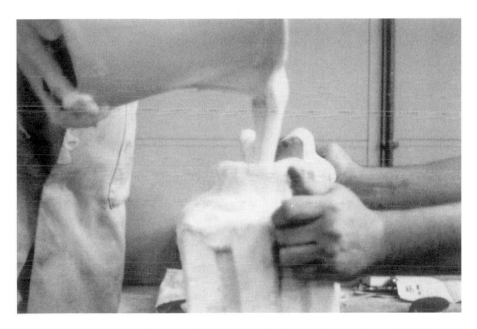

5.04 Pleasure Garden of the Utilities, A Public Art Project for Hanley, Stoke-on-Trent, 1997/1999.

These could be the hands of the person who made the plate you ate your dinner from. Two ceramic patterned benches have been made in collaboration with the fire clay production team at Armitage Shanks in Stoke. These will become part of the street landscape, alongside silver birch trees, white roses and a video. The constellation of these pieces will make a social space of repose shared between the activities of shopping and going out at night.

LF: At Stoke a tension emerged over where collaboration stops and starts. Autonomy was a key question, both amongst the partners, and the fabricators of a project, and also the question of how, or whether, a project might be autonomously situated. So the project has been designed for a space, and also for the making of an object and for the making of a work.

KC: The proposal was that the making of an object would effectively be consultative research. By working in a local factory we learned loads about the place: it gave us a precision and allowed us to work reciprocally, refine the proposal, dissolved the gap between the representation of the idea in the drawing and the idea embodied. The project was in Hanley, designated the centre of the Five Towns, famous for their potteries in Central England. The proposal was to make a social place from a piece of the street. The brief from the local authority asked for a hinged barrier because they wanted to stop ram-raiding: art's really good at stopping ram-raiding. Gradually through talking to the commissioner the brief became less over-determined: there hadn't in fact been any ram-raiding for four years. Art could only be legitimised if it was utilitarian, but in the course of the project they got the confidence to realise that they could commission something and just let it be art.

5.05 Pleasure Garden of the Utilities, A Public Art Project for Hanley, Stoke-on-Trent, 1997/1999.

I was intrigued when I went to Stoke that the evidence of all that industry beavering away is really invisible: the person you sit next to on the bus, their hands could have been the hands that made the plate that you ate your dinner off. We wanted to give a visibility to the thing that people spent all their time doing. We spent three weeks with factory workers making the plaster form for the bench. It was amazing working beside them because they were deeply skilled. One worker involved is going to retire in three years time and has spent his whole life refining this one process: they have an apprenticeship of about ten years. And we were doing it for three weeks. They were deeply supportive of what we were doing, without having any idea about what it was: gradually working with them, they came to understand what the project was and where it was going. People would come into the modelling shop, and everyone would start to claim the project as theirs, saying "I'll be able to say, I made that". So the way the benches were made in a local factory has in itself made a whole set of relationships within a larger, public collaboration: the factory workers are also the people who will sit on the bench. This gave the work a sense of embeddedness which worked in a similar way on our project in Southwark.

5.06 Southwark Street, London, 1 km of Urban Improvement for Southwark Council, 1996/2000.

"As if the foreshore of the Thames had turned inland." A five-point strategy developed in consultation was tested in a pilot project before full implementation for the year 2000. The design makes more space for the simple pleasure of walking to and from work or school. As you walk along the street, parallel panels of pavement flex and expand making a shared ground for the interiors of buildings to spill out onto. Street furniture alters to accommodate different situations, trees and planting drift in from side streets as green windows and directional signs are embedded in the ground.

LF: A continuing conversation has been how to articulate that you value the process of refining and making a proposal quite often as a thing in itself. Sometimes the object of the brief, as described by the client is a by-product rather than end product of that process of refining and making.

At Southwark Street in South London, another project to expand public space involved acknowledgement that you were working in a social structure rather than just a physical built structure.

JB: The process of making the object becomes for us a way of positively engaging with that social structure. At Southwark this worked in an ad hoc way to begin with: Katherine Clarke's film of *100 Desires for Southwark Street* made the diverse points of view of those living and working there become quite explicit. From the initial observations it felt like there weren't many spaces for children, so we decided to continue the consultation with them, as they don't get to vote or have a voice during the official consultation period.

We struggled with how this could work. We replaced their teacher on Friday morning; they all behaved really badly during the Friday afternoon and got detentions (they were eight-year-olds). We told them about what we were doing and what other people do: Katherine showed them a lot of art.

They wanted a fun-fair and the Spice Girls to come to Southwark Street. The children designed environments, paving slabs and so on for these things to happen – a paving slab for Posh Spice to stand on. In the end we incorporated a space for a miniature Posh Spice on the bench.

LF: Formal negotiations took place with the building owner: getting him to make changes in his design to move the vehicle entries of his new development and make them one so that there would be more pavement to spill out onto. It was a bit like the way tramps made marks on people's gates: the children were leaving a tag for other children who might visit the place. Another element in the making of this place was the difficulty of building on the site of someone else who was also a player in Katherine's *100 Desires* video.

JB: In the same way that Posh Spice got a tag, he got a mat of concrete for a potential cafe in the forecourt, cut into the asphalt, an inflection of an internal cafe.

5.07

LF: In making this project called *Shared Ground*, we were trying to share that process of what the ground should be as much as possible.

KC: This sharing of how the ground was made allowed the children we worked with to have privileged knowledge: they knew about the project first and could claim ownership of it – in a similar way to Stoke.

JB: This became a method of making work. Research which could be described as "site investigation" includes who's there – it identifies who the partners are, who the expanded client is, and who you are then in dialogue with. Having identified that the client is more than the chief officer of the council, the question is how do you then continue the dialogue with that expanded client? The reasons for this approach shift between a search for an accuracy of the proposal, and expediency: if people know what you are doing you encounter less hostility – Katherine Clarke's film exposed that much hostility came from not knowing what was planned for the place.

LF: The process at Southwark and Stoke was most important in dispelling *muf*'s anxieties about putting something on the streets; we felt a lot of people knew us but it was only 30 children at Southwark out of the entire population, and only 20 at Stoke. The time spent in this intensive way gives a confidence and an *aide memoire* to remind one, constantly, who the client is.

KC: I felt it was more than that: they become your ambassadors. But does it
mean in the case of all our work, we would have made it pink because
someone said make it pink?

JB: How is public work apprehended anyway? Is it like choosing the new
sofa for a private client's apartment?

KC: Are we trying to offer the client new clothes or tell them they already
look really nice?

LF: Isn't it more about a two-way exposure and a constant awareness on our
part that research is not separated from a proposal because the
research is ongoing, allowing the proposal to be refined.

KC: Consultation is the wrong word: the proposal is made in the sense of
refined, but it is not actually created through the conversation. The
consultation we do is not to design the object.

5.08 Scratton Farm A13 Artscape, The London Borough of Barking and Dagenham, 1998.

*At a barbecue during the 1998 football World Cup we invited people living in Scratton
Farm who were not formally represented to record their experience of living there.
Some commented on the longevity of people who live overlooking the A13, while children described the places they played on the wild edges of the estate. A video played
back and magnified these different recollections.*

JB: The Southwark children were effectively like witnesses to that making: so instead of fantasy you have some real idea about what the project might be like from someone else's point of view.

LF: There is in any case a restraint in our work for the public realm. While there are moments that could be described as exuberant, whether it is the cutting in of the sofa into the bench in Southwark Street, the presence of the child or the willow pattern ceramic on the bench in Stoke – it's almost like if you don't like it you can always look somewhere else.

LF: In Southwark Street if you raise your chin you can't see the project, because everything is pressed into the ground.

5.09 The Museum of Woman's Art, London, 1994.

The Museum of Woman's Art, London, aims to make historic and contemporary work by women artists more visible and to lift work from the basements of the National Collections. The paradox of opening up a hidden cannon only to enclose it again in another institution was inherent in this project. The design proposal was for a site of exhibition which would remain in a constant state of flux: through adjacencies between the historic and the contemporary, art and everyday life and the building and its neighbourhood.

LF: Another key theme, the expansion of public space, emerged in our very first project together, for a proposed Museum of Woman's Art, where the perimeter was pushed and nudged so as to include the public realm. The project also held a set of notions of our belief in the relationship of art to everyday life.

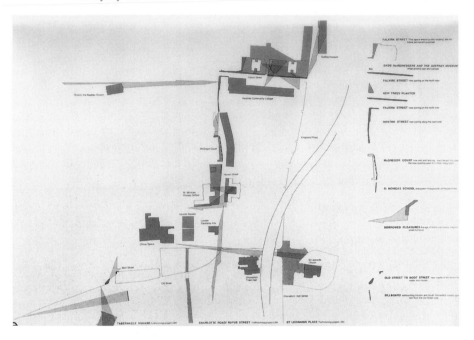

5.10 Borrowed Pleasure, The London Borough of Hackney, 1997/9.

We commissioned six independent artists to make work to surface the culture of Hoxton and South Shoreditch. Meanwhile we were also awarded a commission by Hackney Council to guide the tourist across this territory. In the emerging dialogue about what art can do, the brief for an interpretation board and sculpted flagstones transformed into a digital map and a series of physical interventions in the existing infrastructure, each one serving the resident population and the visitor as a borrowed pleasure.

This was expanded in a project for the London borough of Hackney. We were asked to look at a strategy for public art in public space. The diagram of the visitors' cone of vision explicitly takes in more than we had been asked to look at. We offered back that image as a proposal, giving us more to look an that just the public highway, looking at an expanded public realm.

The digital map resulted in urban strategies for a number of places, including Hackney.

> *JB:* The Millennium Dome is a sad story in a way, but it has given us a clear vision of what we will and won't do.
>
> *KC:* There was not much Shared Ground in the *New Millennium Experience Co.* We now only work with people who share something, who we get on with.
>
> *LF:* We won the project on an initial proposal to spend the money on "locals" outside the Dome and simply bring back a jigsaw of pieces to form the new local inside the Dome. We got the impression the *New Millennium Experience Company* thought this was all very well, but now we had got the commission, couldn't we bring out "some project we had made earlier".

We would arrive at client meetings saying, "We have been asking what the Dome's for?" to be met with "Never mind what it's for: will the Sun reader understand it?" There was no room for conversation. And so we went looking for that conversation elsewhere. That led us to Matthew Pike, the director of the Scarman Trust. The *Can Do* initiative seemed to coincide with our project for the Dome's "local". The jigsaw inside the Dome which we called *The Everyday Made Amazing* was to come from projects throughout the country initiated by the Trust. After our sacking we made a commitment to carry on working with the Trust regardless, unpaid. We have now worked on three pilot projects in Birmingham.

5.11 Recreation Ground, Shard End, Birmingham, Daniel Rogan and The Scarman Trust, 1998.

> *a.* There always seem to be problems that never get sorted out. So I figured that to try and solve one of the problems, that when kids are bored and not doing something, they, usually always end up doing something dangerous or against the law.
> *Daniel Rogan.*

b.   *Youth Network. A cycle route links existing public buildings and unofficial spaces for hanging out, connecting across a landscape formally designated for recreation. The network is always open unlocking partial access to buildings out of hours.*

c.   *Constantly shifting mobile amenities allow different uses to occur in different places at different times.*

5.12

5.13

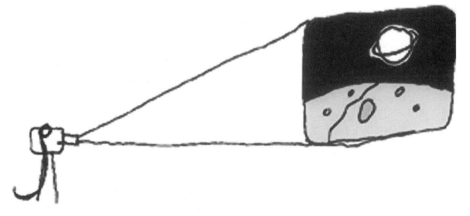

5.14

5.15

LF: *Can Do* starts with a freephone number. The population of Britain, region by region, is asked to respond to three questions: what's going on, what could happen and what will you, the person telephoning, do about it? Working together, we went tentatively. The question was what can the professional, the architect or artist bring, if anything to this situation?

JB: Daniel Rogan is twenty-one, living with his girlfriend and two small children. He can remember his own time hanging out on the streets, and has a younger brother in Borstal. He is worried about what will happen in the future, if his brother continues to be on the streets in the way he has been in the past. He wanted to do something: he didn't know how. We started talking to him, and mapped what he saw as the territory of the young people living in that area.

Daniel took films of the areas he knew and the areas he walked around and sent them back to us. We started looking into his question of there being nothing to do in Shard End. There were two territories: unofficial and official. We made an inventory and assessment of all the public buildings which were supposed to serve local young people but which they didn't use. From his hints we talked to other people and some girls in secondary schools.

The sense was of activity going on in houses: making music and hanging out at home and watching videos, in contrast with all these empty activity clubs and youth clubs that usually weren't open. The young men's territorialising of the street also affected the girls as it meant they could only stay at home. Huge areas of green space had been designated recreation ground just after the war. There were ten public buildings including five schools, all closed at 5 o'clock.

The proposal was not an actual design but more *how* you might do something, to hold the different desires for a young territory. We proposed connections between all the public buildings, shifting the clock and making things open at unconventional hours and a mobile youth club with different sites at different times by different groups: parents and toddlers, youth club, and so on.

Daniel was ambivalent about doing anything, because he is thought of as a bit of a dreamer; he felt if he launched himself into this thing he would have no support. But when he came to the exhibition of the *Can Do* projects he was enthused.

> LF: And as a research project this experience has fed into the methodology
>   of the *Can Do* project. We now know the first thing you have to do is
>   map the resources and have a set of telephone numbers so that when
>   you meet the Daniels there isn't the expectation that they will have to go
>   it alone. *Can Do* is about shifting power. It gives people the confidence
>   of the upper middle classes, that you can change things. It's a question
>   of which six telephone calls you make. To begin to move things. The
>   reciprocity is that the limits of our London EC1 existence are expanded.

A single mother with two children under five living on an estate next to public housing rang the *Can Do* line: there were no child play facilities within three miles. The site is along the M6 motorway – there is sound pollution, overhead pylons, electro-magnetic radiation, a contaminated river and strange pieces of open land.

Her brief to us was to help her make a playground there, she had a petition of 300 names. We were aware of the pitfalls of architects and planners moving cornflake packets around a model. How much things cost and how much it would take to do something are the underlying considerations. Our role was two-fold: a fluency as professionals to talk to those in authority in their other language: but also to find a way to share the knowledge of using Spons building price index.

As she was match funded, £2000 for £2000, the councils initial response to "Can there be a playground?", was "No", because playgrounds cost £70 000. In

Play Strip, Bromford, Birmingham, Elaine Bill and The Scarman Trust, 1998.

5.16 Sometimes you need to get out of the house so the children can play and you can meet other people. Elaine Bill.

5.17 How much playground do you get for £4000?

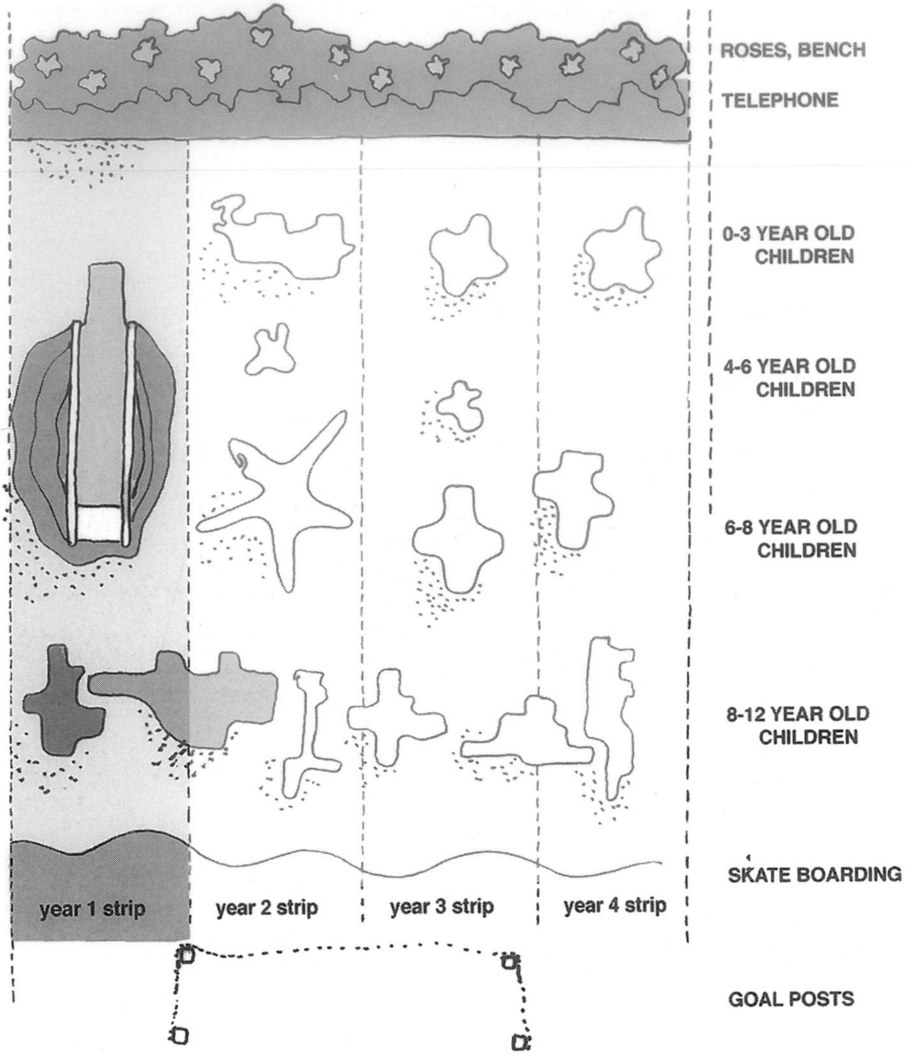

ROSES, BENCH

TELEPHONE

0-3 YEAR OLD
CHILDREN

4-6 YEAR OLD
CHILDREN

6-8 YEAR OLD
CHILDREN

8-12 YEAR OLD
CHILDREN

SKATE BOARDING

year 1 strip year 2 strip year 3 strip year 4 strip

GOAL POSTS

5.18 Five year plan.

response, the question "How much playground can you get for £2000" became overtly stated by making a drawing of the playground in £2000 strips. That drawing then became a proposal for a playground, built incrementally, gradually growing, like not opening all your presents at once on Christmas Day. You get an element of ownership and testing of success before the next strip is bought.

We took this to a member of Birmingham's chief executive. There was an enjoyment of how a micro-example could be a model for macro-policy. So a modular buying-in of public space, or the improvement of public space in place of the tabular rasa approach, meant that transformation emerged as a possible general strategy. An audit of existing resources often only requires a sleight of hand to turn it into a proposal.

Law, Leisure and Learning, Handsworth, Birmingham, L, L & L and The Scarman Trust, 1998.

5.19 Never question it, just carry on doing it. On this particular one: Law, Leisure and Learning, he knew it would need a lot of dedicated people. So he sent them along one by one until we built up a good strong team.

John Holcroft.

KC: *Law, Learning and Leisure* is an amalgam of people who have taken over a burnt-out factory in Handsworth, with a plan to turn it into a resource centre for the local community. The services that they offer generate revenue to support the building: an economically autonomous enterprise.

5.19 Employ, Trim, Rent.

It is particularly interesting that all the people involved in the project have been marginalised in some way: they had either been in prison, or mentally ill. Through friendship and pooling of their vision they had supported one another to give back to themselves a sense of autonomy and power in starting to operate a small business.

5.20 First projection. Handsworth.

There is a creche, there is a boxing club, there is an arts and crafts room: a 24-hour restaurant serving ethnic food, shifting round-the-clock English breakfast and Caribbean in the middle of the night.

They had a dislocated relationship with authority: in one sense they totally fitted the bill, but they were too maverick, and outside the norm.

The normal way of doing things is to do a business plan and a feasibility study before you start. But they had rented the building: the skills were available to them to get on with renovating the building immediately. They had installed a perfect sauna in working order, but there was no roof on half of the building, and leaks in the roof that did exist.

LF: Depending on your description of this project it is either chaotic or
      extremely rigorous and pragmatic. It could become a model for
      regeneration projects. The first thing you to do is not dig foundations or
      make a business plan but install a sauna because it raises the stakes: it
      makes concrete and explicit what sort of place this is going to be. The

5.21 Next projection. Birmingham, Council House.

donated boxing ring already brings in revenue because they can rent it
out: the revenue allows the next thing to happen.

Our role here is:

1   give value to the project and allow it to be disseminated and
2   to amplify the presence and importance of this project to Central Birming-
        ham.

KC: It's not necessarily important to make a project other than a proposal for
          a voice and an exemplary status. In order to get in the mainstream you
          do not have to be like the mainstream. The mainstream is big enough to
          contain both.
KC: Not everybody likes what we do. That isn't necessarily the point. It isn't
          that if you follow all the steps in the right way you end up making the
          perfect project. Through making the work you realise that can't happen.
          However much you seek to include precision, in the end we
          acknowledge you are only refining a precision in relation to your own
          authorship.

So defined by our own practice today, both art and architecture practice are fluid and soft: more it is one's ambition which defines what it means to be an artist or an architect. Together we have extended our own individual remits as practitioners.

Moving

Chapter 6

Open transmission
Krzysztof Wodiczko

The city operates as a monumental stage and a script in the theatre of our way of life, perpetuating our preconceived and outdated notions of identity and community, preserving the way we relate to each other, the way we perceive others and ourselves. An intense presence of historic monuments, advertising, communication media and urban events merge with our own daily personal performance into one uniform aesthetic practice dangerously securing the continuity of "our" culture. Media art, performance art, performative design: they must interfere with these everyday aesthetics if they wish to contribute ethically to a democratic process.

6.01 Alien Staff, first variant, initial test (Xenobacul) Barcelona, 1992. Photo Raimon Ramis/Fundació Tàpies.

6.02 Alien Staff, in use, Warsaw, 1995. Photo Miroslaw Stelmach.

They must interrupt the continuity of existing social relations and perceptions well entrenched in the theatre of the city. Such arts, using the words of Simon Critchley in *Ethics of Deconstruction*, should "interrupt the *polis* in the name of what it excludes and marginalises". To preserve democracy one must challenge it; one must challenge its symmetry with an asymmetry of ethical responsibility.

The issue of sharing a permanent presence with other people has already been raised here. Permanent presence, or the presence of the other, suggests establishing some kind of communication with another party in order to cross barriers, walls, distances; or breaking down the alienation or estrangement between two different groups. Yet there has not been much said about the actual world in which we live. It would be a great delusion to assume everyone is in an equal position to share, to open up towards the other, to communicate his or her own presence and existence, to learn from somebody else's experience and to accept the presence of the other. This is definitely not the case today, in an era which has been called by the United Nations the "migration era" – an era of international

6.03 Alien Staff, in use, New York, 1993. Courtesy Gallery Lelong, New York.

6.04 Mouthpiece, three variants, Interrogative Design Group MIT, 1995.

xenophobia or a fear of the other. This is also an era of uneven social relations affected by uneven urban development; an era of urban struggles, of survival through resistance as in the situation of the homeless or of street children born into poverty, hopelessness, violence; or of people who live with HIV infection, and many other marginalized and alienated individual beings, groups and populations. These people are definitely not in a position to share or even make their experience publicly known.

If we are talking about technology then we must also think about communications technology. What is the position of communications technologies in the troubled communications breakdown that we are experiencing today? If we are so divided, then what is the meaning of an interactive situation between me and somebody else in order to work together, communicate or share things? If new forms of alienation are emerging today, forms that are yet to be discovered and studied, that's where I see the relation between ethics and aesthetics and technology. The more clearly I see it the more dissatisfied I am with my own work, which definitely still needs to absorb a lot of issues. I realize how behind I am in terms of the technological options we have, and the great possibilities that are there. When I speak with my colleagues in the Media Lab at MIT, I realize how late I came into the field of technology. There is already a new generation of people (especially undergraduate students) who are much better equipped at programming than are graduates or researchers. There is an incredible gap between those opportunities and the new responsibilities that they bring. It is in this situation that I am trying to present my work, which will perhaps inspire younger people to push it much further. I am trying to catch up with them; and they are hopefully trying to catch up with me in this area of art, of technological ethics, an ethics of cyborgs, an ethics of interactive environments and so on.

This photograph was taken by a photographer trying to grasp exactly the problems that are at the centre of my work as a designer – which is how to confront the communication gap, and the absence of, or the need for, something in-between; for example, between the couple on the right-hand side and the person on the left-hand side.

Our strangeness is a strangely familiar secret, an uncanny condition which, when kept in the ideological cave of our subjectivity, can explode against the presence of the actual stranger. For those in transit, the state of being a stranger accumulates as an experience with no form, language, expression, or rights to be communicated. It thus becomes a dangerous psychic symptom as Julia Kristeva has called the 'condition of the migrant'. Between the speechless pain and despair of the actual stranger, and the repressed fear of one's own strangeness (see in the couple on the right), lies the real frontier to be challenged. Can art operate as a revelatory, expressive and interrogative passage to such a frontier? Can it be an inspiration of, a provocation to and an opening act for a new form of communication, a new form for a non-xenophobic community? Can it provide an iconic object, a symbolic environment, an interface, with which to create or design such a reconstructive psychocultural project? Well, it is clear that the person on the left is not equipped to deal with this framing, colonizing, intimidating gaze. Nor is he in any position even to accept his own experience of crossing, trespassing and all the process of ethical and political survival, of living through it all and opening it up to find the form and the language, and to present it, expose it, announce it to this couple on the right, who obviously are not open to hear it.

So some equipment, some "thing" in between him and himself is needed, first as a kind of psychological object, a new form of what D.W. Winnicot might call a "transitional object" – an object that will allow him to play and achieve a distance, perhaps even an ironic distance, from the painful and impossible experience, in order to stand behind or next to his own experience and somehow open it to the couple. The couple need the object as well. For they cannot confront the presence of a stranger any more than they can confront their own strangeness, which is well repressed and hidden in their unconscious. They would prefer to expel the

6.05 The Stranger.

6.06 Alien Staff, New York, 1993.

6.07 Alien Staff, two variants in use, Stockholm, 1994. Courtesy Gallery Lelong, New York.

stranger, rather than accept him and thereby recognize their own strangeness. If, however, there was some kind of strange object between this person and them, they would focus on the strangeness of the object first, somehow putting aside for a moment the presence of a stranger. Perhaps in this intermediate moment, through this intermediate object, they might more easily come to terms with some kind of story or story-telling, some kind of performative experience, some kind of artifice, something artificial enough for them to accept the reality in a step-by-step way. I think that's what Freud and Kristeva meant when they were hoping for an artifice to help people come to terms with "uncanny" strangeness. Of course they would want to establish a playful distance from their own fears through an artefact. That object does not yet exist; or rather, I have not yet managed to construct one successfully. I only attempted to do so and this is an experiment which probably will last quite a long time.

6.08 Alien Staff, three variants (1992, 1993, 1994), Stockholm, 1994. Courtesy Gallery Lelong, New York.

Such an experiment is a risk worth taking. The city is worth nothing if it is not open to strangers or the estranged. Technology or design is worth nothing if it cannot create such an opening. Each time the experience of a stranger is understood and heard, each time such acts occur, the city wakes up and comes back to life. It brings back hope for all of us if the city is a place of hope for the stranger. To heal one estranged speechless soul in the city is to heal the entire city. My role is to contribute to a therapy for the city and for its speechless actors. The instruments that I design are an attempt to do this. My interests in psychology and technology merge as they do at MIT; but somehow social ethics is not yet a powerful component in this merger. At MIT my role is to bring this component as a part of my art and my design.

My first experiment was a very simple attempt to reactualize so-called "primitive" technology. A walking stick, the ancient technology of the transient, the mes-

6.09 Alien Staff, containers with "relics", Paris, 1993. Courtesy Gallery Gabriele Maubrie, Paris.

senger, a migrant or a prophet – a staff with specially-designed code of inter-changeable carvings – could become a symbolic inscription for migratory experience. For example, being deported (expelled from a new country) three times would be articulated through three forms attached to the staff; or if someone spent one year in transitional camps, or someone worked illegally for a year or two, those things could be carved or sculpted on the staff. Of course that idea needed to be abandoned very quickly since all of the Departments of Immigration – which are *de facto* Departments of Anti-Immigration – would have learned very quickly about this "secret" code, and no immigrant would risk using such a walking stick openly.

At the top of this walking stick, called the Alien Staff, there was a video monitor and a loudspeaker which would represent the speaking face and the voice of the stranger. Using this walking speech-act instrument, a stranger, a story-teller, would feel he or she was perceived as a respectful and articulate actor in today's urban landscape. In this way the stranger could be reinforced by his or her "porte-parole", as a companion, a confidant. There would now be two of them: the stranger as a character and as an actor. The prerecorded and well-edited speech – the story-telling – could be broadcast with the disturbing, comically disturbing presence and speech of the actual person who recorded it. The relation between the stranger, his or her media image and anybody on the street – the interlocutors – would pos-sibly create a complicated discourse in which the stranger could disagree with what was prerecorded, because every time the story-teller speaks, the story would be dif-ferent. The interlocutor could then ask questions related to the lower part of the Alien Staff – the history of displacement inscribed there – and the third person would come and start responding to the discourse with larger questions, question-ing the questions, questioning the discourse and speaking on behalf of "we" rather than only "me" and the "other". This would create a political, critical and ethical field where both the interlocutor and the stranger, by referring to what was prerecorded and what was broadcast, could actually take up an external and critical position to it.

At the next stage of the experiment, I realized that I needed to replace the carvings of the lower part of the Alien Staff with interchangeable transparent con-tainers: containers for sacred relics, important documents, objects of historical value for the stranger. The stranger is treated, and at best tolerated, as someone who does not have a history and must use story-telling, magic, song and other forms of performance and entertainment to insert his or her own history into the official culture; to propose himself or herself as a history. The issue is, what kind of history? The history of the time *before* crossing the border, or the history of the time *after* crossing the border – and I am emphasizing the history after one has crossed the border – that is, the history of the entire population, society or nation. This history is a performative kind of story that will eventually be distorted and

6.10 Alien Staff, containers with "relics", 1993, Paris. Courtesy Gallery Lelong, New York.

absorbed by the grand national mythology and the city's monumental narrative, only to be challenged again later by another stranger.

The recollection of past experience infused in the present in part creates a completely new history of the present, a critical history of the present. If I go through all the miseries of the past five or ten years, I must reuse them to imagine that this is going to continue; that the future is going to perpetuate that misery for myself and for my children. Therefore I – an immigrant and a stranger – am announcing what is wrong today. My Utopia is based on a refusal to accept the place in which I am – a new concept of "no place" – as Utopia. Utopia – that is a place that is unacceptable; and the hope that is born from this unacceptable experience is extrapolated into the future as another side of this Utopia – so that the future will not repeat the injustices and catastrophes of the present and of the past. This concept of recollection, of remembrance, of critical reactualization and critical history, is located somewhere in between Friedrich Nietzsche and Walter Benjamin. According to Stephan Moses, Benjamin suggested that the process of progress should be replaced by the process of remembrance and recollection. His Utopia was functioning as the hope lived by the mode of the present, rather than

6.11 Alien Staff, in use, Paris, 1993. Courtesy Gallery Gabriele Maubrie, Paris.

as a projection of an ultimate social solution. I understand all immigrants as prophets, as prophetic peoples who through their disturbing performance and rec- ollection of their present experience are each day announcing a better world for all of us. "The Messiah interrupts history", says Benjamin.

These are the relics of a Polish exile living in Brooklyn who went through hell working day and night without documents and as a slave, as a domestic labourer, for a woman, the oppressor. The exile had no choice, terrorized to the point where she entertained the idea of committing suicide, or giving up the job and going back to Poland, all of which were equally impossible solutions for her. She survived this but she kept it to herself or to be precise, to her unconscious. She never really spoke about all of this with anybody. When I suggested this instrument to her she rejected the possibility of "using it" on the spot. Mentally she needed "to destroy" this instrument – the Alien Staff – in order later to accept it step by step and perhaps In the end even to become addicted to it. At first it was a perplexed reac- tion on her part. She rejected this project and at the same time she was allured by the possibility of exposing the history of her experience to a world ignorant of it.

6.12 Alien Staff, immigrant relics in the process of selection, New York, 1993. Courtesy Gallery Lelong, New York.

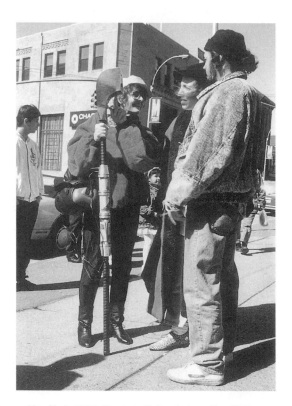

6.13 Alien Staff in use, New York, 1993. Courtesy Gallery Lelong, New York.

She also felt a need to share this with somebody, as well as with herself and even with her own consciousness. The process of video recording – of recalling details, trying to find documents and other relics, editing the story, translating very often from one language to another, speaking in two languages to the video camera – finally began. The same stories are different when spoken in different languages and on different days. To put it together, to concretize it in some synthetic way, is also to release the incredible load of speechless pain and responsibility for carrying all of this inside as a secret, as a uselessly hidden testimony to truth. Once the story is next to her, her strangeness is estranged from her in a healthy way; she sees and hears it now at a distance. She can know now that her anger and aliena-tion are contained there (the psychological container is important here) and now she can be open. She can be very polite, she can negotiate between herself, her prerecorded double, the other person and the third person. She can also reserve her right to disagree with her double – her Alien Staff – at any time. As one rabbin-ical scholar said: "The one who believes the story is a fool but the one who denies the story is a wicked non-believer."

6.14 Alien Staff in use, Stockholm, 1994. Courtesy Gallery Lelong, New York.

It is a myth that immigrants can understand each other. In fact there is a world of disagreement and antagonism between them as much as there is a world of disagreement and antagonism inside of each immigrant. The boundaries and demilitarized zones inside the mind of the migrant are in the process of shifting; they are unstable, so in a way the possibility of internal conflict is as close as the possibility of external conflict among the different ethnic groups, and of course between each of them as individuals and the rest of society as well. This is why I am thinking that the Alien Staff can be expanded and absorb more contemporary technology, allowing strangers – their "operators" – to communicate with each other electronically when they "broadcast" and speak. At the same time they could provide a communication service as social aid for the larger immigrant population and everybody else, assuming that, for example, some of the operators, immigrants, would become agents, "angels" *("l'ange' ou "l'agent")* or messengers who could then visit or explore different areas of the city where immigrants live. Such "angels" would not only open up their own experience using the Alien Staff but also establish a trust – play and trust are interconnected according to Winnicot – to such a point that they could then transmit back and forth questions and advice; the questions would usually be legal ones, but could also be ethical ones to the communication base (the xenological base run by xenologists – immigrant experts on displacement), existential philosophers and legal advisers. Such an Alien Staff as a network is probably a very important option since many of the immigrants are not in any psychological, economic and social position to seek help or advice on their own and take advantage of their rights, if they still have any.

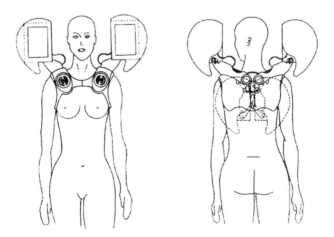

6.15 Aegis, the equipment for strangers, 1998. Courtesy Gallery Lelong, New York.

Alien Staffs were used in Barcelona, Warsaw, Helsinki, Rotterdam, Houston, Brooklyn, Marseilles, Paris – used by many people in many places even though there are only six of them. They can be shared and their containers and video-tapes are interchangeable. Confidence is a very important result of many of the conflicts, once one is prepared to open up all of this within the situation of the studio. A video camera is very patient. But then to accept this is another story. Once all of this is accepted it opens a new possibility: of thinking about one's own identity and participating in an experience and a life that are much richer, much more complex, than is the case for those who never cross the borders. Then the confidence and respect become a motivation for an action, or a speech-act, which is much more critical and demanding or provocative. It might perhaps reach the point (as in this case) where the person is invited to a TV station and appears on the national news. On occasions (and it has already happened twice), immigrants appeared on the official TV screen armed with their personal televisions, with both virtual and actual well-prepared statements, stories and visions.

6.16 Alien Staff in use, Huston, 1992. Courtesy Gallery Lelong, New York.

So those are the three models historically lined up. The next generation of immigrant instruments, called *Mouthpiece* or *Le Porte Parole*, is not for everybody – but only for those who really want to use it. This is not an artifice positioned next to the stranger. This is a cultural prosthesis which can help the stranger him – or herself to become a powerful artifice, perhaps a cyborg. This equipment is to be

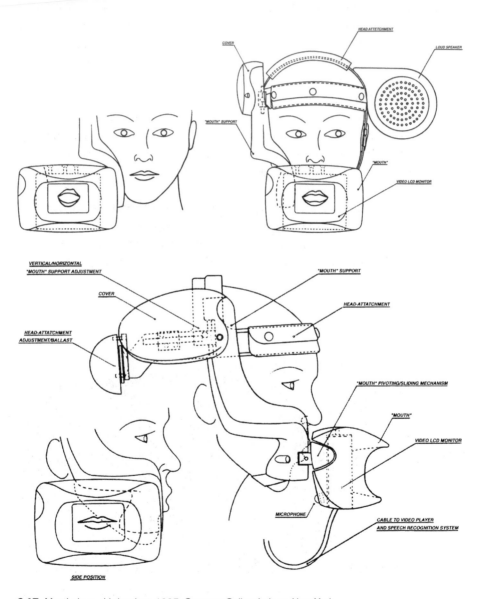

6.17 Mouthpiece, third variant, 1997. Courtesy Gallery Lelong, New York.

used by those who are extremely angry and determined to speak. But also by people that feel more "cyborgian" than others. A "cyborg" is a cybernetic organism, a hybrid of machine and organism – a creature of social reality as well as a creature of fiction. Social reality is linked to social relations, our most important social construction, and to the world of change and technological development where, as Donna Harraway was saying, the "distinction between science fiction and social reality is an optical illusion". On this basis the immigrant is, in fact, partially artificial and partially natural. It is also possible to say that once one becomes or is forced to operate this way, then maybe, as she said, "dehumanisation is so inevitable that we might as well learn to like it". If we can.

Of course the emphasis here is a prosthetic device. A prosthetic device not only is like an additional part or a replacement for a lost body-part, but also empowers or extends the ability of a human or an animal. In this sense the "cyborg" analogy is very close to the experience of migrants, and, as Donna Harraway also suggested, to women and other groups that are marginalized, silenced and oppressed. There is no way back to the "lost land" or "paradise". In the proposed *Mouthpiece* the combination, at the same time, of the deprivation of rights – speech rights – and the reinforcement of speech ability is ironic enough to let us find some kind of analogy to Donna Harraway's concept of the cyborg, which she called an "ironic metaphor". This gag – this loudspeaker like a cyborg – takes irony for granted.

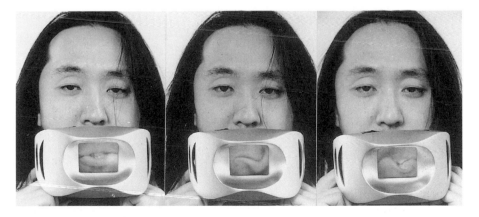

6.18 Mouthpiece, second variant (speech digitally transformed), Interrogative Design Group, MIT, 1996. Courtesy Gallery Lelong, New York.

These are my hopes and my ideas. My design and organizational projections have not begun to materialize yet, but more and more is possible. Right now at MIT we are experimenting with a version of the new Alien Staff that is further developing or creating possibilities for artistic virtuosity. Gesture is of course a very important part of what is happening around this "sacred object". Strangers assume "baroque personalities" according to Kristeva: overemphasizing things, accentuating, full of gestures, in order to compensate for the lack of adequate communication and abilities. And "locals" seem to be immobile, completely opposite, making no attempt even to exchange a gesture. As the stranger becomes a non-stranger, the non-stranger must become the stranger, and somewhere half-way a new communication, a new community, is possible. Coming back to the new version of Alien Staff the antenna here is probably not necessary but is an "ambient" and important symbol of the possibility of a transmission between or among each of the instruments and the base. The larger form of the head of this instrument is something to do with the need to reinforce sound – the large speaker, which can actually be more effective in an urban environment. Also new containers are being tested, so one could show or conceal what is inside: there are two options. But most import-

6.19 Mouthpiece, third variant, Trelaze, 1996. Courtesy Gallery Lelong, New York.

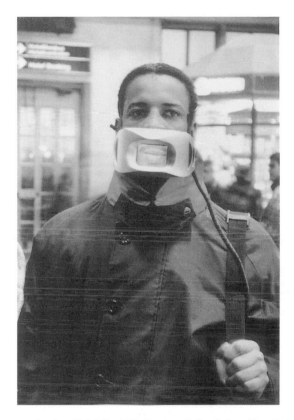

6.20 Mouthpiece, second variant, Helsinki, 1995. Courtesy Gallery Lelong, New York.

antly there are electric sensors being used here. This means that hand gestures towards each container can speed up speech "switching" on the particular story related to particular personal relics. It can modulate in a variety of ways to make it more or less hysterical, comical or strange, depending on the virtuosity that it demands on the part of the stranger – *performative* virtuosity. Those metal components are actually functioning sensors – all of this technology was developed in the 1930s by the Russian inventor Theremin who invented an electronic musical instrument named after him and operated by gestures. The Media Lab at MIT has further developed this system using new minicomputers, programs and micro-chip technology in this and other new instruments to increase performative quality. Story-telling will become new art and new craft. It took many months for Joshua Smith of the Media and Physics Group at MIT to complete the program for this

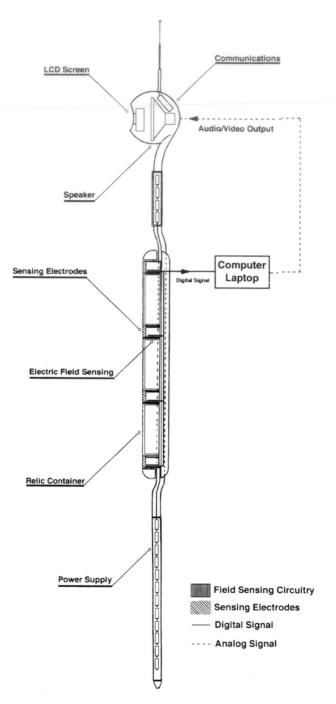

6.21 Alien Staff, gesture responsive variant, Interrogative Design Group and the Media Lab, MIT.

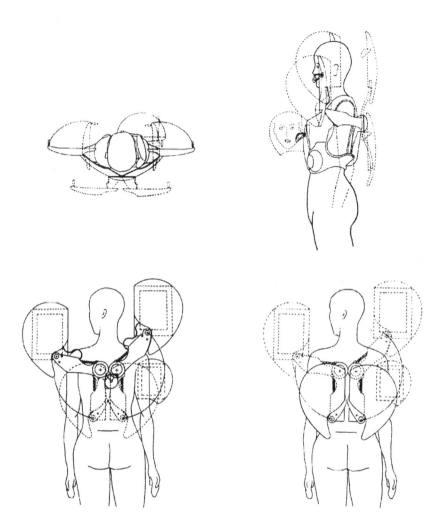

6.22 Aegis, The equipment for strangers, Interrogative Design Group, MIT, 1998.

instrument. I realize only now how long it takes to work with this new technology and new research. Two years is a very short time when it comes to programming and experimenting with new interactive equipment. So I am behind my schedule! But the new instrument, the new Alien Staff responds with its stories and their variations to many gestures already. The Prophet's Prosthesis is coming soon!

Chapter 7

Country dance
Graeme Miller

It's the split second of waking, silver-pink grey rolling on purple-grey dawn. Canary Wharf tower blinks three times before my mind kicks in. It feeds into my unprepared senses with no name. Singular, it is a ladder-moment; the unsupported ladder that will teeter long enough to climb enough rungs to see through the low-level pollution – the mental smog. It is Wittgenstein's ladder – how he describes his momentary and teetering understanding of his own Tractatus. Here it is, but without the Tractatus bit. Dawn. London, England. Real-time and truly happening, but funnily more dreamlike than my dreams. My whirring mechanical dreams.

Because for over a week I have been working deep into the night at a computer, over-riding sleep: adapting my cortex to the system of dragging and dropping, cutting and pasting, stacking and opening folders. Folders within folders, files within folders. Windows in windows have been my window on the world. As the weeks of relentless mousing and staring, caffeine and tannin have gone by, my brain is adapting quickly to this way of thought and instead of sleep, I lie awake and buzz, half-man, half-Mac and flickering images of files and folders dance on my eyelids all night. Here's one . . .

DOGS. click open. DOGS Snappy Yappy. Click. SHIVERY-TOO SMALL. DOGS SLOBBERY-TOO BIG, click DOGS I KNOW. PRINCE click RUN VIDEO foxy coat, expression of patient experience, waving red flag of a tail. Run anecdotes. BITING HIS WAY THROUGH A DOOR. PRINCE IN COURT – Saved by Testimonial from Sheep Murder Death Penalty. Prince Old. Prince has a tumour. Prince is dead. "I love to go a-wandering with Handsome Prince the Dog, He likes a stick, he likes a twig, a branch or a log . . . Epping Forest, about this time of year."

I am remembering the curious sensation of watching an animal watching you – the undeniable strangeness of separate being, separate mammal consciousness – unguarded, uncatalogued reality. It shocks. A kind of dawn.

Clicking down through the layers of doghood is a journey from cliché to subtlety, from stereotype to crass generalisation, through useful bunching, to singular, ineffable experience. The waking apes in the city around me are hard-wired for stereotype and any would-be artist hoping to work to free us from cultural stereotyping must remember this. To function, the infant blur sees a half-open door and a closed one; each makes a different shape, but they are quickly bunched together into a folder. CLICK "doors, windows and apertures". DOORS-hinged, DOORS sliding, revolving . . . out we go into life, into London Town. Past a bloke who has a two-folderish air about him. Click. Me and my Mates. Click. Wogs, queers and Other People. I get the feeling that I fit into his second folder, but I might be wrong and really, must be wrong. Most often I will be more wrong than right even as a twenty-folderish kind of guy, my mind has made these same little bins to cope with the rampant complexity of other things, objects and creatures, but mostly, other people. Clicketty click-click, clicketty click-click, clicketty click click click: the rhythm of the city checking itself out.

Turn right here, down Pearson Street. Friends and neighbours. I know 300 per cent more black people now than I did four years ago. Infinitely more Turks, Vietnamese – exponential. All right? This corner of this City seems to suit purposes I am only just forming. Yeah. Not bad. Singular experiences with and among people in this low-privacy zone, happen daily with a resulting reordering and reshuffling of my people folders that never catches up. And never should it. I know less artists than I did four years ago, but more of just about everyone else. Click ARTIST – Male drunk bastards, YOUNG – Special Glasses – Clubby Clothing, (a local speciality), ESTABLISHED LOFT-LIVING ARTISTS. ARTISTS – Vocational/Confused CLICK male, black polo-neck, middle class/aged/English/white. Oh my God, it's me. A MASS of UNCATALOGUED FILES. Type – Suburban Driven. Kick-started from Mediocrity. Desire to be useful – member – of – village confused with need for attention. Desire to stand apart as a documentarist confused with need to enact dramas of personal melancholia. A WHOLE SPECIES. I am not alone.

THE SOUND OBSERVATORY, Birmingham, 1990. 30 points in the City, in sacred mathematical pattern, inhaled and imported into a space at the centre of the pattern. HEAR THE CITY – an aural equivalent of a high tower – a place of contemplation of reality. REALITY is REALLY HAPPENING. OTHER PEOPLE have CONSCIOUS, SEPARATE LIVES and EXIST. PLACES are REAL. PROFANE COMPLEXITY of LIVES REVEALED in SACRED, ELEVATED FORMALITY.

ARTIST MIDDLE MALE/CLASS/ENGLAND as MAPMAKER . . . *The Desire Paths* 1992 – an A–Z on Stage; three weeks of walking the streets of Birmingham shuffled into a Theatre of Memory. *Feet of Memory, Boots of Nottingham* – a walking map of a day, a city. Seventy people from Nottingham trained in the Art of Memory call up their own streets over one day. The result is set to music and broadcast back into the City. "What am I walking on?" "Glass" "What's that I can smell?" "Pizza". 1994, with my wife Mary Lemley, *Listening Ground, Lost Acres*, A treasure trail of glass, music and words over 100 square miles. Make your own sense of place DO IT YOURSELF – A PSYCHIC ATLAS. HIDDEN CITIES – a dowsed route through the city for a bus trip of live mixed texts and music. *The M11*

Monument – an epitaph to 500 homes removed for a road in constant radio broadcast – a cross-section of intertwining privacies (scuppered after two years of
preparation by lottery funding collapse). Oh well … I like these works I did for
themselves but also for what I hoped was their usefulness AND my useful member
of the villageness. Works of Civil Engineering. Enablers and Reminders. Enabling
an encompassing view in which your own narrative might fit. Reminding that your
narrative takes place in real-time and real place that is too much and too many to
understand, but none the less real. I still think it a useful job – village observatory
maker.

Aloof aloft – the map's perspective. Aloof aloft, the chart-maker of British
now culture has fallen into the map. Click – RUN VIDEO.

I am walking down the road with my son Gabriel. He is eleven years old and
standing at the roadside rocking backwards and forwards with excitement at the
traffic. Other people are soon aware and react visibly.

Clicketty click, staring-glaring, smiling. The summary need to categorise this
strange traffic dancing boy is visible in the extreme. Clicketty SCARY, clicketty-
OTHER, clicketty POOR LITTLE THING. P'leease! Caring for Gabriel, Mary and I
have become the fast-readers of this file management, have learnt, as the grafted-
on sidekicks of this person to deal with misreading, dismissal, and learned to prefer
the benign amusement of uncategorised curiosity to pity of any sort and have
learned to walk tall, speak loud, dress up. It's a kind of fancy dress that as it gets
bolder becomes more invisible that suits this whereabouts where we have fallen
into the map and have adopted tactics to deal with misreading and dismissal for
race, gender, sexuality, whatever. It has taught me that the stereotype can be
adapted as a kind of costume – a sort of Disabled Camp to wear out and about
which allows you to be visible, but protected. As a Carer with Attitude we make a
kind of theatre. Being in control of this whoever you are, makes you an artist.
Which, really, makes everyone an artist. Is that where this is leading? Turn back.

Theatre works, music, surrender to rhythm. Ordinary Ecstasy – the Shaman's
ladder. Ladder Moments teetering with the Gods alongside Pants Down Moments,
struggling with the laundry. DUNGENESS, THE DESERT IN THE GARDEN 1987,
A GIRL SKIPPING 1990. Teetering on the ladder of artist as mediator of spirit
world. Fall to Earth.

I have fallen into the map of the Inner East End where 90 per cent are poor
enough, or newly-enough arrived, or suppressed enough to know how to talk loud
or melt away. I have fallen into the map and turn the corner, "All right?" It's Elsie
next-door who used to danoo in the streets here. Someone would get a piano out
of a house, drag it into the street and they would dance. I didn't know that. Two
doors away from the teenage boys whose booming bass she tolerates, she lives –

the quiet queen of Street Dance Past. The next-door boys are the callers of Street Dance Present. I am the orphaned son of a danceless culture sandwiched between the last flicker of Kneesup and the verbal arts of New Black Britain. But no one actually dances. In Barcelona, they dance. In New York and Washington DC. The dancelessness of my native island worries me. It worried the revivalists, ramblers and socialists who tried to resuscitate a social culture. Suddenly, the small city corners of Old England Town seem to be teetering on the edge of its first steps of a new Country Dance. Right here, an estranged Englander, with my estranged American partner and my strange son I feel more at home than I ever have. There are somehow enough fallow spaces, enough cheap housing, enough council spending to allow a place of complex weave and clash of difference to emerge.

I look back at my work as cartographer, not with regret, but with a change of attitude. Earthbound, faces and buildings demand my response and force my participation. I have come to the party but not sure what as. I look back through this to a clearer and clearer understanding of my Anglo-Saxon culture that has done its colonising with the special and cruel tenacity of farmers gone mad in five continents where a special kind of cunning has allowed it to hold the balance of power to this day. It explains the quiet brutality of the landscape in which I was born and in which I live and the vacuum it has created at its own hearth. As its blood descendant, facing the world, this history streams behind me. A history of disguise – a gift to Native Americans of small-pox infected blankets – disguised; humiliation and suppression as gratitude and protection. It was at the time of Colonial expansion that peasant dances became popular at court – the vernacular was another continent from which to import, and through the seventeenth and eighteenth centuries the vernacular weakened to peter out in the great self-colonising of the Industrial Revolution. Even then a flicker of resilience – clogging on cobbles. The low culture was made high. Aloof. Above. Mapmakers. Map-owners.

The map-owner's son has fallen into the streets that to the clicketty click of trying to categorise its changing each-otherness is in a slow dance of sussing-out. He has arrived in a costume that can only be worked out by others' reactions. It worries me this dancelessness. Dancelessness creates a culture of worried introspection. Of hunger. Of worried, guilty hunger that will acquire, but not surrender to other cultures. Personally, I feel it is easier to stand aside than join in, but that, in itself is an almost stereotypic reaction for my background. I sometimes imagine these streets to be flooded with rhythmic time that generates a compulsive beat so strong that it will force the dance . . . and, I guess, force my participation

Rainy and dim, a car passes pounding bass. The driver is Turkish and twenty. Underfoot a letter on the pavement . . .

Dear Sir/Madam,

I am an artist. How can I best function to disperse cultural stereotypes and . . .?

Dear Artist,

Get a job in T.V. Write Soap. Cast, Produce, wield money, sail the corridors of the stereotype factory, click down through the layers. Alter a single glib multicultural-ism. Give voice. Complexify a single character. Employ tactics. Employ, tactically. People are doing this, have done this and have created change. For the factory in its different departments that publish and transmit on schedules that eternally empty as fast as they fill, does more than anything else to generate mental scenery. Scenery with face-holes and openings for hands and feet. Twentieth Century Stocks. Tools of oppression.

Nights are fair drawing in. T.V. light shines from flat windows on Shoreditch and lights up a shanty town of scenery. Ethnic groups, grannies, market cockneys. It's a video for a pop group. A dance track with a sampled voice. A Black voice. A woman's voice. FREEDOmmmmmm. A deep secret – something passed down since it was wept in the woods and now bought for a £200 session. A dangerous cul-tural dance. Called by a worried and acquisitive master. Who calls the tune? Who pays the piper? Who owns the label? Next single they think it might be cool to have in a Gospel Choir. Two white boys got into sampling at Art School. ARTISTS. p.s. if not TV, get into schools, housing, spaces, places, conversation. Enable your-self or enable someone else. Climb an unsupported ladder. If not step down. If not, just provoke, engage, converse. If not, simply, honestly, participate. Live Pants-Down, Wig-Off. TV off. CLICK.

Common sky scudding overhead. My same fascination for real places happening in time. Boom-mobile a couple of streets off now. It's a wrap. Paddy jackets get into cars. Blue film lighting returns to yellowy streetlight, but the scenery is left to its inhabitants. A nightmare identity prison to struggle out of, an ill-fitting costume, at best – a roof over your head. For there are those who have not. Not even a cliched identity – who are ex-directory. Somalis, recent arrivals, Turkish women, the long-term mentally ill. A stereotype can be a kind of shelter. It can be adapted into a kind of disguise, its parts can be cannibalised, repainted, made into a useful home, a rain-hat or just chopped for firewood. I see people adapt from the raw material of stereotype a public way of being of their own making.

Two teenage girls dressed the-same-but-different are of their own making. It is a dance step of agreed conformity. Self-xerox. A theory. Two teenage girls dressed the same-but-different must occur in every culture at every time. But these two are sat in the stairwell sharing a tin of beer and singing. But singing close harmony. Sweet strong singing girls generating something for nothing, backed in my mind by ghostly piano dragged out onto the street, Elsie, and Joe (who died this year), young and roaring their heads off. Usually someone just pisses in these stairs but this night they are singing. The other day there were five. Soul singing mixed-bag of girls and boys, 15–17, three black, two white, one Turkish. The hollow places have formed a kind of sounding board. Perhaps that might be true of the hollows of this Kingdom. Perhaps that is why the Iraqi postgraduate driving a cab, who had lived in exile in many cities said he felt most comfortable in London – because the politeness and the respectful distance, however insincere, that I imagine to be an unbearable coldness, creates for him a kind of space in which he can operate as someone different. He likes it here. He has a greater freedom. Perhaps it is appropriate that the hollows of the coloniser should become the sounding boards of the colonised. A kind of tissue culture, strangely available to be shaped and formed by new genetic input. I don't mind the idea that we should continue to be blandly tolerant. On the other hand I really wouldn't mind throwing myself into the whirling core of the jig in a sweating frenzy of divine madness. I want to be seventy years old and waist-deep in my own Culture even if it is completely invented. I mean, who invented the Catholic Mass? Someone did and that has worked pretty well for some years now. Skas, Shimmies, Reels and Jigs, Tap and the lost Juba dance are as made up as Funeral Rites, Wedding Services and Soccer Rules were good ideas agreed upon then sort of passed on. I'm 42 and I want to wallow before I get too old. Come on. Someone just make something up.

That's why I love the singers on the stairs. They promise me salvation from an evening of line dancing followed by a meal at a Harvester Restaurant. Even line dancing, with its slightly insipid C&W, despite my worries about Redneck culture, works. It gets people together in real-time and place. It allows people to dance without a partner. It is quick to learn. When I arrived at Nottingham station a posse of Line Dancers were inhabiting the concourse, strangely solemn as if they sensed the ritual in their public flaunt. It has its good points. The Harvester Restaurant doesn't.

Amongst the young here it runs to a Black Beat, Bangra-Muffins, White Wiggers and Turkish Tiggers, Vietnamese, Somalis, all facing a lot of struggle but strangely easier moving from grouping to grouping making their world. Same-but-different kids in their hormone years accidentally inventing a kind of sanity. They are in each others' pockets, pathologically social and filling the void. And yes, it doesn't spread far beyond these few streets and soon disperses in the suburbs and the bland counties beyond, but it almost catches fire. It almost begins ... it could be the beginning of a made-up Country Dance for New England.

A few blocks away now, the artists' zone. Artists in the East End. The Judas Lambs of Property Development who have led the Property Marketeers to the next zone ripe for loft living. It could have been me, but for fateful hardship. The artzone is least aware of its identity in this neck of the woods. I don't believe that it is aware of its strange monoculture 20–40, almost entirely white, clubby, ironic and individual. Aloof, aloft. A loft. A scrap of paper underfoot reads ...

Dear Sir/Madam,

I am an artist. How can I get a solo show before I am 24? Who should I hang out with?

Why is it the Artzone is the least connected and most introspective area? The second biggest Ghetto after The City. I suspect insider-trading is the common factor. Having paced around the perimeter of a world which I questioned little and have spent years away from, I sense a yawning gap between Art and Culture. The City is built on the vernacular of shopping and now, Art is too. Art needs to be built on a thriving culture, not on its own ironic view of its own market place. Culture is the thick layer, Art the thin – the curious and beautiful distillation. The sooner Art gets itself a Culture on which to rest, the sooner it will feel good to be an artist and the less important whether you are one or not. The neighbourhood in which I have fallen is a grade I Site of Cultural interest – a drizzly grey rain forest. It has diluted the tired dominant culture sufficiently to create the right circumstances for rapid evolution. Deliberate housing policy has broken down the racist introspective blocks and freed up the entrenched Cockney from retreat to Rainham to be the complex people they are. Traders. But be careful. Alter one too many elements of the environment and this will die back. One of THE worst changes is to raise the property values and start a chain reaction that hoovers up the cheap housing, workspace, mouseholes and tunnels of semi-legit activity that new culture loves. It may be the voice of envy that I didn't get a lifestyle, but it would make some sense for the Artzone, in the cause of long-term survival for future generations to sell up their spaces at rock-bottom prices with a 1000 year lease, as an act of mass suicide. You could say it was an Artwork. Sell up to the African car repair business that squatted the railway arches behind my flat and was tidied away. Give to families, squatters. Convert converted warehouses into ... warehouses. It might take some persuading, I admit, but I dread seeing this turn into what Bastille became in

Paris after artists moved in because it was interesting and cheap. Where now its former residents inhabit the numbing housing projects beyond the Peripherique.

I cross back into my own manor; over the border down Texaco Way. All right? Yeah pretty good. I feel as if I have stretched this metaphor of dance beyond decency. I've dragged it around these streets for purposes I don't yet understand. I will make for home. I will make the odd map to keep checking out what's what. To remind that there is complex and subtle life out here. To reveal the singular, ineffable bits. And I will trust that a new County Dance can emerge. I remember a short snip of black and white film of the Tarantella danced in a square in Italy. A short middle-aged woman ran around the square where her friends and neighbours had gathered in a circle. Bitten by the spider she was running off the poison. Running closer and closer to the edge of the crowd who held her with a hundred hands as she charged round. She collapsed, in a trance into the waiting arms. Her girl-like run and her surrendering collapse and the tender arms of her neighbours who held her strike a deep chord in me. Up ladder and down. Ordinary Ecstasy. The next day she was back to normality. In the mythology of the dance the dancers allow themselves to be bitten by the tarantula whose poison makes them dance. The dance itself is a kind of antidote for all concerned. Ordinary life generates a kind of poison. Conformity, struggle, oppression, responsibility, grief and desire are everyday toxins. The city generates its need to dance these off. So just as someone made up the Tarantella, just as they made up The Catholic Mass and Tap Dance, I like to think that the necessary dance will inevitably get made and that dance will contain clod hopping, staggering, faltering moments to the Cicketty click-click, clicketty click-click of sussing itself out. A lot of yelling in the night, strains of fiddle and boom mobile, sweet song on the stairs – it will be its own culture of its own invention. There is nothing it need not use, no borrowing or stealing, no mixing of trash and sublime to make its music or its steps. It is a metaphoric dance and music I speak about to make a point. But dance and music are metaphoric. More precisely, they are analogues and equivalents of other forms and shapes. Everything is language and makes its own shapes and squiggles. The landscape throws out rushes of calligraphy and is constantly writing itself. Every moment we are composing ourselves and our world. A social culture is strings of these compositions which are agreed to be shared. Dance and its music, the music and its dance, exist by consent between players and dancers between players and players, dancers and dancers, players and listeners, dancers and onlookers. Layers and layers. Clicketty-click. Dance and music are at the beginning of thought, a kind of dawn, and this may be why they emerge at the beginning of cultural change – the first visible signs. Poison and Antidote are close cousins and part of the dynamics of a culture. I see Britain an antidote culture – that is why it is big on privacy, stasis, definition. Cautious, privet-hedging its bets. It fears poison. It craves poison. It needs the poison to go a bit mad as historically it occasionally does. (10 000 people gathered on a Yorkshire hilltop in the eighteenth Century to hear priests deliver tirades of blasphemy and exhort them to unburden themselves with sin – sin and fornication all to get closer to God). I think the New British Country dance will need a level of craziness to regain its balance. It will exist only by consent, but we are consenting adults, and children, and old people. We are self-stereotyping animals. The same-but-different; the call of biological evolution "The same, the same, the same, different. The same the same the same different", the call of the dance too in a culture of tolerant difference. Hidden in the crates of colonial import is the cultural tarantula that might just release this sad-sack island that might just shake it into life.

Artists are meant to be that bit more resourceful, that bit better at lateral thinking, quicker to react and they could have a useful role to play in the tiny acts of micropolitics that make a difference or the macropolitics that make a difference. They could be great contributors, but I am not sure that the culture that British artists have generated for themselves to live in is very promising. It seems to have forgotten to participate. Its individualism and culture of eternal youth are engineered by people older – my age and older – and cultivates a curious conservatism: a culture of irony and distance; a culture of antidote. It doesn't really matter; this will change. The artworld will change. It's just that right now a few too many people have shown up in the costume of "not dressing up" and won't dance.

Metaphoric dance may turn to real dance. It is in my lifetime that new social dance and music has emerged from a Western City Landscape I love the beauty of its dance, music and attitude. Hip-hop. Serious play. It has the beauty of invention from expedience. Its ability to pull itself into life from its surrounding fragments is due to its timing and angle of approach, its Attitude. It is a Frankenstein's monster of great subtlety allowing the individual free rein by consent. It is social dance lit by individualism. It is a cultural comet that only rarely happens. It happened . . . *is* happening. Its particular stuff may get stolen, adapted, lost or forgotten. Its principle of vitality and proof of the inevitability of culture that can be invented by consent anytime anywhere is what I love and what resonates to the depths of my mid-British boots. It is the same but different incarnate. It says copy me. Copy for the wrong reasons and you will get it wrong; for the right reasons, right.

Revealing

Chapter 8

Speech sites
Alan Read

Walking west from Hammersmith Bridge, along the north bank of the Thames in London, you will encounter unlikely neighbours. Jostling between the paupers' graves beneath Furnival Gardens, the Dove public house and the boat house of the "Men of the Thames" is a single Georgian building of architectural and historic distinction, and a squat two-storey workshop of unprepocessing charm. Here is a speech site where a history of orality reveals something more than oral history, a

8.01 The Coach house and Kelmscott House, 26 Upper Mall, Hammersmith.

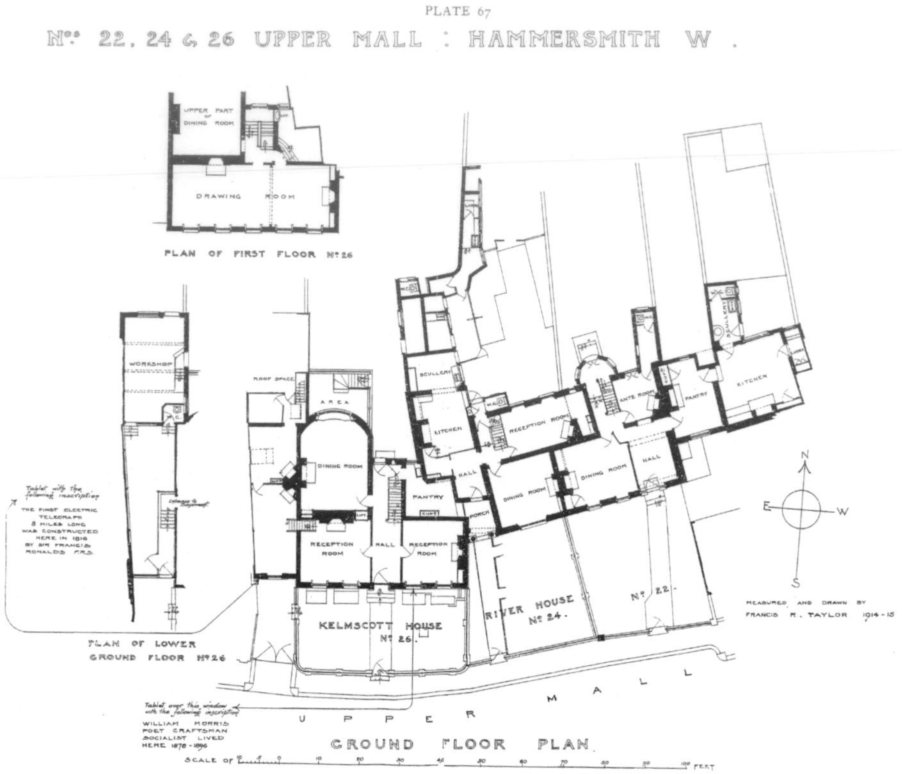

PLATE 67

Nᵒˢ 22, 24 & 26 UPPER MALL : HAMMERSMITH W .

8.02 Plan of Kelmscott House, from London Survey.

location where locution might be amplified in order to discern an ethics of speech for an emerging metropolis.

Kelmscott House greets you first, for that is the sign at the gateway to five storeys of symmetry and elegance that, in the nineteenth century, once housed William Morris and his London-based works. Let us turn away from its neighbour for a moment in order to read between the lines of a stone that records: "William Morris Poet, Craftsman, Socialist lived here 1878–1896". From here Morris, the writer and designer, conducted his interdisciplinary enterprise. His company, known first as "The Firm" and then "Morris and Co" worked in glass, ceramics, wallpaper, typography, and Morris himself moved between poetry and politics informed by a tension between revolutionary concerns and nostalgic romanticism.

Morris was an uneasy but inveterate public speaker, concerned equally with politics, art and the environment. His holistic views on architecture and design, expressed most notably in lectures such as "Gothic Architecture", might not seem too distant in their organicism from some of the concerns of this book, purporting to address questions of architecture, art and the everyday. Morris did after all say: ". . . a work of architecture is a harmonious co-operative work of art, inclusive of all the serious arts . . ."[1] However, in the same speech are serious reservations as to the possible relations such architecture might have with technologies or constructions of the future of any kind. Indeed the absence of what Morris called an "Art of Architecture" signified a ". . . transference of the interest of civilised men from the development of the human and intellectual energies of the race to the development of its mechanical energies."[2]

The plaque which carries the name Kelmscott House is executed in a faux Gothic script and points to a history of the site that would seem to root it in the romantic associations of an outworn socialism, the long lost celebration of craft, and bespoke ideals rooted in a specific location. The plaque simultaneously endorses the stereotypical view of Morris' work as bedded in Gothic eclecticism while announcing in a more pragmatic font the privacy of the site one is facing.

The lease on the house is now, once again, held privately, following acrimonious disputes as to its appropriate use in recent years following the tenancy of the playwright Christopher Hampton and the efforts by Faye Dunaway in the early 1980s to secure it for her London home. But the freehold is still retained by the William Morris Society which works at the reinvention of his potential meanings for the present from a subterranean basement of the house. Since the centenary of

8.03 Kelmscott House, 1892, with men watching Oxford and Cambridge Boat race from roof.

Morris' death in 1996, marked by major exhibitions at the Victoria and Albert Museum in London, that work has redoubled as though to outlast the overriding impression of a man whose work was too thickly spread across a vast array of productive activities of questionable quality.

The script circumscribes a complex reality, more difficult to maintain under the duress of these simplifications, which is the modernity of Morris. His influence extended from architects such as Walter Gropius, and the town planner Lewis Mumford, and their contemporary concerns to the complex juxtapositions of the garden-city movement. Indeed, on arrival in London, Morris had located himself on the edge of its first garden suburb, Bedford Park, in an area that in its title, Turnham Green, underscored the rural margin of this city. His move to Kelmscott House in 1878 coincided with just the moment in the life of this metropolis where the suburban was being enveloped by the urban. Hammersmith had just become connected to the newly-built underground system of subway trains linking the western fringes of the city to its centre. As a writer in works such as *News from Nowhere*, Morris was as preoccupied with this long future towards the city as the medieval past away from it.

News From Nowhere is a utopian work with a contemporary social purpose which through its multi-layered disorientations in time and space project the personal as political in ways reminiscent of a much more contemporary critique. First produced in a serial form for the journal *Commonweal*, the narrative is structured through two river journeys, one East into London, from Hammersmith, the other out of London, West towards Oxford and Morris' other riverside dwelling Kelmscott Manor. In an ironic self-portrait, William Guest, the protagonist of the story, is rowed downriver by Dick the boatman through a sequence of urban villages surrounded by green and space. This is a dream-work where in a post-revolutionary state Marxist processes of history (towards the city) are offset against instinctive needs (towards the country). While the power of roots is never far from Morris' itinerary, there is little real challenge to the power of place; indeed, Morris' own indifference to machinery denies the narrative any technological dimension which might have threatened the bonding power and persistent claims of the priority of place over the vectors of space. It was not that Morris could be described as a Luddite, indeed given the central place of patterning in all his work, and specifically in wallpaper and carpet design, this would be contradictory. But rather that for Morris the role of machinery and technology within the workplace might threaten the relationship between the worker and their product which, for Morris, was to be one of joy if it was to be of value.

However, before we are irretrievably lost to the claims Morris makes as the favoured son of this site, we should avert our eyes just to the left. Attached to the side of the site for Morris' work is something of an anomaly. A squat two-storey coach house grows from the side of the house as though flying in the face of its freehold. The coach house carries its own legends. In the upper part a stone is inlaid and inscribed: "The first electric telegraph eight miles long was constructed here in 1816 by Sir Francis Ronalds F.R.S." The modernity of this inscription is its first appeal. Here was produced for the first time a practical means of conveying messages instantaneously through space. Here was manufactured the prototype for the device through which humankind might precede themselves in space, arriving orally before they appeared physically. And here begins a history of cultural complexity and hybridity with peoples knowing about you before you appeared. The stereotyped and simplistic meetings beloved of children's books, of Captain Cook and the Aborigine, Amerigo Verspucci and the Amerindian, on their respective pristine shorelines, are superseded by a hyperspeeded version of that classic meeting of familiars: "Dr Livingstone I presume". It is all jungle from now on – a twisted braid of knowingness that intertwines identities and colombines previously distinct national boundaries.

And then there is the inscription's contradictory expansiveness, its evocation of an object eight miles long within a workshop barely 20 feet by 40 feet. How could that be, and why is this apparently arbitrary distance worth recording for posterity? It is doubly ironic this message to modernity should sit above the portal of a home for the previous apotheosis of communication. The coach was the last means of transport prior to the train that made equal demands on each of its travellers. Horses and passengers would arrive shaken at their destinations, having felt the distance of anything more than the most modest routes. The coach was the means of cross-country delivery of mail and the fastest secure physical communication link between one voice, in script, and another. Indeed Morris' wife, Jane Burden, was said to have taken the presence of the coach house as a distinct attraction, given her lover Rosetti's ambivalence to her plans to relocate so close to the damp of the river, and perhaps as the daughter of a groom, a clear statement of her raised social standing. But, within weeks of taking the lease on Kelmscott House, Morris had filled the coach house with looms, it became the site for the production of his celebrated "Hammersmith" carpets, and he subsequently converted it to the lecture room for the local branch of the Hammersmith Socialist League. This was a coach house which never housed a coach, which had once been a workshop which never housed the wire that was to supersede the coach. The telegraph was, in fact, manufactured in the garden, to the rear of the house, and as each resident comes and goes the turning of the soil reveals another section of that historic remainder to voice-throwing.

If Morris' biography is somewhat familiar, Ronalds' is now almost completely eclipsed by the prior claims of Morse in the United States and Wheatstone and Cooke in England to the invention of the first telegraph. A simple technical resistance has removed Ronalds from the place in this history he deserves – a faith in static electricity that was to become unfashionable, and then unworkable, with the rise of constant current and the use of the battery that his competitors espoused. A library of electrics compiled through his European travels, two small monographs, a portrait in the National Portrait Gallery in London and the stone on the coach house are what record his endeavours. So what were they?

Having studied physics in the east London suburb of Walthamstow, which was also coincidentally the family home of Morris, he had conducted his first experiment in North London: "the blowing up of a large hydrogen gasometer in the breakfast room of No 1 Highbury Terrace", from where he transferred his studio to a small cock-loft over the coach house: "Here through a round hole or window, in the south wall, I introduced one end of a long wire extended down the fields towards Holloway . . . I made a few unimportant observations . . . and only mention them because I think that the idea of transmitting intelligence by discharging an insulated wire at given intervals first occurred to me while thus occupied." In the end, Ronalds discontinued the work: ". . . because the neighbours were occasionally affrighted by very loud detonations and said that they should be killed by 'the Lightning which I brought into the place'. In fact two or three of my neighbours were killed; but these were only unprincipled rats, experimented upon, dwellers in the Hay Loft, devourers of my poney's corn."[3]

So Ronalds' early work accounted for one of the first crosses between vivisection and execution, an initiation of electricity's complex with discipline, death, and "famous last words", that was to prevail in language from there on. At this time, in 1813, Ronalds now sited at Upper Mall acknowledged that he had moved to a "more elegant hay loft". It was during this year and the next that he experimented with Deluc's "dry column" obtaining discharges between the smallest possible conducting masses, and, with the help of a watchmaker, adapted Deluc's system with a pawl and ratchet mechanism through which the movements of a pendulum caused the rotation of a pointer round a dial. Here Ronalds was establishing the first means to read the discharge of electricity down a wire, as text.

Ronalds describes himself among "scoffs and jeers and a few imputations of insanity" constructing his first electric telegraph in the garden of Upper Mall. The garden, now truncated by the pulsating A4 road west from Hammersmith towards Heathrow, was at that time 600 feet long. Ronalds transformed this into eight miles by suspending his overhead wire on multiple lattices suspended by silk from hooks in horizontal bars. His generator was a frictional cylindrical machine and at the end of each line was an electroscope and balls which collapsed when the line was dis-

8.04 The "8 Mile Telegraph", from F. Ronalds, *Descriptions of an Electrical Telegraph*, 1823.

charged. Dials were set at the sending and receiving stations which rotated synchronously by clockwork. Each was marked with the alphabet covered by plates with a single letter-sized aperture. When the desired letter appeared on the disc the operator discharged his line, the receiving station noted the visible letter as his electroscope collapsed.

Ronalds' first overhead construction, which had created distance in concentrated parallels, was then superseded by a subterranean experiment where a trench 525 feet in length, and four feet deep, was dug down the garden, secured with a trough of wood in which was laid glass tubes carrying the conducting wires. It was this experiment which has emerged piece by piece over the years, in 1862 the first sections were dug up and passed via the Pavilion at Brighton to the Science Museum in Kensington.

These were the experiments, what of their implications? One extraordinary outcome is the degree of bureaucratic ambivalence shown to an invention which preceded the eventual emergence of the telegraph in the hands of Wheatstone and Cooke a full 20 years later. Ronalds had communicated his invention to Lord Melville, First Lord of the Admiralty on 16th July 1816 and received a reply from his secretary on 5th August: "... telegraphs are now [i.e. at the end of the French War] totally unnecessary and no other than the one in use [i.e. semaphore] will be

8.05 Text discs and subterranean cable, from R. Ronalds, *Descriptions of an Electrical Telegraph*, 1823.

adopted." Considering that as late as 1843 the Parliamentary return of the 2nd May showed that, during the three years previously, it was impossible to use semaphore from Admiralty in London to Portsmouth on 323 days due to inclement weather and fogs, this seems a dubious retention of the flawed communications of the day. Semaphore was the only rapid means of conveying intelligence between headquarters and the principal naval station and was costing at that time the not inconsiderable sum of £2000 per annum. But once established, the status quo of the gaze as the prevalent means of reception was impossible to dislodge from common perception.

Ronalds was surprisingly *laissez faire* about this attitude, recording simply that he held no resentment as he well understood that telegraphs have "long been great bores at the Admiralty".[4] He knew well and trusted the implications of his work writing in his one published record of the experiment:

> ... electricity may actually be employed for a more practically useful purpose than the gratification of the philosopher's inquisitive research, the schoolboy's idle amusement, or the physicians' tool ... it may be compelled to travel as many hundred miles beneath our feet as the subterranean ghost which nightly haunts our metropolis, our provincial towns, and even our high roads; and that in such an enlightened country and obscure

climate as this its travels would be trial productive of, at the least, as much public and private benefit. Why has no *serious trial* yet been made of the qualifications of so *diligent* a courier? And if he should *be* proved competent to the task, why should not our kings hold councils at Brighton with their ministers in London? Why should not our government govern at Portsmouth almost as promptly as in Downing Street? Why should our defaulters escape by default of our foggy climate? And since our piteous inamorati are not all Alphei, why should they add to the torments of absence those dilatory tormentors, pens, ink, paper, and posts? Let us *have electrical conversazione offices*, communicating with each other all over the kingdom, *if we can.*[5]

The evocation of a state, shrouded in Dickensian fog, through which the new means of communication would cut, the potential flexibility for government and jurisdiction of such a means of signalling, might have the feel of Michel Foucault's panopticism about it if it were not for Ronalds' prescient invitation to free speech in electrical conversation offices throughout the land.

The loss of convicts and robbers in the fog is a persuasive metaphor which returns in Ronalds' writing when he considers the limitations to the subterranean carriage of the telegraph. His over-riding fear of the liability of his system is that the apparatus might be injured by an enemy "or by mischievously disposed persons".[6] For invasions and civil wars, Ronalds recommends more "smokers" (ships) to prevent invasions and "kings that love their subjects enough to prevent civil wars". To repel the rogues, Ronalds' recommends deeper trenches taking different routes to the same location and if this is not sufficient to deter them: "Hang them if you can catch them, damn them if you cannot" and as always the vermin are just behind: "Should mischievous devils from the subterranean regions (*viz* the cellars) attack my wire, condemn the *houses* belonging thereunto, which cannot *easily* escape detection by running away."[7]

Indeed, a quarter of a century after Ronalds' prophetic link of the telegraph to the fate of escaped criminals, one of the first practical uses of the telegraph of Cooke and Wheatstone (which did more than anything to popularise telegraph) was its employment in effecting the capture of the Quaker Tavell for a murder at Salthill. And again, as Stephen Kern and Scott McQuire have reminded us, the spectacular publicity gained by the wireless in 1910 was owed to its role in bringing about the arrest of Dr Hawley Crippin, who had been accused of murdering his wife, while on board the ocean liner "Montrose".

Ironically both Cooke and Wheatstone, from Brentford in West London and Upper Mall respectively, had visited and observed Ronalds' garden experiments as teenagers and the first patent was granted to them both in 1837 for. "Improvements in giving signals and Sounding Alarums in distant places by means of electronic currents transmitted through electric circuits". By this time Ronalds had long "taken leave of science" having, in the writing up of his work in 1823, "bid a cordial adieu to Electricity" and setting off for European travels, the invention of instruments for "accurately and conveniently sketching from nature" and a "machine for drawing in perspective architectural and other subjects", before finally returning to the spectral fringes of the emerging sciences of photographic record on the assumption of the post of Director and Superintendent of the Kew Meteorological Observatory. There, for the first time, he adapted photography to register meteorological and magnetic observations.

When William Gladstone, the prime minister of the day, conveyed a knighthood on Ronalds, in 1870, just before he died, W.F. Cooke wrote to him: "It is a singular fact that Brentford would have furnished two of the men who were most practical in their original views, I might say, *the only two men* who up to the year 1837 realised ... the electric telegraph as a *future fact*."[8] That Cooke had long been in dispute with Wheatstone about their respective contributions to the invention of the telegraph, with both latterly according Ronalds the decisive influence, this geographical loyalty might be read with a certain scepticism.

The coalescence of the signatures on this site here become confused and interlaced. Morris was concerned in the nineteenth century with the colonial implications of the Stanley explorations in Africa and resolutely opposed their triumphalism in print and speech. Stanley's adventurism in Africa in the 1870s and 1880s occurred to Morris as the brutal act of colonising capital bolstering the capitalist system in Britain. The celebration of Stanley's London speaking engagements by the press were anathema for Morris. Yet the communication conditions for Stanley's mission to the Congo, to the "heart of darkness" with the illuminating force of Christianity coupled with colonial geography, had been set by the invention of the telegraph. On his returns to Europe, Stanley was able to perpetuate myths of his endeavours through the media of his day and to prey on the residual jingoism of a nation that had in reality tired of his brutalist exploits in the name of their nation. Indeed, Stanley's adventurism was itself constructed with the funds and complicity of print journalism. *The New York Herald* had funded his expedition to "find Livingstone" and The *Daily Telegraph* to follow the course of the Lualaba in a monumentally ill-conceived expedition.

If cultural hybridity starts from the eclipse of coach-bound communication by the wire, so does the demand for a post-colonial anthropology. For if being here and being there are now intertwined through the possibility of speaking to "there" before arriving from "here", an innocent arrival scene, once beloved of anthropologists in the field, is no longer adequate nor possible. From here the journey of the visitor is always one in debt to their host; the guest is known about, thought about, expected and theorised before they can open their mouth. Foretold is forewarned.

The implications of these signs for a history of humanity cannot be underestimated in this virtual age. Nor for the geography and demography of the city. From here there was BT and AT, before the telegraph and after the telegraph. It is not so much the graph in the title that announces the disruption of a logocentric history of communication as the "tele", which alerts us to its electronic means, the fundamental leap from script to electronic analogue code. Where the digital age had already long ago been initiated by the invention of the alphabet (digital refers to information representing a set of fixed symbols such as letters or digits) it was analogue, the means of the electric wire which used a continually varying quantity that more profoundly marked two dynamics of distance.[9] Cities now could co-exist as relational concentrations of communications platforms, by-passing the hinterlands between that once had to be crossed in a grounded reminder of the root of the word country, that is "contra", against and in distinction to the urban.

This audio revolution, in broader terms what Paul Virilio called "the last vehicle" had technically begun with the first experiments in telegraph in 1794, and following Ronalds' work was to continue with the telephone of 1876, the phonograph of 1877 and the radio of 1894, revolutionising what could be considered the means of communication.[10] As we have seen, visual systems had previously predominated with Robert Hooke's demonstration of visual telegraphy to the Royal Society in 1684, setting the dynamic of signing which reached its apotheosis in Claude Chappe's 1852 system of 556 semaphore stations across 4800 kms of France. These towers bore signs which were telescopically viewed at relative speed, but although 500 miles could be covered in three minutes, this was not the zero point of instantaneous communication that was so sought after.

While the earliest telegraphy system was proposed in 1753, static electricity was more widely used at the time to entertain philosophical gatherings of friends than it was considered a serious contribution to communications. It was a common amusement to transmit a shock through 30 or 40 persons, each holding hands with the next, by means of a simple magnetic device. This experiment was repeated on a grand scale by Abbé Nollet when a shock was passed around a one-and-a-half kilometre circumference circle of 200 Carthusian monks linked by iron wire lengths. What these amusements *did* prepare for was a common understanding of the instantaneity of the medium irrespective of the span of the circuit.

It was this sense of "knowing now" rather than then, or sometime, that shaped the geography of speech. The instantaneity of the telegraph set the model and pace for what might after its inception have been considered the speed of speech. One response to this acceleration of speech might be to wonder at the loss of space, the contraction of the world, the "death of distance" as Frances Cairncross has called it. Another would be to accept that throwing one's voice does nothing to annihilate distance but reinforces the very separation of subject and discourse; it literally brings peoples together in mutual misunderstandings. As a pamphleteer, a typographer and public speaker, Morris was himself, in the midst of this technological revolution, reinventing the relations between political writing and speech. But for him, living to the side of a lecture hall and above a drawing room theatre, *proximity* was the essence of meaning. What constituted the "with" of communication, talking *with* someone, what constituted the history of that "with", and its possibilities for social change, did not allow Morris to recognise the potential power of the technological means that lay beneath his garden, despite the fact that the very means of this revolution would have, from time to time, emerged in the top soil of his vegetable patch.

Morris' scriptural energies travelled by other means. While it might be anomalous to think of him enduring the pollution of the early London subway system, recording with some delight his thoughts about the novelty of travelling by under-

8.06 Kelmscott House, drawing room.

ground train, he considered tapestry weaving itself a kind of movement therapy, what he described as "the dear warp and weft of Hammersmith". His Hammersmith carpets, produced in the coach house next to Kelmscott House, were only part of a range of responses to designs of the East and Persia which Morris described as "carpeteering", orienteering towards an Eastern model. Each carpet was a textual reminder of a geography of elsewhere, read through motifs of the locality, and in Morris' house, as elsewhere, were not only used to walk, and sit on, but to drape over and surround the whole domestic environment. Morris called himself the "word spinner" and though, as Fiona McCarthy points out, he was verbally inhibited in public, the more one looks at the site itself a different history of his spell-binding emerges.

Below the stone memorial to the telegraph lies another plaque complicating the textual cacophony of this apparently mute site: "GUESTS AND NEIGHBOURS, ON THE SITE OF THIS GUEST-HALL ONCE STOOD THE LECTURE-ROOM OF THE HAMMERSMITH SOCIALISTS. DRINK A GLASS TO THE MEMORY! MAY 1962". The text is from *News from Nowhere*, Morris' futuristic work which, when discovered beneath the modernity of the wire announced above, appears singularly dated. In fact, the plaque was mounted on the coach house in 1962 and though the Red Flag had long flown over Hammersmith Town Hall almost directly north of Morris' house, away from the river, the vision of socialist debate the script promises had passed from the site even before Morris' death in 1896. The history of guests speaking in this venue in the latter years of the nineteenth century reads like a "who's who" of founding socialist voices. As well as George Bernard Shaw, there was Keir Hardie, a miner, and founder of the Scottish Labour Party, Pietr Kropotkin the leading Russian anarchist, and Beatrice and Sidney Webb, all of whom spoke in this long but intensely focused assembly room with a spectral light illuminating its small platform from above and behind. What Donald Sassoon has called "the most anomalous Left" in Europe found its voice here, overwhelmingly middle class, idiosyncratic and divergent from the Social Democratic Foundation and the Fabian Society of the day, the Socialist League was nevertheless unable to outlive Morris' own lifetime. As Morris joked in the opening passage of News from Nowhere: ". . . there were six persons present, and consequently six sections of the party were represented . . ."

William Morris was a consummate storyteller, a romancer from the Nordic tradition of the sagas, and he was above all else, through necessity if not desire, a public speaker. He chose to speak of architecture, art and the city as well as write about it. It occurs to me that choosing to speak about each of these three complex and mutable objects is an invitation to become inscribed within them and responsible to them. The promises of the wire here pale, for the possibility of speaking at a

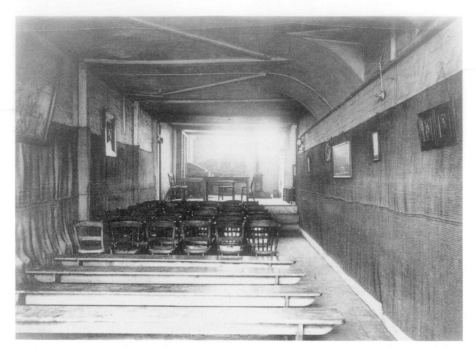

8.07 Coach-house, Kelmscott House, 1896.

distance and with a degree of anonymity *could* be perceived as an unwelcome invitation to remain discreet from questions and their implications. But how might one theorise the question of distance in a more nuanced way, neither noting its death nor submitting to its dominance?

Readdressing this site through the work of that consummate "botanist of the asphalt" Walter Benjamin, in that space between his two, now very familiar texts of the same year, 1936, "The Work of Art in the Age of Mechanical Reproduction" and "The Storyteller" further opens out some of the complications of speech in this location.[11] The shattering of tradition that Benjamin recognised in the mechanical reproduction process, the end of the auratic quality of the live and unique encounter was precisely the potential for the reinvention of artist practice as a mass phenomenon. The historical decline of the aura, most assertively premised for Benjamin in the culture of film, was associated with the masses, urge to bring things "closer", spatially and humanly and in so doing to deconstruct the "distance" on which aura depends. Here Benjamin memorably referred to the masses destroying the aura like "prying an object from a shell". Thus distance was associated with the unapproachability and status of the cult object. For Benjamin, technical reproduction would bring the art object closer to the beholder, meeting the viewer halfway. So far, so Ronalds. Indeed Ronalds' telegraph not only announces the destruction of the "original" encounter, his graphic machines were invented precisely to dispel the aura of the artist as a privileged arbiter of perspective.

But the spectre of Morris returns in the other key text of that year, "The Storyteller", in which Benjamin discusses the disappearance of the storyteller's art. Here space is reversed with Benjamin arguing for the power of the distance inherent in the storyteller's craft. Here perspective was coming to an end, literally the means through which experiences might be exchanged. Thus storytelling is for Benjamin, as for Morris, a fundamental part of subjectivity. There could be no greater contrast with the faith in the technical means of production than this celebration of the individual experience in *communitas*, the significance of dialogue. This well-known and observed dialectic in Benjamin between proximity and distance, reproduction and originality is played out between the two buildings and their inscriptions. And it would seem the one determines the fate of the other.

The end of storytelling is harboured, for Benjamin, in the proliferation of information which gains precedence over intelligence in its infinite revolutions. The class control of the media of communication, including the wire, ensures the responsibility of this information to advanced capitalism. Here Benjamin, perhaps like Morris, distinguishes between information and story: "The value of information does not survive the moment in which it was new. It lives only at the moment; it has to surrender to it completely and explain itself to it without losing any time. A story is different. It does not expend itself. It preserves and concentrates its strength and is capable of releasing it even after a long time."[12] Benjamin proposes something akin to the "slow release" efficacy of a narrative vitamin – a reminder perhaps of why *News from Nowhere* retains its signifying power long after the more copius ministrations of Morris and his Socialist League colleagues have been immersed in history's folds.

The disappearance of the storyteller vacates a space where rumour can flourish. The political word-spinners of Morris' coach house, George Bernard Shaw, Keir Hardie, each worked their own crafting of narrative containers which were themselves socially and politically constructed. These stories, of course were not only describing political process but making movement and practice possible in the first place. To move into a place, there is always the need for a story about it. This goes for the oldest of seafaring legends as it does for the narratives of cyborg culture in cyber space. Stories furthermore by their presence resist the flourishing of rumour: "stories differ from rumours in that the latter are always injunctions, initiators and results of a levelling of space, creators of common movements that reinforce an order by adding an activity of making people believe things to that of making people do things. Stories diversify, rumours totalise."[13] Rumours here begin and revolve around the river. Morris was well aware of the suicidal allure of the river, the nearby bridge as a site for vertiginous valedictions.

To take a trip now on one of the pleasure boats plying their trade on the Thames is to hear a chimera of the truth through a loudspeaker. Just above Hammersmith Bridge you will be told that a small building close to St Paul's School boathouse is where Marconi made his first tests of wireless telegraphy to the general Post Office in St Martins-le-Grand. But this would seem to be the hyperbole of Thames tourism fuelled by the kernel of a telegraphic idea sown on the far bank beneath the garden of Kelmscott House.

On his death-bed on the 3rd October 1896, Morris is reputed to have said: "I want to get the mumbo-jumbo out of the world." This went for everything between discourse and design and returns us to his Hammersmith home. As Shaw said in 1880, on visiting Morris' house: "Nothing in it was there because it was interesting or quaint or rare or hereditary . . ."[14] But of course the eternal contradiction in which Morris is held is the wealth that enabled this paring away of the irrelevant. Morris could do little about the entrance to his house being bordered by Ionic pilasters, and indeed he never liked the house in which he lived. In Morris' lecture at Burslem Town hall in 1881 on "Art and the Beauty of the Earth", he said: "Look you, as I sit and work at home, which is at Hammersmith, close to the river, I often hear go past the window some of that ruffianism of which a good deal has been said in the papers of late. . . . As I hear the yells and shrieks and all the degradation cast on the glorious tongue of Shakespeare and Milton, as I see the brutal reckless faces as figures go past me, it rouses recklessness and brutality in me also . . ." Here Morris recalls the good fortune that began with the inheritance from his wealthy father that has placed him on the far side of the glass among the books and works of art in his library.

But how might one read the gap between Morris and this world, and the sites of injustice today? Again by looking up at the house. Between the two tablets marking Ronalds' and Morris' lives and works is a third, darker, and more solemn tablet etched in classical script noting that: "George MacDonald Poet and Novelist Lived Here 1867–1877". His tenure joins the two ages of Ronalds and Morris. His current obscurity (except among literary fantasists and game theorists for whom he has always been a prophetic figure) invites us to avert our eyes once more. There is little point in seeking a comprehensive biography of this building. That would hardly be possible given that Rosetti in three days here was said to have fallen so intensely in love with a sixteen-year-old that he would have given the whole of the rest of his life for that stay at Kelmscott again. Indeed what kind of temporality to the site does such an adventure imply? What is more, it is said that Lewis Carroll wrote *Alice Through the Looking Glass* here; but where, as that is the claim of a

8.08 William Morris' library, Kelmscott House, 1896.

realtor who may declare an interest in softening the hum of the traffic that now overwhelms the garden? But rather the task might be to reflect back on the two modes of speech we have already been examining with the entry of a third voice.

MacDonald is the biographical, historical and conceptual link between the two worlds of speech I have been discussing so far. MacDonald was a poet–preacher, religious novelist, modern mystic and future fantasist from the Scottish congregational church background of radical non-conformism. In works such as *Robert Falconer* he awakened a new popular interest in what working among and "for" those people in poverty might be and he was one of the few writers of his generation to turn the reading classes' heads Eastwards towards the slums at the edge of the city.

At "The Retreat", as the house was then called, he came into the city circle of Burne-Jones who, at the Grange in nearby Fulham, was to become a close associate and working partner of Morris. MacDonald believed in the growing reform of the stage and as Joseph Johnson notes in his hagiography of 1906 "the elevation of the public taste by the introduction of pure plays performed by acts of high character". Here fantastical "juvenile tales" were dramatised by his children and acted out in the drawing room with its natural proscenium break, and annually these

8.09 Garden from interior of Kelmscott House.

occasions became an opportunity to gather large numbers of people together from across the social divide. Each winter there was an open day for Octavia Hill's "model dwellings for the poor" at which the MacDonald children acted out plays and ended their celebrations with bouts of country dancing. These were gatherings of the impoverished alongside intellectual and artistic philanthropists such as the Reverend Samuel Barnett, the founder of Toynbee Hall.[15] In 1868, Ruskin, Morris' mentor, had attended the first of these receptions. These amusements were said to blend and almost imperceptibly grow into reverential service. The garden played host to a visit of the American Jubilee Singers and Mark Twain also visited the house around this time.

MacDonald was known in his day as "the Interpreter" and there is a sense in which his work in fantasy such as the "faerie romance" *Phantastes*, and *The Princess and the Goblin* (enduring through the work of C.S. Lewis and Maurice Sendak) is as persuasive a medium as Morris' social tracts or Ronalds' technologies as a means to imaginative transformation. Here the hermeneutic link between two modes of speech might be worked through. It is MacDonald's mystical allegories that have become the ubiquitous architectural structuring device for digital play, it is his non-conformist apocalyptic overtones coupled to grass-roots social observation of injustice that seems most closely echoed by today's eco-warriors whose environmentalism might once have been expected to mimic the secular Marxism of Morris' speeches. In the labyrinthine warrens of those environmentalists, Animal and Co, zig zagging beneath England's "green and pleasant land" through the turn of a century, there has been at work one of the only visible resistances in Britain to the spoiling power of capital that this Millennial moment can summon. But the means of resistance in this subterranean network, its baroque filigree, and rococo languages of resistance, is conducted "through the wire", "with" the enemy of nature, "between" comrades through the erudition and weaving of fantasy and fact drawing precisely on the technologies and traditions of speech afforded by MacDonald as much as the medium of Ronalds and the political pedigree of Morris.

Is there not something to be gained then in the interests of complexity from rereading these signs of the street as a dialogue with each other, a sedimentation of pasts and futures, rather than a contradictory impasse to thought? They are already, and anyway, in states of mutual coalescence for the dates are strangely inconsequential, or even misleading. The house dates from the 1790s, Morris bought the lease after the decade of MacDonald and brought it to commercial life in 1878; the stone in its classical antiquity speaking of the future of communications is dated 1816; the socialist message is inscribed in a text of 22nd November 1892 while looking forward to the final meeting of a socialist group in 1962 which may or may not have occurred. The apparent nostalgia of a socialist ideal here becomes the more up-to-date message, while the true future in the form of telecommunications predates this rootedness by almost a century.

If there was a living image of what Jurgen Habermas describes in his resistance to the facile announcement of the end of modernity, this site might provide its most fruitful illustration. What price the baton charge of history when faced with this accretion of reversals to fortune? The story would appear to run: first there was the word, and the word was made electronic and man needed no more to travel to be heard, except when the other did not listen to his threats. Or, first there was the word, and the word was made locally and confusion reigned under the guise of universal emancipation for all those who could not understand each other but felt that their oppression might be shared.

Between these two apparent poles is a spectrum of positions from which one might construct a politics of the location of locution, that neither lionises stability nor celebrates the insecurities of hybridity. Walter Benjamin understood this tension when, in speaking about the art of the storyteller, he characterised the archaic representatives of the genre: the resident tiller of the soil and the figure destined to travel returning with stories from afar. Characteristically nuanced, Benjamin avoids settling with either, understanding the dynamic was as likely to be that of the complex figure whose sense is never one of being quite at home.

There is only one record of Morris' engagement with Ronalds: towards the end of his life in 1896 and after Ronalds' own death in 1873. It is recorded, in a single source, and there is no verification of this in Morris' letters. A man called W. Kemp approached Morris with the aim of placing a memorial stone to Ronalds on the house: "The suggestion met with wrath. Morris declared that for their brutalising influence upon humans, telegraphs were as much to be blamed as railways."[16] Modernity prevailed, however, and with Morris' "full approval" the tablet was placed on the coach house, where it is to be seen now complicating and confusing any pedestrian's sense of the past as "back then" with a present sense of "here now" and "where to?".

Notes

1   William Morris, *News From Nowhere and Other Writings* Clive Wilmer (ed.) London: Penguin 1993) 331. I have drawn on the introduction and notes to this volume for points of context included here.

2   ibid. 331–2.

3   Francis Ronalds quoted in Rollo Appleyard, *Pioneers of Electrical Communication* (London: Macmillan and Co 1930) 303–4.

4   Francis Ronalds, *Descriptions of an Electrical Telegraph* (London: R Hunter 1823) 24.

5   ibid. 2–3.

6   ibid. 16.

7   ibid. 17.

8   A.J. Frost, *F. Ronalds, Biographical Memoir* (London: Ronalds Catalogue, Society of Telegraphic Engineers 1880).

9   Prof. D.A. Turner, University of Kent, *Guardian* (Newspaper, London edition) letters page, 21, Tuesday November 10, 1998.

10   See Scott McQuire, "Pure Speed – From Transport to Teleport", in Jeremy Millar and Michiel Schwarz (eds), *Speed-Visions of an Accelerated Age* (London: Photographers Gallery et al. 1998) 26.

11   Walter Benjamin, *Illuminations* Hannah Arendt (ed.), trans. Harry Zohn (New York: Schocken Books 1969).

12   For a fuller discussion of this theme, see Alan Read, *Theatre and Everyday Life: An*

Ethics of Performance (London: Routledge 1993) 162–7, and Walter Benjamin, op. cit. 90.

13   Michel de Certeau, *The Practice of Everyday Life*, trans. Steven Rendall (Berkeley: University of California Press 1977) 107.

14   See Fiona McCarthy, *William Morris: A Life For Our Time* (London: Faber 1994) 397.

15   ibid. 392.

16   Appleyard, op. cit., 331.

Credits: All photographs except 7, Hammersmith and Fulham Archives; No. 7: The William Morris Gallery, Walthamstow, London.

Chapter 9

Battle lines: E.1027
Beatriz Colomina

> Anger is perhaps the greatest inspiration in those days when the individual is
> separated in so many personalities. Suddenly one is all in one piece.
> Eileen Gray, 1942

E.1027. A modern white house is perched on the rocks, a hundred feet above the
Mediterranean Sea, in a remote place, Roquebrune at Cap Martin in France (Figure
9.01). The site is "inaccessible and not overlooked from anywhere."[1] No road leads
to this house. It was designed and built between 1926 and 1929 by Eileen Gray
for Jean Badovici and herself. Gray named the house E.1027: E for Eileen, 10 for J
(the tenth letter of the alphabet), 2 for B and 7 for G. Gray and Badovici lived there
most summer months, until Gray built her own house in Castellar in 1934. After

9.01 Eileen Gray. E.1027, Roquebrune, Cap Martin, France. 1926–9. View from the sea. Source: Peter
Adam, *Eileen Gray: Architect/Designer.*

Badovici's death in 1956, the house was sold to the Swiss architect Marie Louise Schelbert. She found the walls riddled with bullet holes. The house had clearly been the scene of some considerable violence. In a 1969 letter, she commented on the state of the house: "Corbu did not want anything repaired and urged me to leave it as it is as a reminder of war."[2] But what kind of war? Most obviously, it was World War II. The bullet holes were wounds from the German occupation. But what violence was there to the house before the bullets, and even before the inevitable relationship of modern architecture to the military? And anyway, to start with, what was Le Corbusier doing here? What brought him to this isolated spot, this remote house that would eventually be the site of his own death?

"As a young man he had traveled in the Balkans and the near East and had made sketches of strange, inaccessible places and scenes. It was perhaps through a natural, anti-romantic reaction of maturity that later, as a Purist, he proposed to paint what was duplicable and near-at-hand."[3] We will have to go back to Le Corbusier's earlier travels, to the "strange, inaccessible places and scenes" that he had conquered through drawing – at the very least, to Le Corbusier's trip to Algiers in the spring of 1931, the first encounter in what would become a long relationship to this city, or in Le Corbusier's words, "Twelve years of uninterrupted study of Algiers."[4] By all accounts, this study began with his drawing of Algerian women. He said later that he had been "profoundly seduced by a type of woman particularly well built," of which he made many nude studies.[5] He also acquired a big collection of colored postcards depicting naked women surrounded by accoutrements from the Oriental bazaar. Jean de Maisonseul (later director of the Musée National des Beaux-Arts d'Alger), who as an eighteen-year-old boy had guided Le Corbusier through the Casbah, recalls their tour:

> Our wanderings through the side streets led us at the end of the day to the rue Kataroudji where he [Le Corbusier] was fascinated by the beauty of two young girls, one Spanish and the other Algerian. They brought us up a narrow stairway to their room; there he sketched some nudes on – to my amazement – some schoolbook graph paper with colored pencils; the sketches of the Spanish girl lying both alone on the bed and beautifully grouped together with the Algerian turned out accurate and realistic; but he said that they were very bad and refused to show them.[6]

Le Corbusier filled three notebooks of sketches in Algiers that he later claimed were stolen from his Paris atelier. But Ozenfant denies it, saying that Le Corbusier himself either destroyed or hid them, considering them a "secret d'atelier."[7] The Algerian sketches and postcards appear to be a rather ordinary instance of the ingrained fetishistic appropriation of women, of the East, of "the other". Yet Le Cor-

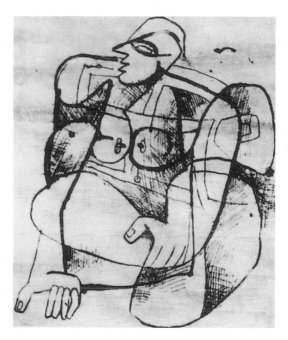

9.02 Le Corbusier. *Crouching Woman, Front View* (after Delacroix's Les Femmes d'Alger). N.d. Watercolour on transparent paper, 19 5/8 × 12 7/8 in. Private collection, Milan.

busier, as Samir Rafi and Stanislaus von Moos have noted, turned this material into "preparatory studies for and the basis of a projected monumental figure composition, the plans for which seem to have preoccupied Le Corbusier during many years, if not his entire life."[8]

From the months immediately following his return from Algiers until his death, Le Corbusier seems to have made hundreds and hundreds of sketches on yellow tracing paper by laying it over the original sketches and redrawing the contours of the figures. (Ozenfant believed that Le Corbusier had redrawn his own sketches with the help of photographs or postcards.[9]) He also exhaustively studied Delacroix's famous painting *Les Femmes d'Alger dans leur appartement*, producing a series of sketches of the outlines of the figures in this painting, divested of their "exotic clothing" and the "Oriental décor" (Figure 9.02).[10] Soon the two projects merged: he modified the gestures of Delacroix's figures, gradually making them correspond to the figures in his own sketches. Le Corbusier said that he would have called the final composition *Les Femmes de la Casbah*.[11] In fact, he never finished it. He kept redrawing it. That the drawing and redrawing of these images became a lifetime obsession already indicates that something was at stake. This became even more obvious when in 1963/64, shortly before his death, Le

9.03 Le Corbusier. *Three Women (Graffite à Cap Martin)*. 1938. Mural in Eileen Gray's house E.1027, Roquebrune, Cap Martin. Source: Alfred Roth, *Begegnungen mit Pionieren* (Basel and Stuttgart 1973) 119.

Corbusier, unhappy with the visible aging of the yellow tracing paper, copied a selection of 26 drawings onto transparent paper and, symptomatically for someone who kept everything, burned the rest.[12]

But the process of drawing and redrawing the *Les Femmes de la Casbah* reached its most intense, if not hysterical, moment when Le Corbusier's studies found their way into a mural that he completed in 1938 in E.1027. Le Corbusier referred to the mural as *Sous les pilotis* or *Graffite à Cap Martin*; sometimes he also labeled it *Three Women* (Figure 9.04).[13] According to Schelbert, Le Corbusier "explained to his friends that 'Badou' [Badovici] was depicted on the right, his friend Eileen Gray on the left; the outline of the head and the hairpiece of the sitting figure in the middle, he claimed, was 'the desired child, which was never born.' "[14] This extraordinary scene, a defacement of Gray's architecture, was perhaps even an effacement of her sexuality. For Gray was openly gay, her relationship to Badovici notwithstanding. And in so far as Badovici is here represented as one of the three women, the mural may reveal as much as it conceals. It is clearly a "theme for a psychiatrist", as Le Corbusier's *Vers Une Architecture* says of the

9.04 Le Corbusier. Cabanon. 1952. Cap Martin. Credit: Fondation le Corbusier.

nightmares with which people invest their houses,[15] particularly if we take into account Le Corbusier's obsessive relationship to this house as manifest (and this is only one example of a complex pathology) in his quasi-occupation of the site after World War II, when he built a small wooden shack (the Cabanon, Figures 9.04, 9.05) for himself at the very limits of the adjacent property, right behind Gray's house. He occupied and controlled the site by overlooking it, the cabin being little more than an observation platform, a sort of watchdog house. The imposition of this appropriating gaze is even more brutal if we remember that Gray had chosen the site because it was, in Peter Adam's words, "inaccessible and not overlooked from anywhere". But the violence of this occupation had already been established when Le Corbusier painted the murals in the house (there were eight altogether) without Gray's permission (she had already moved out). She considered it an act of vandalism; indeed, as Adam put it, "It was a rape. A fellow architect, a man she admired, had without her consent defaced her design."[16]

The defacement of the house went hand in hand with the effacement of Gray as an architect. When Le Corbusier published the murals in his *Oeuvre Complète* (1946) and in *L'Architecture D'aujourd'hui* (1948), Gray's house was referred to as "a house in Cap-Martin"; her name was not even mentioned.[17] Later on, Le Corbusier actually got credit for the design of the house and even for some of its

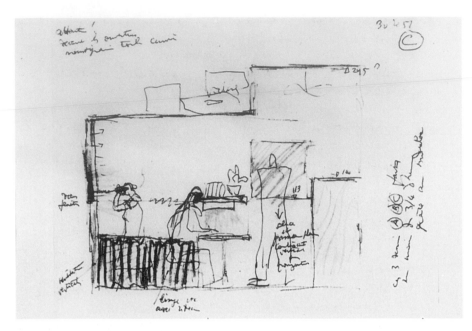

9.05 Le Corbusier. Early sketch for the *Cabanon*. December 30, 1951. Source: Le Corbusier, Modular I and II, Cambridge, Mass: Harvard University Press, 1986, 241. Fondation le Corbusier.

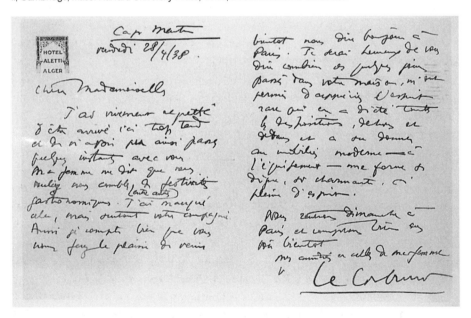

9.06 Letter from Le Corbusier to Eileen Gray, in which he praises E.1027. Cap Martin, April 28, 1938. Note the letterhead: Hotel Aletti Alger. Source Peter Adam, *Eileen Gray*, 310. Credit Eileen Gray Archives, London.

furniture.[18] Today the confusion continues, with many writers attributing the house to Badovici alone or, at best, to Badovici and Gray, and others suggest that Le Corbusier had collaborated on the project. Gray's name does not figure, even as footnote, in most histories of modern architecture, including the most recent and ostensibly critical ones.

"What a narrow prison you have built for me over a number of years, and particularly this year through your vanity," Badovici wrote to Le Corbusier in 1949 about the whole episode (in a letter that Adam thinks may have been dictated by Gray herself).[19] Le Corbusier's reply is clearly addressed to Gray:

> You want a statement from me based on my worldwide authority to show – if I correctly understand your innermost thoughts – to demonstrate "the quality of pure and functional architecture" which is manifested by you in the house at Cap Martin, and has been destroyed by my pictorial interventions. OK, you send me some photographic documents of this manipulation of pure functionalism.... Also send some documents on Castellar, this U-boat of functionalism; then I will spread this debate in front of the whole world.[20]

Now Le Corbusier was threatening to carry the battle from the house into the newspapers and architectural periodicals. But his public position completely contradicted what he had expressed privately. In 1938, the same year he would go on to paint the mural *Graffite à Cap Martin*, Le Corbusier had written a letter to Gray, after having spent some days in E.1027 with Badovici, in which he acknowledged not only her sole authorship but also how much he likes the house:

> I am so happy to tell you how much those few days spent in your house have made me appreciate the rare spirit which dictates all the organization, inside and outside, and gives to the modern furniture – the equipment – such dignified form, so charming, so full of spirit.[21] (Figure 9.06)

Why, then, did Le Corbusier vandalize the very house he loved? Did he think that the murals would enhance it? Certainly not. Le Corbusier had repeatedly stated that the role of the mural in architecture is to "destroy" the wall, to dematerialize it. In a letter to Vladimir Nekrassov in 1932, he wrote: "I admit the mural not to enhance a wall, but on the contrary, as a means to violently destroy the wall, to remove from it all sense of stability, of weight, etc."[22] The mural for Le Corbusier is a weapon against architecture, a bomb. "Why then to paint on the walls ... at the risk of killing architecture?" he asked in the same letter, and then answered, "It is when one is pursuing another task, that of telling stories."[23] So what, then, is the story that he so urgently needed to tell with *Grafitte à Cap Martin*?

9.07 "Femmes kabyles", postcard bought by Le Corbusier in Algiers in 1931.

We will have to go back once more to Algiers. In fact, Le Corbusier's complimentary letter to Gray, sent from Cap Martin, April 28, 1938, bears the letterhead, "Hôtel Aletti Alger". Le Corbusier's violation of Gray's house and identity is consistent with his fetishization of Algerian women. One might even argue that the child in this mural reconstitutes the missing (maternal) phallus, whose absence, Freud argues, organizes fetishism. In these terms, the endless drawing and redrawing is a violent substitution that required the house, domestic space, as prop. Violence is organized around or through the house. In both Algiers and Cap Martin, the scene starts with an intrusion, the carefully orchestrated occupation of a house. But the house is, in the end, effaced − erased from the Algiers drawings, defaced at Cap Martin.

Significantly, Le Corbusier described drawing itself as the occupation of a "stranger's house." In his last book, *Creation Is a Patient Search*, he wrote: "By working with our hands, by drawing, we enter the house of a stranger, we are enriched by the experience, we learn."[24] Drawing, as has often been noted, played a crucial part in Le Corbusier's appropriation of the exterior world. He repeatedly opposed his technique of drawing to photography:

When one travels and works with visual things − architecture, painting or sculpture − one uses one's eyes and draws, so as to fix deep down in one's experience what is seen. Once the impression has been recorded by the pencil, it stays for good – entered, registered, inscribed. The camera is a tool for idlers, who use a machine to do their seeing for them.[25]

Statements such as this have gained Le Corbusier the reputation of having a phobia for the camera – despite the crucial role of photography in his work. But what is the specific relationship between photography and drawing in Le Corbusier?

The sketches of the Algerian women were not only redrawings of live models but also redrawings of postcards (Figure 9.08). One could even argue that the construction of the Algerian women in French postcards, widely circulated at the time,[26] would have informed Le Corbusier's live drawings in the same way that, as Zeynep Çelik notes, Le Corbusier precisely re-enacted the images of foreign cities (Istanbul or Algiers, for example) constructed by postcards and tourist guides when he actually entered these cities. In these terms, he not only "knew what he wanted to see,"[27] as Çelik says, but saw what he had already seen (in pictures). He "entered" those pictures. He inhabited the photographs. The redrawings of the *Les Femmes d'Alger* are also more likely to have been realized, as von Moos points

9.08 Le Corbusier, Deux Femmes Enlacées. c. 1932. 24.5 × 32cm. Pencil and pastel on cardboard. (Fondation Le Corbusier 114)

out, from postcards and reproductions than from the original painting in the Louvre.[28] So what, then, is the specific role of the photographic image in the fetishistic scene of the *Femmes de la Casbah* project?

The fetish is "pure presence," writes Victor Burgin, "and how many times have I been told that photographs "lack presence," that paintings are to be valued because of their presence!"[29] This separation between painting and photography organizes the dominant understanding of Le Corbusier's relationship to photography. What these accounts seem to ignore is that here the drawing, the hand-crafted artistic meditation, is done "after" the photograph: the art reproduction, the postcard, the photograph.

In fact, the whole mentality of the *Femmes de la Casbah* drawings is photographic. Not only are they made from photographs but they are developed according to a repetitive process in which the images are systematically reproduced on transparent paper, the grid of the original graph paper allowing the image to be enlarged to any scale. This photographic sensibility becomes most obvious with the murals at Cap Martin. Traditionally, they have been understood as paradigm of Le Corbusier the painter, the craftsman detached from mechanical reproduction, an interpretation to which Le Corbusier himself has contributed with the circulation of that famous photograph of him, naked, working at one of the murals (Figure 9.09). This is the only nude image of him that we know, and that it had to be here, in this scene, is telling. What is normally overlooked is that *Graffite à Cap Martin* was not conceived on the wall itself. Le Corbusier used an electric projector to enlarge the image of a small drawing onto the 2.5 × 4 metre white wall where he etched the mural in black.

It is said that in using black Le Corbusier was thinking about Picasso's *Guernica* of the year before, and that Picasso, in turn, was so impressed with the mural at Cap Martin that it prompted him to do his own versions of the *Femmes d'Alger*. Apparently Picasso drew Delacroix's painting from memory and was later "frappé" to find out that the figure that he had painted in the middle, lying down, with her legs crossed, was not in the Delacroix.[30] It was, of course, *Graffitte à Cap Martin* that he remembered, the reclining crossed-legged women (inviting but inaccessible), Le Corbusier's symptomatic representation of Gray. But if Le Corbusier's mural had so impressed him, why did Picasso choose not to see the swastika inscribed on the chest of the woman on the right? The swastika may be yet one more sign of Le Corbusier's political opportunism. (We must remember that the mural was done in 1938.) But the German soldiers, who occupied the house during World War II, may not have seen the swastika either, for this very wall was found riddled with bullet holes, as if it had been the site of some execution.

The mural was a black and white photograph. Le Corbusier's fetish was pho-

9.09 Le Corbusier painting one of the murals in E.1027. Source: *Le Corbusier une encyclopedie* 275.

tographic. Photography, too, has been read in terms of the fetish. Victor Burgin writes:

> Fetishism thus accomplishes that separation of knowledge from belief characteristic of representation; its motive is the unity of the subject. The photograph stands to the subject-viewer as does the fetished object.... We know we see a two-dimensional surface, we believe we look through it into three-dimensional space, we cannot do both at the same time – there is a coming and going between knowledge and belief.[31]

So if Le Corbusier "entered the house of a stranger" by drawing, could "the house" be standing in for the photograph? By drawing he entered the photograph that is itself a stranger's house, occupying and re-territorializing the space, the city, the sexualities of the other by reworking the image. Drawing on and in photography is the instrument of colonization. The entry to the house of a stranger is always a breaking and entering – there being no entry without force no matter how many invitations. Le Corbusier's architecture depends in some way on specific techniques of occupying yet gradually effacing the domestic space of the other.

Like all colonists, Le Corbusier did not think of it as an invasion but as a gift. When recapitulating his life work five years before his death, he symptomatically wrote about Algiers and Cap Martin in the same terms: "From 1930 L-C devoted twelve years to an uninterrupted study of Algiers and its future. . . . Seven great schemes (seven enormous studies) were prepared free of charge during those years"; and later, "1938/39. Eight mural paintings (free of charge) in the Badovici and Helen Grey house at Cap Martin."[32] No charge for the discharge. Gray was outraged; now even her name was defaced. And renaming is, after all, the first act of colonization. Such gifts cannot be returned.

P.S. In 1944, the retreating German Army blew up Gray's apartment in Menton, having vandalized E.1027 and Temple a Paiella (her house in Castellar). She lost everything. Her drawings and plans were used to light fires.

P.P.S. On August 26, 1965, the endless redrawing of the *Femmes de las Casbah* still unfinished, Le Corbusier went down from E.1027 to the sea and swam to his death.

P.P.P.S. In 1977, a local mason in charge of some work in the house "mistakenly" demolished the mural *Graffitte*.[33] I like to think that he did so on purpose. Gray had spent almost three years living on the site in complete isolation, building the house with the masons, having lunch with them every day. She did the same thing when building her house at Castellar. The masons knew her well; in fact, they loved her and they hated the arrogant Badovici. They understood perfectly what the mural was about. They destroyed it. In so doing, they showed more enlightenment than most critics and historians of architecture.

P.P.P.P.S. Since then, the mural has been reconstructed in the house using photographs. It re-emerged from its original medium. The occupation continues.

Notes

1   Peter Adam, *Eileen Gray: Architect/Designer* (New York: Harry N. Abrams Inc. 1987) 174.

2   Letter from Marie Louise Schelbert to Stanislaus von Moos, February 14, 1969, as quoted by von Moos in "Le Corbusier as Painter," *Oppositions* 19/20 (1980), 93.

3   James Thrall Soby, "Le Corbusier, Muralist," *Interiors* (1948) 100.

4   Le Corbusier, *My Work*, trans. James Palmes (London: The Architectural Press 1960) 50.

5   Samir Rafi, "Le Corbusier et 'Les Femmes d'Alger,' " *Revue d'histoire et de civilisation du Maghreb* (Algiers) (January 1968) 51.

6   Letter from Jean de Maisonseul to Samir Rafi, January 5, 1968, as quoted by Stanislaus von Moos in "Le Corbusier as Painter," op. cit. 89.

7   From several conversations of both Le Corbusier and Ozenfant with Samir Rafi in 1964. As quoted by Samir Rafi in "Le Corbusier et 'Les Femmes d'Alger,' " op. cit. 51.

8   Von Moos, "Le Corbusier as Painter," 91.

9   Conversation of Ozenfant with Samir Rafi, June 8, 1964, as quoted by Samir Rafi in "Le Corbusier et 'Les Femmes d'Alger,' " 52.

10   Von Moos, 93.

11   Rafi, 54–5.

12   ibid. 60

13   In *My Work*, Le Corbusier refers to the mural as *Graffiti at Cap Martin*. In "Le Corbusier as Painter," Stanislaus von Moos labels the mural *Three Women (Graffite à Cap Martin)*, and in "Le Corbusier et 'Les Femmes d'Alger,' " Samir Rafi labels the final composition from which the mural was derived, "Assemblage des trois femmes: Composition définitive. Encre de Chine sur papier calque 49.7 × 64.4 cm. Coll. particulière. Milan."

14   Letter from Marie Louise Schelbert to Stanislaus von Moos, February 14, 1969, as quoted by von Moos, 93.

15   Le Corbusier, *Vers une architecture* (Paris: Crès 1923) 196. The passage referred to here is omitted in the English version of the book.

16   Adam, 311.

17   See Adam, 334–5. No caption of the photographs of the murals published in *L'Architecture d'aujourd'hui* mentions Eileen Gray. In subsequent publications, the house is either simply described as "Maison Badovici" or credited directly to Badovici. The first recognition since the thirties of Gray as architect came from Joseph Rykwert, "Un Ommagio a Eileen Gray – Pioniera del Design," *Domus* 468 (December 1966) 23–5.

18   For example, in an article entitled "Le Corbusier, Muralist," published in *Interiors* (June 1948), the caption of the murals at Cap Martin reads: "Murals, interior and exterior, executed in sgraffito technique on white plaster, in a house designed by Le Corbusier and P. Jeanneret, Cap Martin, 1938." In 1981 in *Casa Vogue* 119 (Milan), the house is described as "Firmata Eileen Gray–Le Corbusier" (signed Eileen Gray and Le Corbusier), and an Eileen Gray sofa as "pezzo unico di Le Corbusier" (unique piece by Le Corbusier), as quoted by Jean Paul Rayon and Brigitte Loye in "Eileen Gray architetto 1879–1976," *Casabella* 480 (May 1982), 38–42.

19   "Quelle réclusion étroite que m'a faite votre vanité depuis quelques années et qu'elle m'a faite plus particulièrement cette année." Letter from Badovici to Le Corbusier, December 30, 1949, Fondation Le Corbusier, as quoted by Brigitte Loye in *Eileen Gray 1879–1976: Architecture Design* (Paris: Analeph/J.P. Viguier, 1983) 86; English translation in Adam, 335.

20 "Vous réclamez une mise au point de moi, couverte de mon autorité mondiale, et démontrant – si je comprends le sens profond de votre pensée – 'la qualité d'architecture fonctionnelle pure' manifesté par vous dans la maison de Cap Martin et anéantie par mon intervention picturale. D'ac [sic], si vous me fournissez les documents photographiques de cette manipulation fonctionnelle pure: 'entrez lentement'; 'pyjamas'; 'petites choses'; 'chaussons'; 'robes'; 'pardessus et parapluies'; et quelques documents de Castellar, ce sous-marin de la fonctionnalité: Alors je m'efforcerai d'étaler le débat au monde entier." Letter from Le Corbusier to Badovici, Fondation Le Corbusier, as quoted in Loye, 83–4; English translation in Adams, 335–6.

21 Letter from Le Corbusier to Eileen Gray, Cap Martin, 28 April, 1938, as quoted in Adam, 309–10.

22 "J'admets la fresque non pas pour mettre en valeur un mur, mais au contraire comme un moyen pour détruire tumultueusement le mur, lui enlever toute notion de stabilité, de poids, etc." *Le Corbusier, Le passé à réaction poétique*, Catalogue of an exhibition organized by the Caisse nationale des Monuments historiques et des Sites/Ministère de la Culture et de la Communication, Paris 1988, 75.

23 "Mais pourquoi a-t-on peint les murs des chapelles au risque de tuer l'architecture? C'est qu'on poursuivait une autre tâche, qui était celle de raconter des histoires." ibid.

24 Le Corbusier, *Creation Is a Patient Search* (New York: Frederick Praeger 1960) 203.

25 ibid. 37.

26 About French postcards of Algerian women circulating between 1900 and 1930, see Malek Alloula, *The Colonial Harem* (Minneapolis: University of Minnesota Press 1986).

27 Zeynep Çelik, "Le Corbusier, Orientalism, Colonialism," *Assemblage* 17 (1992), 61.

28 Von Moos, 93.

29 Victor Burgin, "The Absence of Presence," in *The End of Art Theory: Criticism and Postmodernity* (Atlantic Highlands, N.J.: Humanities Press International, Inc. 1986), 44.

30 Rafi, 61.

31 Victor Burgin, "Modernism in the Work of Art," *20th Century Studies* 15–16 (December 1976). Reprinted in Burgin, 19. See also Stephen Heath, "Lessons from Brecht," *Screen* 15:2 (1974), 106 ff.

32 Le Corbusier, *My Work*, 50–1 (my emphasis).

33 Von Moos, 104.

Conceiving

Chapter 10

Six concepts
Bernard Tschumi

In an article published in January 1991 in *The New York Times*, Vincent Scully, a respected architectural critic and historian, stated that "the most important movement in architecture today is the revival of the vernacular and classical traditions and their reintegration into the mainstream of modern architecture in its fundamental aspect: the structure of communities, the building of towns." Professor Scully's words cannot easily be ignored, especially when, in the same article, he pronounces the rest of the architectural profession to be in "a moment of supreme silliness that deconstructs and self-destructs."

I would like to pursue a short exploration of some of the issues that are addressed by those who, because they do not wish to perpetuate the revival of the vernacular and the classical, are now condemned to that "supreme silliness". I

10.01 Folie P6, Parc de la Villette, Paris 1985.

want to examine some of the concepts that govern the making of architecture and cities at this particular period – a period that cannot easily be recontained within the comforting fiction of an eighteenth-century village.

If we were to characterize our contemporary condition, we could say it is "after simulation", "postmediation". What do we do after everything has been relived at least once, after everything has been presented, re-presented, and re-re-presented? In order to elaborate on this, please allow me to briefly recapitulate our recent architectural past.

Much of architectural postmodernism was developed at a time of general reaction against what was perceived as the abstraction of modernism: abstraction because modernism's glass office buildings were "imageless" and cold, like abstract painting. Abstraction too because, it was said, modern architects were elitist, detached, or "abstracted" from everyday life – from people and, above all, from the community that was not allowed to "participate" while zoning, highways, and high-rise housing (to quote Scully again) "destroyed the very fabric of our neighborhoods". Were Brasilia and Chandigarh beautiful or ugly, social or asocial, historical or ahistorical?

This reaction against the perception of modernity as the abstract reducer dates from the mid-1960s, whether through scholarly texts or through the first organized protests against the demolition of neighborhoods and landmark buildings in the name of progress, from New York's Pennsylvania Station to Paris's Les Halles. Among architects, it is certainly a book, Robert Venturi's *Complexity and Contradiction in Architecture*, published by The Museum of Modern Art, New York, in 1966, that triggered an extraordinary and widespread reappraisal of architectural priorities and values, suggesting that there was more to architecture than the ethereal, abstract formulation of a utopian ideal. Filled with examples that ranged from Borromini's work to "juxtapositions of expressways and existing buildings", Venturi's text concluded by praising "the vivid lessons of Pop Art", for pop art involved contradictions of scale and context "that should have awakened architects from their prim dreams of pure order".

Almost simultaneously, a new area of knowledge was developing that was to prove a formidable instrument in the hands of architects and critics who sought to restore meaning to what they had attacked as the zero degree of modernism. Semiology and linguistics invaded the architectural scene. Often greatly misunderstood, the work of Noam Chomsky, Umberto Eco, and Roland Barthes was to inform new architectural strategies of coding, so that ordinary people and scholars alike could finally decode multiple meanings pasted onto what nevertheless remained neutral sheds. While as early as 1968 Barthes, in one of his rare ventures into urbanism and architecture, had concluded with the impossibility of fixed meanings, postmodern architects and critics developed a most unusual construct of a signifying architecture in which building facades would convey a world of allusions, quotations, and historical precedents.

Particular to these allusions is that they all referred to a very narrow sector of architectural culture: first, they dealt only with the appearance of architecture, with its surface or image, never with its structure or use. Second, a very restricted set of images was being proposed – Roman palazzi, villas, and English vernacular buildings, or what could be described as the Arcadian dreams of a conservative middle class whose homogeneity of taste disproved the very theories of heterogeneity that Barthes and Venturi seemed to suggest. In passing, it should be added that for others who were proposing a new formalist vocabulary instead, the same situation often occurred. The talk was mostly about image, about surface; structure and use were not mentioned. Indeed, the industrial and metropolitan culture of our society was notoriously absent. Rare were allusions to the megalopolis, to factories, power stations, and other mechanical works that had defined our culture for more than a century. In contrast, we were treated to a constant set of images of a preindustrial society – pre-airport, pre-supermarket, pre computor, pre-nuclear.

Of course, developers and builders were as easily convinced by these "classical" architects as by preservationists: the world of nostalgia, of comfort, of *geborgenheit* would be a better world to live in, and more houses could be sold. Despite recent interest in new forms of contemporary architecture, this preindustrial Arcadia constitutes the mainstream of architectural and political ideology in most of the built world. The more ideologically inclined among the apologists of revival argue that at the end of the twentieth century, after hundreds of years of industrial, technological, and social development, it is still possible to return to an earlier lifestyle, ignoring cars, computers, and the nuclear age. And, more important, ignoring the specific social and historical changes that took place during this time. These ideologists claim that the Arcadian "towns" now being developed on the model of holiday villages will, by virtue of their architecture, foster ideal communities where social values and respect for one another will replace difference, conflict, and urban interchange. This kind of community dream (shared by co-op boards and politicians alike) is ironic when proposed in a city like New York, where people move an average of every four years. However, it is symptomatic of a fantasy: that the village of our ancestors – one that we have never known – can be a model for generations to come.

But are modern versus classical or vernacular images really the issue? Pitched roofs against flat roofs? Is it really a key question? Of course not. I would claim that our contemporary condition affects historicists and modernists alike.

PART I

I have always been fascinated by the construction phase of two Manhattan build-ings that were erected simultaneously and side-by-side on Madison Avenue in the Upper Fifties. These two skyscrapers, one designed for IBM and the other for AT&T, are almost identical in their steel structure, function, and office layout. The skins of both buildings are hung onto their structures using the same technique of lattice and clips. But here the similarities end. In the first case, the IBM building is clad with a slick, polished marble and glass facade, with abstract and minimalist detailing. In contrast, the AT&T building has a slightly articulated facade treatment with pink granite slabs cut to resemble Roman and Gothic stonework. The IBM building has a flat roof; the AT&T, a pediment. Until recently, the IBM building was seen as a symbol of a "passe" modernist era, the AT&T building as the heroic statement of the new historicist postmodernism that became the established corporate style of the 1980s. Both buildings are nearly identical in content, bulk, and use. Less than ten years later the same situation was repeated in Times Square, with a proposal for a so-called deconstructivist skin replacing a postmod-ern classical one. Such examples also apply to houses in East Hampton, Long Island where the designs of Robert A.M. Stern and Charles Gwathmey often serve the same programs, and sometimes the same clients. One architect is labeled a historicist, the other a modernist in their manufacture of fashionable images.

Such work on the surface can also be seen in building renovations, as in the Biltmore Hotel in New York, where a 1913 brick facade was replaced 75 years later by a more businesslike curtain wall. Almost simultaneously, the white-tile facade of Columbia University's East Campus dormitories was being replaced by an imitation 1913 brick facade. This comment is not a value judgement: it has become a condition of our time. It should be noted that the administration and trustees of Columbia University agonized over what to do with the building when they found that the falling tiles could not be repaired or replaced, and that the alternative was to find $70 million to build a new dorm. No one is happy about the decision the university had to make – to change the skin – but if it is of any comfort, one can think of that shedding skin as a symptom of our contemporary condition, rather than as a result of faulty construction.

"The triumph of the superficial", as Stuart Ewen calls it in his recent book on the politics of style, *All Consuming Images*, is not a new phenomenon, but archi-tects have yet to understand the consequences of this separation of structure and surface. Until the nineteenth century, architecture made use of load-bearing walls that held the building up. Although it was common to apply decorations of various styles to these surfaces, the walls performed a key structural function. Often there was a connection between the type of image used and the structure of the wall. By the 1830s the connection between image, structure, and construction method was gone. New construction methods employed an inner structural frame that supported the building. Whether in the form of "balloon frame" structures covered by a skin or of "structural frames" covered by curtain walls, these new building techniques meant that walls no longer played a structural role: they became increasingly ornamental. A multiplicity of styles became possible due to the development of prefabricated panels, ready to be shaped, painted, or printed to reflect any image, any period.

With the new disembodied skins, the roles of engineer and architect became increasingly separate: the engineer took care of the frame, the architect the skin. Architecture was becoming a matter of appearances: the skin could be Romanesque, Baroque, Victorian, "regionalist vernacular", and so on. This evolution of the interchangeability of surfaces coincided with new techniques of visual representation. Photography and the mass printing of decorative wallpapers further democratized the merchandising of surface treatments in architecture. Above all, photography increased the power of the image over any structure of substance.

We are talking about the nineteenth century, but things have intensified so much that the quantitative change has led to a qualitative leap. With photography, magazines, television, and buildings designed by fax, so-called superficiality has become the sign of our times. To quote Jean Baudrillard in "Transparency of Evil": ". . . things continue functioning when their idea has long disappeared from [them]. They continue to function with a total indifference to their own content. Paradoxically, they even function better this way."

Looked at in this manner, modernist buildings became "better" in the 1930s when social ideals began to prove illusive and finally vanished. By extension, are not Richard Meier's buildings today more "esthetic" than Le Corbusier's? A generalized form of estheticization has indeed taken place, conveyed by the media. Just as Stealth Bombers were estheticized on the televised Saudi Arabian sunset, just as sex is estheticized in advertising, so all of culture – and, of course, this includes architecture – is now estheticized, "xeroxized". Furthermore, the simultaneous presentation of these images leads to a reduction of history to simultaneous images: not only to those of the Gulf War interspersed with basketball games and advertisement but also to those of our architectural magazines and, ultimately, to those of our cities.

The media appetite for the consumption of architectural images is enormous. And one consequence of the shift of attention toward the surface has been that much of architectural history has become the printed image, the printed word (and their dissemination), and not the actual building. At the time of this writing, influential architectural personalities – Daniel Libeskind for example, or Wolf Prix, Zaha Hadid, or Rem Koolhaas – had built relatively little. Our generation of architects is the subject of countless articles, even though it is only infrequently given the power to build. Still, it dominates media information. The intensity of this information offensive, or what we might call "reality", is such that a single, objective reality is increasingly difficult to conceive. We are familiar with Nietzsche's aphorism in *Twilight of the Idols*: "The real world, finally, will become a fiction." Inevitably, architecture and its perception will become like another object of contemporary reality.

Eclectic classicism, rationalism, neomodernism, deconstructivism, critical regionalism, green architecture, or, in the art world, neo-geo, new expressionism, new abstraction, or figuration – all of them coexist and increasingly provoke in us a profound indifference: indifference to difference. From *The New York Times* to *Vanity Fair*, from *A.D.* to *Assemblage*, we see a multiple reality that is increasingly based on a constant oscillation between trends, theories, schools, movements, and waves. The question is: why oppose this mediated world? Should it be in the name of some solid, unified reality? Should we once again long for a coherent *Gesamtkunstwerk*? But today, the project of the early twentieth century appears as a wish to restore a society in which every element is in a fixed hierarchical relationship with every other – a world of order, certainty, and permanence.

Indeed, if most of architecture has become surface, applied decoration, superficiality, paper architecture (or to use Venturi's celebrated expression, "decorated shed"), what distinguishes architecture from other forms of billboard design: or, more ambitiously, what distinguishes architecture from editions, layouts, graphics? If the so-called contextualisms and typological historicisms are nothing but a set of opportune disguises applied to a ready-made formula – in other words, a skin on a frame that respects or disrupts the bulk of the adjacent buildings – then how can architecture remain a means by which society explores new territories and develops new knowledge?

10.02 North–South Gallery, Parc de la Villette, Paris 1985.

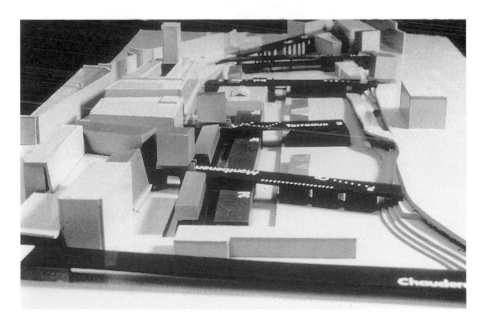

10.03 Inhabited bridges, Lausanne, 1988.

10.04 Inhabited bridges, Lausanne, 1988.

10.05 ZKM, Karlsruhe, Germany, 1988.

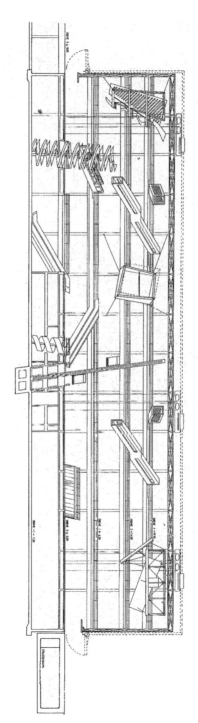

10.0€ ZKM, Karlsruhe, Germany, 1988.

10.07 ZKM, Karlsruhe, Germany, 1988.

10.08 Le Fresnoy, Center for Art and Media, Tourcoing, France, 1991.

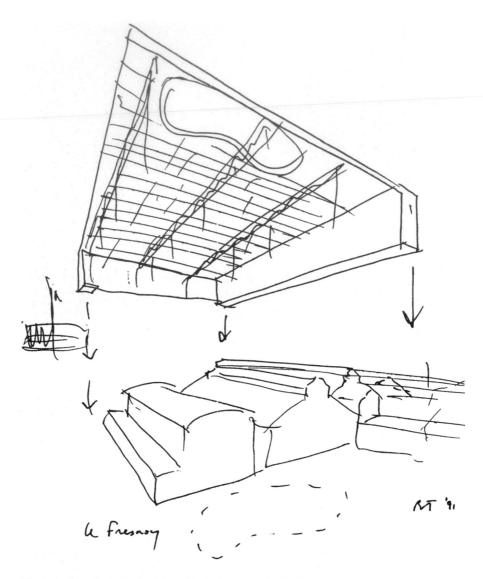

10.09 Le Fresnoy, Center for Art and Media, Tourcoing, France, 1991.

10.10 Glass video gallery, Groningen, the Netherlands,1988.

10.11 Bibliotheque de France, Paris, 1988.

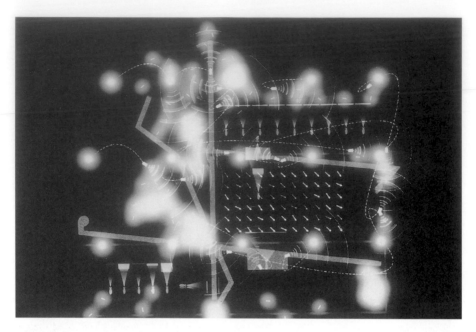

10.12 Le Fresnoy, Center for Art and Media, Tourcoing, France, 1991.

PART II

Concept I: technologies of defamiliarization

In recent years, small pockets of resistance began to form as architects in various parts of the world – England, Austria, the United States, Japan (for the most part, in advanced postindustrial cultures) – started to take advantage of this condition of fragmentation and superficiality and to turn it against itself. The prevalent ideology was one of familiarity – familiarity with known images, derived from 1920s modernism or eighteenth-century classicism – maybe one's role was to defamiliarize. If the new, mediated world echoed and reinforced our dismantled reality, maybe, just maybe, one should take advantage of such dismantling, celebrate fragmentation by celebrating the culture of differences, by accelerating and intensifying the loss of certainty, of center, of history.

In culture in general, the world of communication in the last 20 years has certainly helped the expression of a multiplicity of new angles on the canonic story, airing the views of women, immigrants, gays, minorities, and various non-Western identities who never sat comfortably within the supposed community. In architecture in particular, the notion of defamiliarization was a clear tool. If the design of windows only reflects the superficiality of the skin's decoration, we might very well start to look for a way to do without windows. If the design of pillars reflects the conventionality of a supporting frame, maybe we might get rid of pillars altogether.

Although the architects concerned might not profess an inclination toward the exploration of new technologies, such work usually took advantage of contemporary technological developments. Interestingly, the specific technologies – air conditioning, or the construction of lightweight structures, or computer modes of calculation – have yet to be theorized in architectural culture. I stress this because other technological advances, such as the invention of the elevator or the nineteenth-century development of steel construction, have been the subject of countless studies by historians, but very little such work exists in terms of contemporary technologies because these technologies do not necessarily produce historical forms.

I take this detour through technology because technology is inextricably linked to our contemporary condition: to say that society is now about media and mediation makes us aware that the direction taken by technology is less the domination of nature through technology than the development of information and the construction of the world as a set of images. Architects must again understand and take advantage of the use of such new technologies. In the words of the French writer, philosopher, and architect Paul Virilio, "... we are not dealing anymore with the technology of construction, but with the construction of technology."

Concept II: the mediated "metropolitan" shock

That constant flickering of images fascinates us, much as it fascinated Walter Benjamin in *The Work of Art in the Age of Mechanical Reproduction*. I hate to cite such a "classic", but Gianni Vattimo's recent analysis of the text has indicated aspects that are illustrative of our contemporary condition. When Benjamin discussed the reproducibility of images, he pointed out that the loss of their exchange value, their "aura", made them interchangeable, and that in an age of pure information the only thing that counted was the "shock" – the shock of images, their surprise factor. This shock factor was what allowed an image to stand out: more over, it was also characteristic of our contemporary condition and of the dangers of life in the modern metropolis. These dangers resulted in constant anxiety about finding oneself in a world in which everything was insignificant and gratuitous. The experience of such anxiety was an experience of defamiliarization, of *Un-zu-hause-sein*, of *Unheimlichkeit*, of the uncanny.

In many ways, the esthetic experience, according to Benjamin, consisted of keeping defamiliarization alive, as contrasted to its opposite – familiarization, security, *Geborgenheit*. I would like to point out that Benjamin's analysis corresponds exactly to the historical and philosophical dilemma of architecture. Is the experience of architecture something that is meant to defamiliarize – let's say, a form of "art" – or, on the contrary, is it something that is meant to be comforting, *heimlich*, homely-something that protects? Here, of course, one recognizes the constant opposition between those who see architecture and our cities as places of experience and experiment, as exciting reflections of contemporary society – those who like "things that go bump in the night", that deconstruct and self-destruct – and those who see the role of architecture as refamiliarization, contextualization, insertion – in other words, those who describe themselves as historicists, contextualists, and postmodernists, since postmodernism in architecture now has a definitely classicist and historicist connotation.

The general public will almost always stand behind the traditionalists. In the public eye, architecture is about comfort, about shelter, about bricks and mortar. However, for those for whom architecture is not necessarily about comfort and *Gehorgenheit*, but is also about advancing society and its development, the device of shock may be an indispensable tool. Cities like New York, despite – or maybe because of – its homeless and 2000 murders a year become the post-industrial equivalent of Georg Simmel's preindustrial *Grosstadt* that so fascinated and horrified Benjamin. Architecture in the megalopolis may be more about finding unfamiliar solutions to problems than about the quieting, comforting solutions of the establishment community.

Recently, we have seen important new research on cities in which the fragmentation and dislocation produced by the scaleless juxtaposition of highways, shopping centers, high-rise buildings, and small houses is seen as a positive sign of the vitality of urban culture. As opposed to nostalgic attempts to restore an impossible continuity of streets and plazas, this research implies making an event out of urban shock, intensifying and accelerating urban experience through clash and disjunction.

Let us return to the media. In our era of reproduction, we have seen how the conventional construction techniques of frame and skin correspond to the superficiality and precariousness of media culture, and how a constant expansion of change was necessary to satisfy the often banal needs of the media. We have also seen that to endorse this logic means that any work is interchangeable with any other, just as we accelerate the shedding of the skin of a dormitory and replace it with another. We have also seen that the shock goes against the nostalgia of permanence or authority, whether it is in culture in general or architecture in particular. Over 50 years after the publication of Benjamin's text, we may have to say that shock is still all we have left to communicate in a time of generalized information. In a world heavily influenced by the media, this relentless need for change is not necessarily to be understood as negative. The increase in change and superficiality also means a weakening of architecture as a form of domination, power, and authority, as it historically has been in the last 6000 years.

Concept III: de-structuring

This "weakening" of architecture, this altered relationship between structure and image, structure and skin, is interesting to examine in the light of a debate that has resurfaced recently in architectural circles – namely, structure versus ornament. Since the Renaissance, architectural theory has always distinguished between structure and ornament and has set forth the hierarchy between them. To quote Leon Battista Alberti: "Ornament has the character of something attached or additional." Ornament is meant to be additive; it must not challenge or weaken the structure.

But what does this hierarchy mean today, when the structure often remains the same – an endlessly repetitive and neutralized grid? In the majority of construction in this country today, structural practice is rigorously similar in concept: a basic frame of wood, steel, or concrete. As noted earlier, the decision whether to construct the frame from any of these materials is often left to the engineers and economists rather than to the architect. The architect is not meant to question structure. The structure must stand firm. After all, what would happen to insurance premiums (and to reputations) if the building collapsed? The result is too often a refusal to question structure. The structure must be stable, otherwise the edifice collapses – the edifice being both the building and the entire edifice of thought. For, in comparison to science or philosophy, architecture rarely questions its foundations.

The result of these "habits of mind" in architecture is that the structure of a building is not supposed to be questioned anymore than are the mechanics of a projector when watching a movie or the hardware of a television set when viewing images on its screen. Social critics regularly question the image yet rarely question the apparatus, the frame. Still, for over a century, and especially in the past 20 years, we have seen the beginning of such questioning. Contemporary philosophy has touched upon this relationship between frame and image – here the frame is seen as the structure, the armature, and the image as the ornament. Jacques Derrida's *Parergon* turns such questioning between frame and image into a theme. Although it might be argued that the frame of a painting does not quite equate to the frame of a building – one being exterior or "hors d'oeuvre" and the other interior – I would maintain that this is only a *superficial* objection. Traditionally, both frame and structure perform the same function of "holding it together".

Concept IV: superimposition

This questioning of structure led to a particular side of contemporary architectural debate, namely deconstruction. From the beginning, the polemics of deconstruction, together with much of poststructuralist thought, interested a small number of architects because it seemed to question the very principles of *Gehorgenheit* that the postmodernist mainstream was trying to promote. When I first met Jacques Derrida in order to try to convince him to confront his own work with architecture, he asked me, "But how could an architect be interested in deconstruction? Alter all, deconstruction is anti-form, anti-hierarchy, anti-structure, the opposite of all that architecture stands for." "Precisely for this reason", I replied.

As years went by, the multiple interpretations that multiple architects gave to deconstruction became more multiple than deconstruction's theory of multiple readings could ever have hoped. For one architect it had to do with dissimulation; for another, with fragmentation; for yet another, with displacement. Again, to quote Nietzsche: "There are no facts, only an infinity of interpretations." And very soon, maybe due to the fact that many architects shared the same dislike for the *Geborgenheit* of the "historicist postmodernists" and the same fascination for the early twentieth-century avant-garde, deconstructivism was born – and immediately called a "style" – precisely what these architects had been trying to avoid. Any interest in poststructuralist thought and deconstruction stemmed from the fact that they challenged the idea of a single unified set of images, the idea of certainty, and of course, the idea of an identifiable language.

Theoretical architects – as they were called – wanted to confront the binary oppositions of traditional architecture: namely, form versus function, or abstraction versus figuration. However, they also wanted to challenge the implied hierarchies hidden in these dualities, such as, "form follows function", and "ornament is subservient to structure." This repudiation of hierarchy led to a fascination with complex images that were simultaneously "both" and "neither/nor" – images that were the overlap or the superimposition of many other images. Superimposition became a key device. This can be seen in my own work. In *The Manhattan Transcripts* (1981) or *The Screenplays* (1977), the devices used in the first episodes were borrowed from film theory and the *nouveau roman*. In the *Transcripts* the distinction between structure (or frame), form (or space), event (or function), body (or movement), and fiction (or narrative) was systematically blurred through superimposition, collision, distortion, fragmentation, and so forth. We find superimposition used quite remarkably in Peter Eisenman's work, where the overlays for his 'Romeo and Juliet' project pushed literary and philosophical parallels to extremes. These different realities challenged any single interpretation, constantly trying to problematize the architectural object, crossing boundaries between film, literature, and architecture: ("Was it a play or was it a piece of architecture?").

Much of this work benefited from the environment of the universities and the art scene – its galleries and publications – where the crossover among different fields allowed architects to blur the distinctions between genres, constantly questioning the discipline of architecture and its hierarchies of form. Yet if I was to examine both my own work of this time and that of my colleagues, I would say that both grew out of a critique of architecture, of the nature of architecture. It dismantled concepts and became a remarkable conceptual tool, but it could not address the one thing that makes the work of architects ultimately different from the work of philosophers: materiality.

Just as there is a logic of words or of drawings, there is a logic of materials, and they are not the same. And however much they are subverted, something ultimately resists. *Ceci n'est pas une pipe*. A word is not a concrete block. The concept of dog does not bark. To quote Gilles Deleuze, "The concepts of film are not given in film." When metaphors and catachreses are turned into buildings, they generally turn into plywood or "papier-mache" stage sets: the ornament again. Sheet rock columns that do not touch the ground are not structural, they are ornament. Yes, fiction and narrative fascinated many architects, perhaps because, our enemies might say, we knew more about books than about buildings.

I do not have the time to dwell upon an interesting difference between the two interpretations of the role of fiction in architecture: one, the so-called historicist postmodernist allegiance, the other, the so-called deconstructivist neomodernist allegiance (not my labels). Although both stemmed from early interests in linguistics and semiology, the first group saw fiction and narrative as part of the realm of metaphors, of a new *architecture parlante*, of *form*, while the second group saw fiction and scenarios as analogues for programs and *function*.

I would like to concentrate on that second view. Rather than manipulating the formal properties of architecture, we might look into what really happens inside buildings and cities: the function, the program, the properly *historical* dimension of architecture. Roland Barthes's *Structural Analysis of Narratives* was fascinating in this respect, for it could be directly transposed both in spatial and programmatic sequence. The same could be said of much of Sergei Eisenstein's theory of film montage.

Concept V: crossprogramming

Architecture has always been as much about the event that takes place in a space as about the space itself. The Columbia University Rotunda has been a library; it has been used as a banquet hall; it is often the site of university lectures; someday it could fulfill the needs for an athletic facility at the university. What a wonderful swimming pool the Rotunda would be! You may think I'm being facetious, but in today's world where railway stations become museums and churches become nightclubs, a point is being made: the complete interchangeability of form and function, the loss of traditional, canonic cause-and-effect relationships as sanctified by modernism. Function does not follow form, form does not follow function – or fiction for that matter – however, they certainly interact. Diving into this great blue Rotunda pool – a part of the *shock*.

If shock can no longer be produced by the succession and juxtaposition of facades and lobbies, maybe it can be produced by the juxtaposition of events that take place behind these facades in these spaces. If "the respective contamination of all categories, the constant substitutions, the confusion of genres" – as described by critics of the right and left alike from Andreas Huyssens to Jean Baudrillard – is the new direction of our times, it may well be used to one's advantage, to the advantage of a general rejuvenation of architecture. If architecture is both concept and experience, space and use, structure and superficial image – nonhierarchically – then architecture should cease to separate these categories and instead merge them into unprecedented combinations of programs and spaces. "Crossprogramming," "transprogramming," "disprogramming": I have elaborated on these concepts elsewhere, suggesting the displacement and mutual contamination of terms.

Concept VI: events: the turning point

My own work in the 1970s constantly reiterated that there was no architecture without event, no architecture without action, without activities, without functions. Architecture was seen as the combination of spaces, events, and movements without any hierarchy or precedence among these concepts. The hierarchical cause-and-effect relationship between function and form is one of the great certainties of architectural thinking – the one that lies behind that reassuring *idee recue* of community life that tells us that we live in houses "designed to answer to our needs", or in cities planned as machines to live in. *Geborgenheit* connotations of this notion go against both the real "pleasure" of architecture, in its unexpected combinations of terms, and the reality of contemporary urban life in its most stimulating, unsettling directions. Hence, in works like *The Manhattan Transcripts*, the definition of architecture could not be form or walls but had to be the combination of heterogeneous and incompatible terms.

The insertion of the terms "event" and "movement" was influenced by Situationist discourse and by the 1968 era. *Les evenements*, as they were called, were not only events in action but also in thought. Erecting a barricade (function) in a Paris street (form) is not quite equivalent to being a *flâneur* (function) in that same street (form). Dining (function) in the Rotunda (form) is not quite equivalent to reading or swimming in it. Here all hierarchical relationships between form and function cease to exist. This unlikely combination of events and spaces was charged with subversive capabilities, for it challenged both the function and the space. Such confrontation parallels the Surrealists' meeting of a sewing machine and an umbrella on a dissecting table or, closer to us, Rem Koolhaas' description of the Downtown Athletic Club: "Eating oysters with boxing gloves, naked, on the nth floor."

We find it today in Tokyo, with multiple programs scattered throughout the floors of high-rise buildings: a department store, a museum, a health club, and a railway station, with putting greens on the roof. And we will find it in the programs of the future, where airports are simultaneously amusement arcades, athletic facilities, cinemas, and so on. Regardless of whether they are the result of chance combinations or are due to the pressure of ever-rising land prices, such noncausal relationships between form and function or space and action go beyond poetic confrontations of unlikely bedfellows. Michel Foucault, as cited in a book by John Rajchman, expanded the use of the term *event* in a manner that went beyond the single action or activity and spoke of "events of thought". For Foucault, an event is not simply a logical sequence of words or actions but rather "the moment of erosion, collapse, questioning, or problematization of the very assumptions of the setting within which a drama may take place – occasioning the chance or possibility of another, different setting." The event here is seen as a turning point – not an origin or an end – as opposed to such propositions as form follows function. I would like to propose that the future of architecture lies in the construction of such events.

Just as important is the spatialization that goes with the event. Such a concept is quite different from the project of the modern movement, which sought the affirmation of certainties in a unified Utopia as opposed to our current questioning of multiple, fragmented, dislocated terrains.

A few years later, in an essay about the *folies* of the Parc de la Villette, Jacques Derrida expanded on the definition of *event*, calling it "the emergence of a disparate multiplicity". I had constantly insisted, in our discussions and elsewhere, that these points called *folies* were points of activities, of programs, of events. Derrida elaborated on this concept, proposing the possibility of an "architecture of the event" that would "eventualize," or open up that which, in our history or tradition, is understood to be fixed, essential, monumental. He had also suggested earlier that the word "event" shared roots with "invention", hence the notion of the event, of the action-in-space, of the turning point, the invention. I would like to associate it with the notion of shock, a shock that in order to be effective in our mediated culture, in our culture of images, must go beyond Walter Benjamin's definition and *combine the idea of function or action with that of image*. Indeed, architecture finds itself in a unique situation: it is the only discipline that by definition combines concept and experience, image and use, image and structure. Philosophers can write, mathematicians can develop virtual spaces, but architects are the only ones who are the prisoners of that hybrid art, where the image hardly ever exists without a combined activity.

It is my contention that far from being a field suffering from the incapability of questioning its structures and foundations, it is the field where the greatest discoveries will take place in the coming century. The very heterogeneity of the definition of architecture − space, action, and movement − makes it into that event, that place of shock, or that place of the invention of ourselves. The event is the place where the rethinking and reformulation of the different elements of architecture, many of which have resulted in or added to contemporary social inequities, may lead to their solution. By definition, it is the place of the combination of differences.

This will not happen by imitating the past and eighteenth-century ornaments. It also will not happen by simply commenting, through design, on the various dislocations and uncertainties of our contemporary condition. I do not believe it is possible, nor does it make sense, to design buildings that *formally* attempt to blur traditional structures, that is, that display forms that lie somewhere between abstraction and figuration, or between structure and ornament, or that are cut up and dislocated for esthetic reasons. Architecture is not an illustrative art; it does not illustrate theories. (I do not believe you can design deconstruction.) You cannot design a new definition of cities and their architecture. But one may be able to design the conditions that will make it possible for this nonhierarchical, nontraditional society to happen. By understanding the nature of our contemporary circumstances and the media processes that accompany them, architects possess the possibility of constructing conditions that will create a new city and new relationships between spaces and events.

Architecture is not about the conditions of design but about the design of conditions that will dislocate the most traditional and regressive aspects of our society and simultaneously reorganize these elements in the most liberating way, so that our experience becomes the experience of events organized and strategized through architecture. Strategy is a key word in architecture today. No more masterplans, no more locating in a fixed place, but a new heterotopia. This is what our cities must strive toward and what we architects must help them to achieve by intensifying the rich collision of events and spaces. Tokyo and New York only appear chaotic. Instead, they mark the appearance of a new urban structure, a new urbanity. Their confrontations and combinations of elements may provide us with the event, the shock, that I hope will make the architecture of our cities a turning point in culture and society.

Chapter 11

Rappel a l'ordre: the case for the tectonic
Kenneth Frampton

I have elected to address the issue of tectonic form for a number of reasons, not least of which is the current tendency to reduce architecture to scenography. This reaction arises in response to the universal triumph of Robert Venturi's decorated shed; that all too prevalent syndrome in which shelter is packaged like a giant commodity. Among the advantages of the scenographic approach is the fact that the results are eminently amortisable with all the consequences that this entails for the future of the environment. We have in mind, of course, not the pleasing decay of nineteenth-century Romanticism but the total destitution of commodity culture. Along with this sobering prospect goes the general dissolution of stable references in the late-modern world; the fact that the precepts governing almost every discourse, save for the seemingly autonomous realm of techno-science, have now become extremely tenuous. Much of this was already foreseen half a century ago by Hans Sedlmayr, when he wrote, in 1941:

> The shift of man's spiritual centre of gravity towards the inorganic, his feeling of his way into the inorganic world may indeed legitimately be called a cosmic disturbance in the microcosm of man, who now begins to show a one-sided development of his faculties. At the other extreme there is a disturbance of macrocosmic relationships, a result of the especial favour and protection which the inorganic now enjoys – almost always at the expense, not to say ruin, of the inorganic. The raping and destruction of the earth, the nourisher of man, is an obvious example and one which in its turn reflects the distortion of the human microcosm for the spiritual. [1]

Against this prospect of cultural degeneration, we may turn to certain rearguard positions, in order to recover a basis from which to resist. Today we find ourselves in a similar position to that of the critic Clement Greenberg who, in his 1965 essay "Modernist Painting", attempted to reformulate a ground for painting in the following terms:

> Having been denied by the Enlightenment of all tasks they could take seriously, they [the arts] looked as though they were going to be assimilated to entertainment pure

and simple, and entertainment itself looked as though it were going to be assimilated, like religion, to therapy. The arts could save themselves from this levelling down only by demonstrating that the kind of experience they provided was valuable in its own right, and not to be obtained from any other kind of activity.[2]

If one poses the question as to what might be a comparable ground for architecture, then one must turn to a similar material base, namely that architecture must of necessity be embodied in structural and constructional form. My present stress on the latter rather than the prerequisite of spatial enclosure stems from an attempt to evaluate twentieth-century architecture in terms of continuity and inflection rather than in terms of originality as an end in itself. In his 1980 essay, "Avant Garde and Continuity", the Italian architect Giorgio Grassi had the following comment to make about the impact of avant-gardist art on architecture:

> ... as far as the vanguards of the Modern Movement are concerned, they invariably follow in the wake of the figurative arts ... Cubism, Suprematism, Neoplasticism, etc, are all forms of investigation born and developed in the realm of the figurative arts, and only as a second thought carried over into architecture as well. It is actually pathetic to see the architects of that "heroic" period and the best among them, trying with difficulty to accommodate themselves to these "isms"; experimenting in a perplexed manner because of their fascination with the new doctrines, measuring them, only later to realise their ineffectuality ...[3]

While it is disconcerting to have to recognise that there may well be a fundamental break between the figurative origins of abstract art and the constructional basis of tectonic form, it is, at the same time, liberating to the extent that it affords a point from which to challenge spatial invention as an end in itself: a pressure to which modern architecture has been unduly subject. Rather than join in a recapitulation of avant-gardist tropes or enter into historicist pastiche or into the superfluous proliferation of sculptural gestures, all of which have an arbitrary dimension to the degree that they are based in neither structure nor in construction, we may return instead to the structural unit as the irreducible essence of architectural form.

Needless to say, we are not alluding here to mechanical revelation of construction but rather to a potentially poetic manifestation of structure in the original Greek sense of *poesis* as an act of making and revealing. While I am well aware of the conservative connotations that may be ascribed to Grassi's polemic, his critical perceptions none the less cause us to question the very idea of the new, in a moment that oscillates between the cultivation of a resistant culture and a descent into value-free aestheticism. Perhaps the most balanced assessment of Grassi has been made by the Catalan critic, Ignasi Sola Morales, when he wrote:

> Architecture is posited as a craft, that is to say, as the practical application of established knowledge through rules of the different levels of intervention. Thus, no notion of architecture as problem solving, as innovation, or as invention *ex novo*, is present in Grassi's thinking, since he is interested in showing the permanent, the evident, and the given character of knowledge in the making of architecture.... The work of Grassi is born of a reflection upon the essential resources of discipline, and it focuses upon specific media which determine not only aesthetic choices but also the ethical content of its cultural contribution. Through these channels of ethical and political will, the concern of the Enlightenment ... becomes enriched in its most critical tone. It is not solely the superiority of reason and the analysis of form which are indicated, but rather, the critical role (in the Kantian sense of the term) that is, the judgement of values, the very lack of which is felt in society today.... In the sense that his architecture is a meta-language, a reflection on the contradictions of its own practice, his work acquires the appeal of something that is both frustrating and noble ...[4]

The dictionary definition of the term "tectonic" to mean "pertaining to building or construction in general; constructional, constructive used especially in reference to architecture and the kindred arts," is a little reductive to the extent that we intend not only the structural component *in se* but also the formal amplification of its presence in relation to the assembly of which it is a part. From its conscious emergence in the middle of the nineteenth century with the writings of Karl Bötticher and Gottfried Semper, the term not only indicates a structural and material probity but also a poetics of construction, as this may be practised in architecture and the related arts.

The beginnings of the Modern, dating back at least two centuries, and the much more recent advent of the Post-Modern are inextricably bound up with the ambiguities introduced into Western architecture by the primacy given to the scenographic in the evolution of the bourgeois world. However, building remains essentially *tectonic* rather than scenographic in character and it may be argued that it is an act of construction first, rather than a discourse predicated on the surface, volume and plan, to cite the "Three Reminders to Architects", of Le Corbusier. Thus one may assert that building is *ontological* rather than *representational* in character and that built form is a presence rather than something standing for an absence. In Martin Heidegger's terminology we may think of it as a "thing" rather than a "sign".

I have chosen to engage this theme because I believe it is necessary for architects to re-position themselves given that the predominant tendency today is to reduce all architectural expression to the status of commodity culture. In as much as such resistance has little chance of being widely accepted, a "rearguard" posture would seem to be an appropriate stance to adopt rather than the dubious assumption that it is possible to continue with the perpetuation of avant-gardism. Despite its concern for structure, an emphasis on tectonic form does not necessarily favour either Constructivism or Deconstructivism. In this sense it is astylistic. Moreover it does not seek its legitimacy in science, literature or art.

Greek in origin, the term *tectonic* derives from the term *tekton* signifying carpenter or builder. This in turn stems from the Sanskrit *taksan* referring to the craft of carpentry and to the use of the ax. Remnants of a similar term can also be found in Vedic, where it again refers to carpentry. In Greek it appears in Homer, where it again alludes to carpentry and to the art of construction in general. The poetic connotation of the term first appears in Sappho where the *tekton*, the carpenter, assumes the role of the poet. This meaning undergoes further evolution as the term passes from being something specific and physical, such as carpentry, to the more generic notion of construction and later to becoming an aspect of poetry. In Aristophanes we even find the idea that it is associated with machination and the creation of false things. This etymological evolution would suggest a gradual passage from the ontological to the representational. Finally, the Latin term *architectus* derives from the Greek *archi* (a person of authority) and *tekton* (a craftsman or builder). The earliest appearance of the term "tectonic" in English dates from 1656 where it appears in a glossary meaning "belonging to building", and this is almost a century after the first English use of the term *architect* in 1563. In 1850 the German oriental scholar K.O. Muller was to define the term rather rudely, as "A series of arts which form and perfect vessels, implements, dwellings and places of assembly". The term is first elaborated in a modern sense with Karl Bötticher's *The Tectonic of the Hellenes* of 1843–52 and with Gottfried Semper's essay *The Four Elements of Architecture* of the same year. It is further developed in Semper's unfinished study, *Style in the Technical and Tectonic Arts or Practical Aesthetic*, published between 1863 and 1868.

The term "tectonic" cannot be divorced from the technological, and it is this that gives a certain ambivalence to the term. In this regard it is possibly to identify three distinct conditions:

1   the *technological object* that arises directly out of meeting an instrumental need;

2   the *scenographic object* that may be used equally to allude to an absent or hidden element;

3   the *tectonic object*, that appears in two modes.

We may refer to these modes as the ontological and representational *tectonic*. The first involves a constructional element, that is shaped so as to emphasise its static role and cultural status. This is the tectonic as it appears in Bötticher's interpretation of the Doric column. The second mode involves the representation of a constructional element which is present, but hidden. These two modes can be seen as paralleling the distinction that Semper made between the *structural–technical* and the *structural–symbolic*.

Aside from these distinctions, Semper was to divide built form into two separate material procedures: into the *tectonics* of the frame in which members of varying lengths are conjoined to encompass a spatial field and the *stereotomics* of compressive mass that, while it may embody space, is constructed through the piling up of identical units; the term *sterotomics* deriving from the Greek term for solid, stereos and cutting, *-tomia*. In the first case, the most common material throughout history has been wood or its textual equivalents such as bamboo, wattle and basket-work. In the second case, one of the most common materials has been brick, or the compressive equivalent of brick such as rock, stone or rammed earth and later, reinforced concrete. There have been significant exceptions to this division particularly where, in the interest of permanence, stone has been cut, dressed, and erected in such a way as to assume the form and function of a frame. While these facts are so familiar as to hardly need repetition, we tend to be unaware of the ontological consequences of these differences; that is to say, of the way in which framework tends towards the aerial and the dematerialisation of mass, whereas the mass form is telluric, embedding itself ever deeper into the earth. The one tends towards light and the other towards dark. These gravitational opposites, the immateriality of the frame and the materiality of the mass, may be said to symbolise the two cosmological opposites to which they aspire; the sky and the earth. Despite our highly-secularised technoscientific age, these polarities still largely constitute the experiential limits of our lives. It is arguable that the practice of architecture is impoverished to the extent that we fail to recognise these transcultural values and the way in which they are intrinsically latent in all structural form. Indeed, these forms may serve to remind us, after Heidegger, that inanimate objects may also evoke "being", and that through this analogy to our own corpus, the body of a building may be perceived as though it were literally a physique. This brings us back to Semper's privileging of the joint as the primordial tectonic element, as the fundamental nexus around which building comes into being; that is to say, comes to be articulated as a presence in itself.

Semper's emphasis on the joint implies that fundamental syntactical transition may be expressed as one passes from the stereotomic base to the *tectonic* frame, and that such transitions constitute the very essence of architecture. They

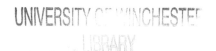

are the dominant constituents whereby one culture of building differentiates itself from the next.

There is a spiritual value residing in the particularities of a given joint that the "thingness" of the constructed object, so much so that the generic joint becomes a point of ontological condensation rather than a mere connection. We need only to think of the work of Carlo Scarpa to touch on a contemporary manifestation of this attribute.

The first volume of the fourth edition of Karl Bötticher's *Tektonik der Hellenen* appeared in 1843, two years after Schinkel's death in 1841. This publication was followed by three subsequent volumes which appeared at intervals over the next decade, the last appearing in 1852, the year of Semper's *Four Elements of Architecture*. Bötticher elaborated the concept of the tectonic in a number of significant ways. At one level he envisaged a conceptual *juncture*, which came into being through the appropriate interlocking of constructional elements. Simultaneously articulated and integrated, these conjunctions were seen as constituting the body-form, the *Korperbilden* of the building that not only guaranteed its material finish of the building, but also enabled this function to be recognised, as a symbolic form. At another level, Bötticher distinguished between the *Kernform* or nucleus and the *Kunstform* or decorative cladding, the latter having the purpose of representing and symbolising the institutional status of the work. According to Bötticher, this shell or *revetment* had to be capable of revealing the inner essence of the tectonic nucleus. At the same time Bötticher insisted that one must always try to distinguish between the indispensable structural form and its enrichment, irrespective of whether the latter is merely the shaping of the technical elements, as in the case of the Doric column or the cladding of its basic form with revetment. Semper will later adapt this notion of *Kunstform* to the idea of *Bekleidung*; that is to say, to the concept of literally "dressing" the fabric of a structure.

Bötticher was greatly influenced by the philosopher Josef von Schelling's view that architecture transcends the mere pragmatism of building by virtue of assuming symbolic significance. For Schelling and Bötticher alike, the inorganic had no symbolic meaning, and hence structural form could only acquire symbolic value by virtue of its capacity to engender analogies between tectonic and organic form. However, any kind of direct imitation of natural form was to be avoided since both men held the view that architecture was an imitative art only in so far as it imitated itself. This view tends to corroborate Grassi's contention that architecture has always been distanced from the figurative arts, even if its form can be seen as paralleling nature. In this capacity architecture simultaneously serves both as a metaphor of, and as a foil to, the naturally organic. In tracing this thought retrospectively, one may cite Semper's "Theory of Formal Beauty" of 1856 in which he no longer grouped architecture with painting and sculpture as a plastic art, but with dance and music as a cosmic art, as an ontological world-making art rather than as representational form. Semper regarded such arts as paramount not only because they were symbolic but also because they embodied man's underlying erotic–ludic urge to strike a beat, to string a necklace, to weave a pattern, and thus to decorate according to a rhythmic law.

Semper's *Four Elements of Architecture* of 1852 brings the discussion full circle in as much as Semper added a specific anthropological dimension to the idea of tectonic form. Semper's theoretical schema constitutes a fundamental break with the 400-year-old humanist formula of *utilitas, firmitas, venustas*, that first served as the intentional triad of Roman architecture and then as the underpinning of post-Vitruvian architectural theory. Semper's radical reformulation stemmed from his seeing a model of a Caribbean hut in the Great Exhibition of 1851 (Figure 11.01). The empirical reality of this simple shelter caused Semper to reject Laugier's primitive hut, adduced in 1753 as the primordial form of shelter with

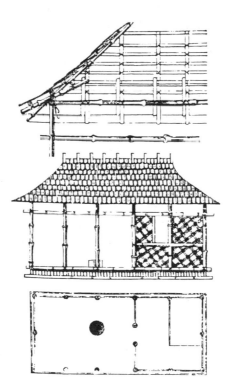

11.01 Gottfried Semper, illustration from *Der Stil in den technischen Kunsten*, 1860–3. The Caribbean hut in the Great Exhibition of 1851.

which to substantiate the pedimented paradigm of Neoclassical architecture. Semper's *Four Elements* countermanded this hypothetical assumption and asserted instead an anthropological construct comprising (1) a hearth, (2) an earthwork, (3) a framework and a roof, and (4) an enclosing membrane.

While Semper's elemental model repudiated Neoclassical authority, it none the less gave primacy to the frame over the loadbearing mass. At the same time, Semper's four-part thesis recognised the primary importance of the earthwork, that is to say, of a telluric mass that serves in one way or another to anchor the frame or the wall, or *Mauer*, into the site.

This marking, shaping, and preparing of ground by means of an earthwork had a number of theoretical ramifications. On the one hand, it isolated the enclosing membrane as a differentiating act, so that the textural could be literally identified with the proto-linguistic nature of textile production that Semper regarded as the basis of all civilisation. On the other hand, as Rosemary Bletter has pointed out, by stressing the earthwork as the fundamental basic form, Semper gave symbolic import to a nonspatial element, namely, the hearth that was invariably an inseparable part of the earthwork. The term "breaking ground" and the metaphorical use of the word "foundation" are both obviously related to the primacy of the earthwork and the hearth.

In more ways than one Semper grounded his theory of architecture in a phenomenal element having strong social and spiritual connotations. For Semper the hearth's origin was linked to that of the altar, and as such it was the spiritual nexus of architectural form. The hearth bears within itself connotations in this regard. It derives from the Latin verb *aedisficare* which in its turn is the origin of the English word edifice, meaning literally "to make a hearth". The latent institutional connotations of both hearth and edifice are further suggested by the verb *to edify*, which means to educate, strengthen and instruct.

Influenced by linguistic and anthropological insights of his age, Semper was concerned with the etymology of building. Thus he distinguished the massivity of a fortified stone wall as indicated by the term *Mauer* from the light frame and infill, wattle and daub say, of mediaeval domestic building, for which the term *Wand* is used. This fundamental distinction has been nowhere more graphically expressed than in Karl Gruber's reconstruction of a mediaeval German town (Figure 11.02). Both *Mauer* and *Wand* reduce to the word "wall" in English, but the latter in German is related to the word for dress, *Gewand*, and to the term *Winden* which means to embroider. In accordance with the primacy that he gave to textiles, Semper maintained that the earliest basic structural artifact was the knot which predominates in nomadic building form, especially in the Bedouin tent and its textile interior. We may note here in passing Pierre Bourdieu's analysis of the

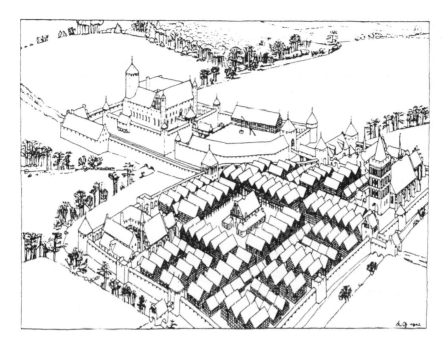

11.02 Karl Gruber, reconstruction of a typical medieval city, 1937.

Bedouin house wherein the loom is identified as the female place of honour and the sun of the interior (Figure 11.03).[5] As is well known, there are etymological connotations residing here of which Semper was fully aware, above all, the connection between knot and joint, the former being in German *die Knoten* and the latter *die Naht*. In modern German both words are related to *die Verbindung*,

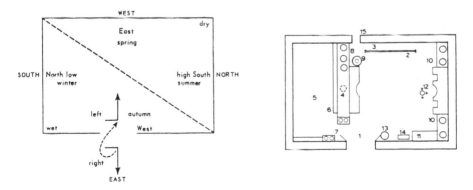

11.03 Berber house, seasonal orientation and internal/external inversion according to the cardinal points: 1. threshold; 2. loom; 3. rifle; 4. thigejdity; 5. stable; 6. trough for oxen; 7. water pitchers; 8. jars of dried vegetables, etc.; 9. hand mill; 10. jars of grain; 11. bench; 12. kanun; 13. large water jar; 14. chest; 15. back door.

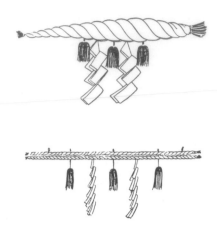

11.04 Shime-nawa. The bound rice straw, apotropaic signs and talismans of Shinto culture.

which may be literally translated as "the binding". All this evidence tends to support Semper's contention that the ultimate constituent of the art of building is the joint.

The primacy that Semper accorded to the knot seems to be supported by Gunther Nitschke's research into Japanese binding and unbinding rituals as set forth in his seminal essay *Shi-Me* of 1979. In Shinto culture these proto-tectonic binding rituals constitute agrarian renewal rites (Figure 11.04). They point at once to that close association between building dwelling, cultivating, and being, remarked on by Martin Heidegger in his essay "Building, Dwelling, Thinking" of 1954.

Semper's distinction between tectonic and stereotonic returns us to theoretical arguments recently advanced by the Italian architect Vittorio Gregotti, who proposes that the marking of ground, rather than the primitive hut, is the primordial tectonic act. In his 1983 address to the New York Architectural League, Gregotti stated:

> ... The worst enemy of modern architecture is the idea of space considered solely in terms of its economic and technical exigencies indifferent to the idea of the site.
>
> The built environment that surrounds us is, we believe, the physical representation of its history, and the way in which it has accumulated different levels of meaning to form the specific quality of the site, not just for what it appears to be, in perceptual terms, but for what it is in structural terms.
>
> Geography is the description of how the signs of history have become forms, therefore the architectural project is charged with the task of revealing the essence of the geoenvironmental context through the transformation of form. The environment is therefore not a system in which to dissolve architecture. On the contrary, it is the most important material from which to develop the project.

Indeed, through the concept of the site and the principle of settlement, the environment becomes the essence of architectural production. From this vantage point, new principles and methods can be seen for design. Principles and methods that give precedence to the siting in a specific area [sic]. This is an act of knowledge of the context *that comes out of its architectural modification* [my italics]. The origin of architecture is not the primitive hut, the cave or the mythical "Adam's House in Paradise". Before transforming a support into a column, roof into a tympanum, before placing stone on stone, man placed a stone on the ground to recognise a site in the midst of an unknown universe, in order to take account of it and modify it. As with every act of assessment, this one required radical moved and apparent simplicity. From this point of view, there are only two important attitudes to the context. The tools of the first are mimesis, organic imitation and the display of complexity. The tools of the second are the assessment of physical relations, formal definition and the interiorisation of complexity.[6]

With the tectonic in mind, it is possible to posit a revised account of the history of modern architecture, for when the entire trajectory is reinterpreted through the lens of *techne* certain patterns emerge and others recede. Seen in this light, a tectonic impulse may be traced across the century uniting diverse works irrespective of their different origins. In this process, well-known affinities are further reinforced, while others recede and hitherto unremarked connections emerge asserting the importance of criteria that lie beyond superficial stylistic differences. Thus for all their stylistic idiosyncrasies a very similar level of tectonic articulation patently links Hendrik Petrus Berlage's Stock Exchange of 1895 (Figure 11.05) to Frank Lloyd Wright's Larkin Building of 1904 (Figure 11.06) and Herman Hertzberger's Central Beheer office complex of 1974 (Figure 11.07). In each instance there is a similar concatenation of span and support that amounts to a tectonic syntax in which gravitational force passes from purlin to truss, to pad stone, to corbel, to arch, to pier and abutment. The technical transfer of this load passes through a series of appropriately articulated transitions and joints. In each of these works the constructional articulation engenders the spatial subdivision and vice versa and this same principle may be found in other works of this century possessing quite different stylistic aspirations. Thus we find a comparable concern for the revealed joint in the architecture of both August Perret and Louis Kahn. In each instance the joint guarantees the probity and presence of the overall form while alluding to distinctly different ideological and referential antecedents. Thus where Perret looks back to the structurally rationalised classicism of the Graeco-Gothic ideal, dating back in France to the beginning of the eighteenth century, Kahn evokes a "timeless archaism", at once technologically advanced but spiritually antique.

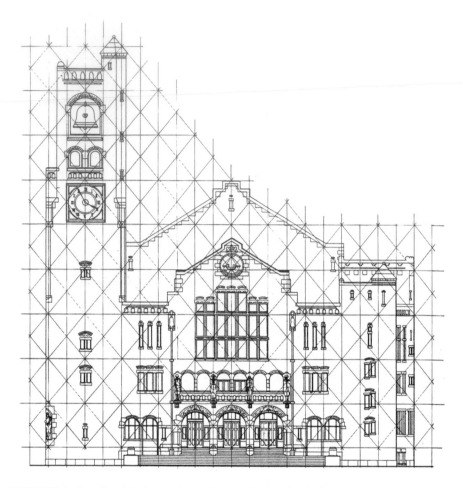

11.05 H.P. Berlage, Stock Exchange, Amsterdam, 1897–1903. South elevation with the system of proportions (1998 drawing).

     The case can be made that the prime inspiration behind all this work stemmed as much from Eugene Viollet-le-Duc as from Semper, although clearly Wright's conception of built form as a petrified fabric writ large, most evident in his textile block houses of the 1920s, derives directly from the cultural priority that Semper gave to textile production and to the knot as the primordial tectonic unit. It is arguable that Kahn was as much influenced by Wright as by the Franco-American Beaux-Arts line, stemming from Viollet-le-Duc and the École des Beaux Arts. This particular genealogy enables us to recognise the links tying Kahn's Richards' Laboratories of 1959 (Figure 11.08) back to Wright's Larkin Building. In each

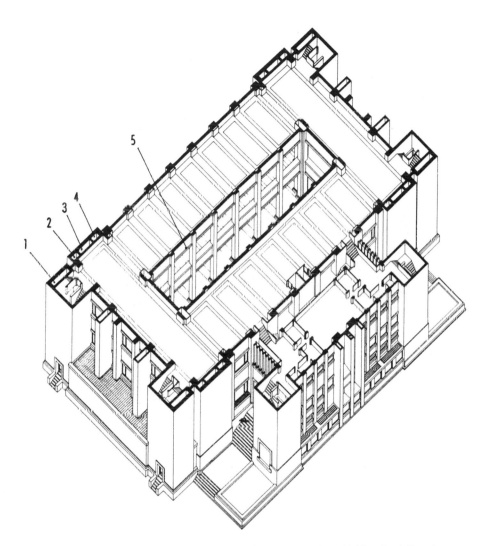

11.06 Frank Lloyd Wright, Larkin Building, Buffalo, 1904. Axonometric at third floor level. Note the service ducts built into the walls of the stair shafts. Numbers indicate built-in services according to the following key: 1. fresh-air intake; 2. utilities; 3. foul air exhaust; 4. miscellaneous ducts and services; 5. tempered air outlets under balcony fronts and ceiling beams.

instance there is a similar "tartan", textile-like preoccupation with dividing the enclosed volume and its various appointments into *servant* and *served* spaces. In addition to this, there is a very similar concern for the *expressive rendering of mechanical services* as though they were of the same hierarchic importance as the structural frame. Thus the monumental brick ventilation shafts of the Richards'

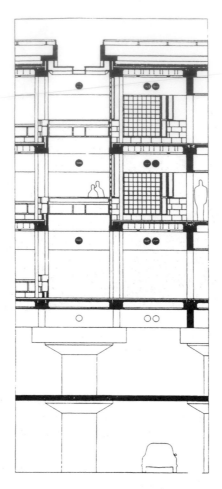

11.07 Herman Hertzberger, Centraal Beheer, Apeldoorn, 1970–3. Section.

Laboratories are anticipated, as it were, in the hollow, ducted, brick bastions that establish the four-square monumental corners of the Larkin Building. However dematerialised there is a comparable discrimination between servant and served spaces, Norman Foster's Sainsbury centre of 1978 (Figure 11.09), combined with a similar penchant for the expressive potential of mechanical services. And here again we encounter further proof that the *tectonic* in the twentieth century cannot concern itself only with structural form.

Wright's highly tectonic approach and the influence of this on the later phases of the modern movement have been underestimated, for Wright is surely the primary influence behind such diverse European figures as Carlo Scarpa, Franco Albini, Leonardo Ricci, Gino Valle (Figure 11.10) and Umberto Riva, to cite

11.08 Louis I. Kahn, Richards' Medical Research Laboratories, perspective sketch from the southwest, 1957 version showing cantilevered and ribbed exhaust stacks.

only the Italian Wrightian line. A similar Wrightian connection runs through Scandinavia and Spain, serving to connect such diverse figures as Jorn Utzon, Xavier Saenz de Oiza and most recently Rafael Moneo, who as it happens was a pupil of both.

Something has to be said of the crucial role played by the joint in the work of Scarpa, and to note the syntactically tectonic nature of his architecture. This dimension has been brilliantly characterised by Marco Frascari in his essay on the mutual reciprocity of "constructing" and "construing":

> Technology is a strange word. It has always been difficult to define its semantic realm. The changes in meaning, at different times and in different places of the word "technology" into its original components of *techne* and *logos*, it is possible to set up a mirror-like relationship between the *techne* of *logos* and the *logos* of *techne*. At the time of the Enlightenment the rhetorical *techne* of *logos* was replaced by the scientific *logos* of *techne*. However, in Scarpa's architecture this replacement did not take place. Technology is present with both the forms in a chiastic quality. Translating this chiastic presence into a language proper to architecture is like saying that there is no construction without a construing, and no construing without a construction.[7]

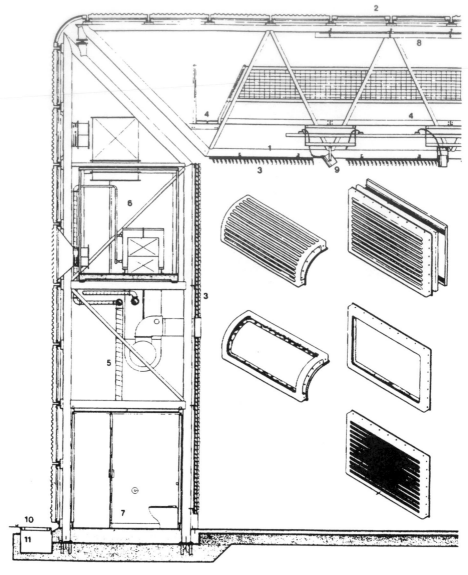

11.09 Foster Associates, Sainsbury Centre for the Visual Arts, University of Norwich, England, 1977. Wall Section.

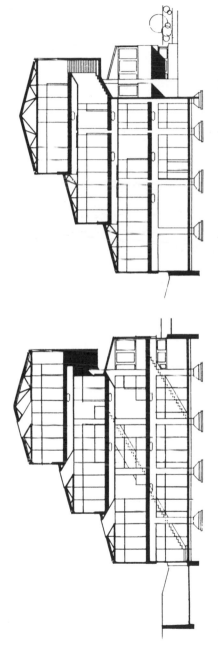

11.10 Gino Valle, factory for Zanussi Rex, Pordenone, 1961.

Elsewhere Frascari writes of the irreducible importance of the joint not only for the work of Scarpa but for all tectonic endeavours. Thus we read in a further essay entitled "The Tell-Tale Detail":

> Architecture is an art because it is interested not only in the original need for shelter but also in putting together, spaces and materials, in the meaningful manner. This occurs through formal and actual joints. The joint, that is the fertile detail, is the place where both the construction and the construing of architecture takes place. Furthermore, it is useful to complete our understanding of this essential role of the joint as the place of the process of signification to recall that the meaning of the original Indo-European root of the word *art* is joint ... [8]

If the work of Scarpa assumes paramount importance for stress on the joint, the seminal value of Utzon's contribution to evolution of modern tectonic form resides in his reinterpretation of Semper's "four elements". This is particularly evident in all his "pagoda/podium" pieces that invariably break down into the earthwork and the surrogate hearth embodied in the podium and into the roof and the textile-like infill to be found in the form of the "pagoda", irrespective of whether this crowning roof element comprises a shell vault or a folded slab (cf. the Sydney Opera House of 1973 and the Bagsvaerd Church of 1977) (Figure 11.11). It says something for Moneo's apprenticeship under Utzon that a similar articulation of earthwork and roof is evident in his Roman archaeological museum completed in Merida, Spain in 1986. As we have already indicated, the tectonic lies suspended between a series of opposites, above all between the *ontological* and the *representational*. However, other dialogical conditions are involved in the articulation of tectonic form, particularly the contrast between the culture of the heavy-*stereotomics* and the culture of the light-*tectonics*. The first implies load-bearing masonry and tends towards the earth and opacity. The second implies the dematerialised a-frame and tends towards the sky and translucence. At one end of this scale we have Semper's earthwork reduced in primordial times, as Gregotti reminds us, to the marking of ground. At the other end we have the ethereal dematerialised aspirations of Joseph Paxton's Crystal Palace, that which Le Corbusier once described as the victory of light over gravity. Since few works are absolutely the one thing or the other, it can be claimed that the poetics of construction arise, in part, out of the inflection and positionings of the tectonic object. Thus the earthwork extends itself upwards to become an arch or a vault, or alternatively withdraws first to become the cross wall support for a simple light-weight span and then to become a podium, elevated from the earth, on which an entire framework takes its anchorage. Other contrasts serve to articulate this dialogical movement further, such as *smooth* versus *rough*,

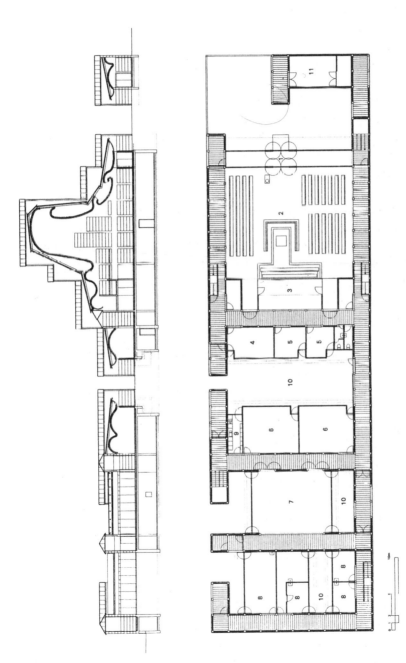

11.11 Jorn Utzon, Bagsvaerd Church, Copenhagen, 1976. Section and plan. Plan key: 1. entrance; 2. church; 3. sacristy; 4. waiting room; 5. office; 6. candidate's room; 7. parish hall; 8. meeting rooms; 9. kitchen; 10. atrium garden; 11. chapel.

at the level of material (cf. Adrian Stokes) or *dark* versus *light* at the level of illumination.

Finally, something has to be said about the signification of the "break" or the "dis-joint" as opposed to the signification of the joint. I am alluding to that point at which things break against each other rather than connect; that significant fulcrum at which one system, surface or material abruptly ends to give way to another. Meaning may be thus encoded through the interplay between "joint" and "break" and in this regard rupture may have just as much meaning as connection. Such considerations sensitise the architecture to the semantic risks that attend all forms of articulation, ranging from the over-articulation of joints to the under-articulation of form.

POSTSCRIPTUM: TECTONIC FORM AND CRITICAL CULTURE

As Sigfried Giedion was to remark in the introduction to his two-volume study, *The Eternal Present* (1962), among the deeper impulses of modern culture in the first half of the 20th century was a "transavantgardist" desire to return to the timelessness of a prehistoric past; to recover in a literal sense some dimension of an eternal present, lying outside the nightmare of history and beyond the processal compulsions of instrumental progress. This drive insinuates itself again today as a potential ground from which to resist the commodification of culture. Within architecture the tectonic suggests itself as a mythical category with which to acquire entry to an anti-processal world wherein the "presencing" of things will once again facilitate the appearance and experience of men. Beyond the aporias of history and progress and outside the reactionary closures of Historicism and the Neo-Avant-Gardism, lies the potential for a *marginal* counterhistory. This is the primaeval history of the logos to which Vico addressed himself in his *Nuova Scienza*, in an attempt to adduce the poetic logic of institutions. It is a mark of the radical nature of Vico's thought that he insisted that knowledge is not just the province of objective fact but also a consequence of the subjective, "collective" elaboration of archetypal myth, that is to say, an assembly of those existential symbolic truths residing in the human experience. The critical myth of the tectonic joint points to just this timeless, time-bound moment, excised from the continuity of time.

Notes

1   Hans Sedimayr, *Art in Crisis: The Lost Centre*. (New York and London: Hollis and Carter Spottiswoode, Ballantyne & Co., Ltd. 1957) 164.

2   Clement Greenberg, "Modernist Painting", 1965. Republished in *The New Art* Gregory Battcock (ed.) (New York: Dalton Paperback 1966) 101–2.

3   Giorgio Grassi, "Avant-Garde and Continuity", *Oppositions* No. 21, Summer, 1980
     IAUS & MIT Press, 26–7.

4   Ignasi Sola Morales, "Critical Discipline", *Oppositions* No. 23. Winter 1981. IAUS &
     MIT Press, 148–50.

5   Vittorio Gregotti, "Lecture at the New York Architectural League". *Section A*, Vol. 1.
     No. 1, Feb/Mar, 1983. Montreal, Canada.

6   Marco Frascari, "Technometry and the work of Carlo Scarpa and Mario Ridolf", Pro-
     ceedings of the ACSA National conference on Techndoom, Washington, 1987.

7   Marco Frascari, "The Tell-Tale Detail", *VIA No. 7*, University of Pennsylvania.

8   See Joseph Mali, "Mythology and Counter-History: The New Critical Art of Vico and
     Joyce".

Constructing

Chapter 12

No-man's land
Lebbeus Woods

This is the first time I have accepted the title given by someone else to a talk I was invited to give, and, what is more, a title given without asking me. But there are two reasons why I like "No-man's land". One, it suggests a land that is no longer "man's," therefore charged with a potential to become more human than "man" ever was. Second, this "no man's land", a term and condition taken from the First World War, refers to a zone between entrenched positions that is extremely difficult and yet extremely necessary to inhabit.

There are an increasing number of such zones in our present cities and in many parts of the world. They are no longer only the slums of a perennial economic underclass that our society maintains at the edge of survival, but also the spaces of a new kind of ambiguity, an uncertainty of meaning that haunts our contemporary condition and cuts across every social class. Today, they include the uncertain living and working spaces of the newly marginalized: skilled workers whose factories have been closed; managers who have been downsized out of their corporate jobs; technicians whose hi-tech industry has moved elsewhere, university graduates who have been trained for jobs that no longer exist. These and others comprise a new category of displaced people who no longer see themselves as members of established and secure social groups. They can no longer identify with spaces these groups erect as symbols of their presence, strength, stability. They exist wherever there's been some eruption in the global economic landscape, wherever there's been a war, or some form of abrupt shift in political power, or any other disruption of a status quo that suddenly creates a void where only yesterday there was community, livelihood, meaning.

I think of these voids as spaces of crisis. Within them, and in a sense, because of them, the entire elaborate superstructure of social and personal relationships, built up over lifetimes, is called into question. We are no longer sure of the intentions that have created these spaces, and do not know how to either act or react within or to them, and yet we must continue to act nonetheless. Their strangeness already determines that they are not spaces for everyone. Universality and typicality do not pertain to or issue from them. Like Tolstoy's "unhappy families," they are each unique. As for the happy families, which are the very justifi-cation of social order, and which are supposed to be "all alike," it is true there are many people today – though I hesitate to say most – who are snugly installed in comforting spaces of the familiar, where the idea of crisis is confined to peoples and events so distant that they appear only as ghosts on the nightly news. Still, the dynamics of contemporary life are such that crisis, and its discomfiting spaces of uncertainty and anxiety, is drawing ever nearer to the core of our common experience. Is there a no-man's land next door? If not, maybe you are already in one.

Architecture is a field largely devoted to valorizing the normal. Even when extraordinary buildings are built, they more often define the limits of the normal than confirm the potential of the extra-normal; that is, of domains beyond the ones con-trolled by secure social groups. From the standpoint of these groups, this is as it should be. However, for those living on the outside, in the no-man's lands of the "others", "extraordinary" takes on an urgent meaning. It is with this meaning in mind that I shall discuss three projects designed not only to valorize three extraordinary domains, but also to activate their potential in human terms.

The first of these is in Berlin, or, I should say, in the Berlin of 1990, barely a year after the re-unification of the city. The second is in the Sarajevo of 1993 and today, a city tormented then and now by fierce uncertainties. The third is in Eind-hoven, Holland, a city in which the uncertainty provoked by change is well-managed, so far, but will remain so only if it is increasingly acknowledged.

BERLIN AND THE INVENTION OF FREESPACE

The concept of freespace emerged in late 1990 from questions arising about the re-unification of Berlin and the role architecture would and could play in the process. It was plain to see then, and even more so now, that new building pro-jects would become primary instruments for installing a near-total cultural, political, and social program in the reconfigured center of the city. This would be a kind of soft totalitarianism catering to business and political interests, but would be near-fatal to the new forms of creative development latent in the very condition of "re-unification." I reasoned that if the potential for new forms of various kinds in the dynamics of re-defining and re-structuring the center of an important capital were to be activated, then there must be new kinds of spaces built alongside the typical monuments – office building complexes, museums and restored palaces that were sure to come.

At the same time, I realized there were no clients, in the traditional sense, for these new kinds of spaces. Today's investors have little interest in supporting in a

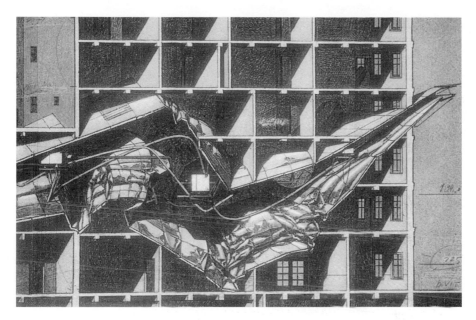

12.01

material way the risky ambiguity involved in trying untested ideas on a civic scale. I took the position that it is up to architects to not only design the new kinds of spaces, but to propose them. In this way they would be exercising the social agency inherent in the idea of architecture (a social art) and its design (a political act). I acknowledge, however, that this is very much a minority view.

My initiative in Berlin in 1990 was to propose a new type of space, which I called "freespace." What made it new was not its utter lack of programmatic content, which is one implication of the term "free." It can be argued – and I have vigorously done so elsewhere[1] – that all architectural space is abstract and without inherent meaning or purpose. Nor is its newness tied to an especially urgent need to provide such space in Berlin. Every city – even the ultra-orderly capital of the German state – will inevitably produce some left-over or abandoned places, spaces which were once useful and now are not. They wait in darkness and silence, "free" of content, poised for some re-occupation, some re-definition in human terms, or for the wrecking-ball that will abruptly end their latency and potential. Rather, the newness of freespace resided in its resistance to use in normal terms. Like primordial landscapes placed in the innards of conventional buildings, they are of a form and materiality alien to them, spaces of strangeness, challenge, potential.

I'll note only briefly here that by proposing these sorts of interventions, I

12.02

became a kind of hero of urban "viruses" and other forms of cultural/social subversion, at least for those architects and others who propose, for various reasons, to undermine prevailing social systems. My aims — whatever my views of these systems — were far more modest. What I hoped to achieve in Berlin, then later in Zagreb, and much later in Havana, was an expansion of potentials, a widening of possibilities of the ways that space might be inhabited in these self-transforming cities. Far from wanting to see the prevailing systems collapse, these projects actively depend on the viability of existing infrastructures of all kinds, even as they aim to expand, or, in some cases, transcend them. But in one sense the proponents of subversion are right: the truly strange, the transformative unknown, is accessible only within the terrain of the familiar.

SARAJEVO AND THE CONSTRUCTION OF THE SCAR

Of all the sites I saw in the besieged city of Sarajevo in the misty, dark November of 1993, none struck me as more poignant than the ruins of the old tobacco factory in the sector of the city known as *Marijin dvor*. Believe me, there was plenty of competition. The city's venerable mosques were being shelled from the mountaintops above, and were badly damaged. The National Library, which was built long ago as a city hall, and whose destruction had become a worldwide symbol of the savagery of the city's besiegers, was still emitting the smoke of burned Medieval manuscripts. People were running behind improvised sniper-screens on the main streets, hoping only to find their way home alive, and once getting there, to find that their homes and families had survived the rain of mortar and artillery shells continuously falling on the city. There was little food and water, no electricity, no heat. This is not the place to discuss the heroism of the people of Sarajevo in those terrible times, which means their refusal to despair in the face of sheer desperation. Still, the subject cannot be entirely avoided. Especially when we come to *Marijin dvor*.

This cultural significance of this part of Sarajevo derives from the fact that it is the western limit of the Austro-Hungarian development of the city, which ended in 1914. Even further to the west, in Novo Sarajevo, extending some ten kilometers to the airport, there were already hectares of new housing blocks, shops, and

12.03

communities built with drab socialist vigor. *Marijin dvor* was a potential space occupied by a potpourri of scattered, but significant, buildings: the Parliament of Bosnia and Herzegovina, the Unis Towers, the Holiday Inn hotel, built for the Winter Olympic Games of 1984 and, not least, the old tobacco factory.

During the siege of Sarajevo, which lasted from 1992 to 1995, and which took more than 10 000 human lives and devastated a unique culture, there was a joke told in the city which reveals something about Bosnian humor, and about the old tobacco factory. It went like this: "There's enough tobacco stored in the factory to make cigarettes for four years. When that is gone, we will surrender." Because the tobacco factory, which was built by the Austrians, was reduced to a ruin by artillery fire early on in the siege, the tobacco store was moved and cigarettes were actually manufactured elsewhere for the duration of the siege. Still, the old site retained its symbolic significance. To appreciate the joke, and this story, you must understand that there is nothing Sarajevans enjoyed more than sitting in outdoor cafes, sipping kava, talking to one another, and smoking. The joke underlines a serious civilizational premise, which has more to do with an idea of style than with smoking per se, yet cannot do without it. When the tobacco runs out, the city is lost.

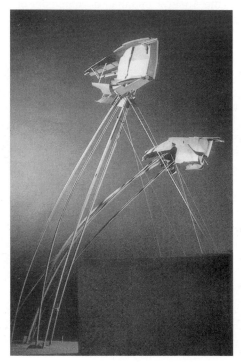

12.04

This is a long, Sarajevan, way of telling why I found the site in *Marijin dvor* more poignant than the shattered mosques and the smoldering library, which – indispensable as they are – have more to do with culture as epic than with the texture and feel of everday life. In this site, it was not the past that was being attacked, nor the future, but exactly the present.

It was no surprise, then, that when, some months later, I began to think seriously about the reconstruction of Sarajevo, this site was one of the first I considered. For it I proposed the High Houses.

Built on tall, flexible columns made of scavanged steel beams welded end-to-end, the two houses – precisely two – rise above the devastated site. Fixed to it by cables that pull the columns like catapults into tension, the houses are stabilized by their strong impulse to move. They reclaim the space that was for so long dominated by the arcing mortar and artillery shells that destroyed this and many others places in the city. But more, by their physical presences they address a particularly Sarajevan improbability: the desire to fly and the desire to be rooted to one place, both at the same time.

After the siege ended, and even from the perspective of that desperate November more than two years earlier, it was clear that reconstruction of this site or any other, when it came, could not be a simple matter of restoration. Yes, it is always technically possible to rebuild things to their pre-siege condition, and many

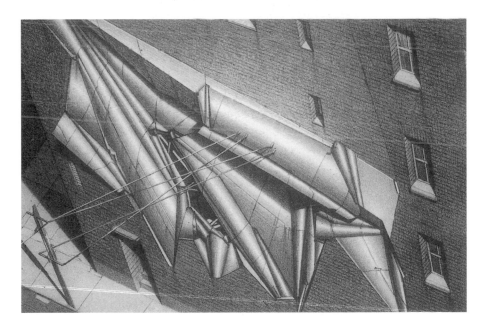

12.05

people would like it to be so. They think it will be a way of erasing the destruction and degradation the siege had imposed upon them. But the fact is that none of it can be erased, but only transcended. And this cannot occur in a game of pretense that everything will be restored to normal. Things will never be restored to normal, and cannot be. Things must move on from what they actually are, continually becoming, continually redefining themselves. That is the rule of life anywhere, and nowhere more so than in the city where life has been so threatened, so disrupted, and so abruptly transformed. The pre-siege Sarajevo, cosmopolitan, multi-cultural, and innocent of the violence incubating within it, is now a closed chapter, a completed history.

The new Sarajevo can only emerge from the great depth of its private and collective experiences, painful though they may have been and in some ways remain. I will put it in more vulgar terms. From deep wounds come scars. The scar is not a monument to the wound, nor the circumstances that caused it. On the contrary, it is a manifestation of the wound's healing that at the same time incorporates what flesh has learned. The scar is new tissue, a sign of life transforming itself, a signal of hope that the past has been overcome, and that existence has once again been victorious over itself.

EINDHOVEN AND THE INSTALLATION OF THE HERMIT

Who is the hermit, and how does he or she fit into the idea-picture I've been making here? How also does the hermit contradict this picture, or at least expand its frame?

Well, it is clear that the hermit is a person who is not only alone, but who has chosen to be alone. He is Nietzsche, gone up to the Oberengadine to commune with his spirit. She is Emily Dickenson, withdrawing to her room in her father's house to write poems and struggle with her God. He is also William Burroughs, locked into his "room of terminal addiction", in the Casbah, scribbling visionary nonsense onto soiled bits of paper. He is the Unabomber, hiding in a remote rural cabin, feeding his bitterness towards the world. He and she are the recluses and agoraphobiacs hiding behind lowered shades in the very midst of the urban tumult, thinking God knows-what. Their choices have been made for many reasons, but their essential condition is the same.

On the surface, we can say that the hermit demands to be left alone, but that is only the surface. Beneath this demand is a request that is almost a plea: to be accepted on his or her own terms. The keyword here is acceptance. The hermit retreats from the society of others as a way of joining it. The terms of joining are, for most, extreme: accept me for who and what I am, even if that means one who

12.06

refuses to accept you on your terms. This is far from the efforts of most people to be nice, fit in, follow the rules, play the game. Nietzsche, like his Zarathustra, came down from the mountain to propogate his world-destroying, world-creating visions. Dickenson published her poems, somehow knowing her inner life would find its corresponding outer reflections. Burroughs' scraps became a book that influenced a generation, making him the cult hero of its rebellious uncertainty. The Unabomber used the postal system to send out his deadly messages. As for the uncounted others locked deep in the city's heart, or bowels, we have not heard from them – yet. If we never do, it will be our fault as much as theirs. Like Kafka's Hunger Artist, whispering from beneath the dirty straw of his ultimate cage, they will not have found the food they liked to eat, the nourishment of our unconditional acceptance.

In Eindhoven, Holland, we – a group of architects, engineers, and constructors – decided to create a "hermitage" in a significant public space in the city center, the atrium entrance of a renovated building known as de Witte Dame.[2]

12.07

Something more than a symbolic gesture, but something less than a complete dwelling, it is a temporary space installed in a more permanent landscape. Like the "freespaces" in Berlin and the "scars" in Sarajevo, the hermitage in Eindhoven is a challenge and an act of conciliation, working in both directions. It tests the limits of tolerance of this most liberal of self-professed democracies, by taking liberties with its already-established rules. At the same time, it presents a difficult space for the would-be hermit to conquer, one demanding active engagement, not passive retreat. Conciliation between the extremes of the need to be alone and the need to be together can only occur in the no-man's land between entrenched notions of the public and the private, the very space created by an architecture deeply questioning both.

12.08

Finally we can turn to this interpretation of the lecture's title: the land that belongs to no man.

The idea of ownership is potent enough to have sustained itself for the whole of human history, and to have caused millions of individuals to relinquish their lives in its name. Ownership by the nation, represented by the state. Ownership by the rulers of the state, the stewards of the nation, its land, the culture that thrives upon it, and its wealth – the kings and queens, aristocrats, presidents, prime ministers and CEOs. The idea of private ownership has played its role, too. The farms, the dwellings, the shops . . . but here the story gets much more complex and far less clear.

Returning to the hermit, we can see that in the most immediate sense he and she have made a claim against the ostensible owners of the land, the property, the houses, against the few who actually hold them but only by the tacit consent of the many. The essence of the claim is this: space exists not by fiat, but only by virtue of action, and choice is action's highest form. The liberation of choice is the creation of space.

Notes

1   Woods, Lebbeus, "The Question of Space," *Cyberculture and Technoscience*, Aronowitz, Menser, Matinsons (eds) (New York: Routledge 1996).

2   "The White Lady" is a popular local name for an immense white factory building built for Phillips Electronics in the 1920s and abandoned by them in 1990. The excellent reformation of the building by architect Bert Dirrix, for a private/state consortium, provides Eindhoven with a new "cultural center". The team formed to design and build the Hermitage consisted of myself, Jos Bosman and Dwayne Oyler, architects; Leon Mavis, engineer; and Werner Schippers, fabricator. The project was strongly supported and funded by the MU Art Foundation, Ton van Gool, Director.

Chapter 13

Internal terrains
Zaha Hadid

INTRODUCTION

The idea of the relationship between the Ground and a new, emancipated formulation
of the Plan has existed throughout my work. The Ground organizes space, which in
turn organizes social relations, political structures and the very fabric of everyday life. It
is at once mundane and sublime. The Plan is the architectural vehicle for the manipulating of the ground, its multiplying, renewing, intensifying and re-naming. The projects
we will describe here reflect recent work in the field of the Arts, and have been
grouped according to certain thematic strains that are recurrent. There are many
others, but those identified here share the notion of internalizing "landscape" concepts. By "*landscape*" I do not infer traditional Arcadian visions of Garden cities, but
instead use it to connote an ideological plane of open and continuous space. It could
be said that it is a kind of "pastoralism" that has by some surreal default melded with
urban reality. It is a hybridized encounter, a new version of the plastic architectonic.
Synthesizing external and internal realms as a play of surface and interstitial places, the
Internal Terrain offers a generosity of spatial quality and unbounded delight in a liber-
ated, fluid architectural experience for spectator, visitor, worker or accidental tourist.

CONTOURING

A number of projects exploit the idea of "landscape" whereby the fundamental
organizational patterns are rendered as emerging from the very strata of the existing ground condition. It is as though there is a pregnant potential inherent in the
topography of the site. This, in play with the characteristics of its planometric
delimitation (or sometimes, the lack of), give rise to an architectural order consist-
ing of the interaction between synthetic plate tectonics or artificial and expansive
landforms reminiscent of geological effects

For the Cardiff Bay Opera House Project (1993–6), the site was a former
active harbor that had become swamped. The city had ambitious plans for Cardiff
to become more metropolitan. It had a boulevard-like route called Bute Avenue,
which in the city-councilor's dreams, would become the Champs d'Elycee of
Cardiff. Bute Avenue stretched from the city center to the harbor site, directly into
the Oval Basin, the allocated site for the Opera House.

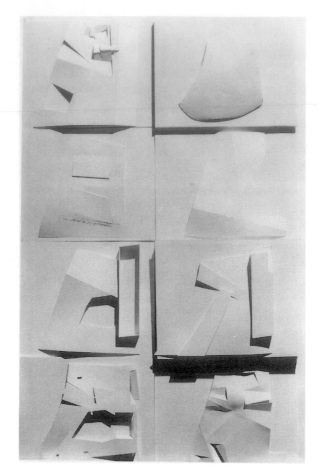

13.01 Cardiff Bay Opera House: ground studies. © Zaha Hadid.

The boulevard notion gave an urban scale to the project, forcing some kind of negotiation with the city center and this more peripheral condition. The question was how to urbanize this hinterland.

The program, though complex and large, could roughly be divided into those spaces that were serviced and those that provided the servicing, or more specifically, performance and ancillary program. Taking the idea of the linear boulevard as a kind of urban spine, we imagined the ancillary program to be a service strip from which the performative spaces were suspended. This we called an "inverted necklace". We folded this ensemble to fit the site outline, giving a configuration of a lifted perimeter block and a cluster of "jewels" in the middle, which were the performance spaces. This at once provided a solution for the organizational prob-

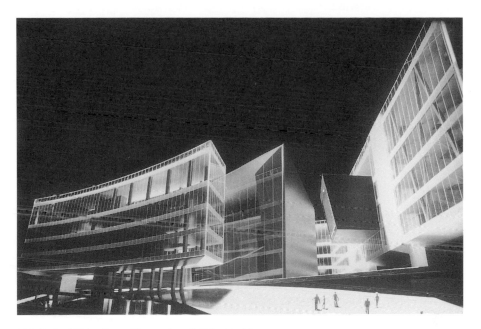

13.02 Cardiff Bay Opera House: view. © Zaha Hadid.

lems and a formal, spatial story containing an array of gaps and elisions. The residual spaces between the "jewels" provided extensive views into the Bay, and into
each other. The idea of an "incomplete" composition is a recurrent theme, whereby
one programs a certain degree of *unprogrammed* space. These interstitial
moments, often at an urban scale, enliven a dialogue with the immediate surroundings and instill a counterpart to the clear, crystalline depiction of form.

The main entry to the building would have been into a place that we called
"The Bubble". This was the ground lobby level, manifested as a peel or bulge of
the existing ground, leaving space underneath (the covered Lobby leading to the
other places in the building, a kind of orientation space), and making a lifted external ground condition, which is the space between the jewels, as mentioned above.
This "peeling" of an existing groundplate renders a new condition in which the
ground level splits into a continuous surface, blurring boundaries between inside
and outside, providing for a multitude of spatial and visual experiences within an
ambivalent environment. The "inverted necklace" configuration would sit on top of
the "Bubble", at once hiding it and giving it expression in acute views. One's
journey, therefore, would be to enter *into* the ground from the waterside, and
ascend into the various pieces of the Opera House from this huge public, covered
square. "The Bubble" negotiates between the public urban character of the city

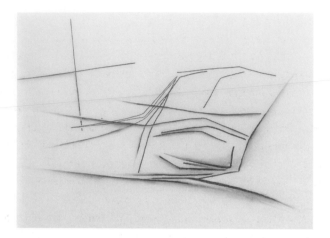

13.03 Luxembourg Concert Hall: sketch. © Zaha Hadid.

and the more private domain of the theatre, which in itself, is a more explicitly-charged space taking its cue from the drama of the Operatic performance.

The Competition for a Philharmonic Hall, Luxembourg (1997) offered a similar programmatic content: a major Concert Hall and a smaller Chamber Music Hall, with the requisite amount of public lobby space and ancillary function. The site overlooked Luxembourg's city center, and was planned as a new locus for cul-

13.04 Luxembourg Concert Hall: view. © Zaha Hadid.

tural activity, with a Museum designed by I.M. Pei planned next to our plot. The neighboring buildings were generic glass-curtained 1960s administrative blocks.

Without a striking architectural context to play off, we looked at the topographical situation, which began to give some clues. The Kirchberg plateux was an artificial plane, surmounting a serpentine route of steep slopes and dramatic drops. The design develops its tectonic language as an interpretation and extension of the animated topography of the Kirchberg. "Slopes, cliffs and valleys" articulate a program with diverse sectional requirements – the entry points of various terraced seating, the performance circulation, service routes, etc. The two main event spaces – the Concert Hall and the Chamber Music Hall stand out in sharp relief as the main scenic features. The rehearsal spaces announce themselves indirectly. A large plate lifts up to give space underneath. The whole coheres into an artificial mountain crowning the plateux of the Place de l'Europe. The public arriving at the plateux ascend further to the raised foyer level of the concert hall. Upon entry, the halls themselves are then expressed as valleys one descends into. A rupture or a canyon as it were, carves a public circulation route in between the two concert halls, which allows for crossing the building without accessing its ticketed areas. This idea of interweaving public routes with programmatically-restricted areas is one that will re-emerge in the Landesgartenschau project, as we will see below.

This theme of a simulacrum of existing topographical features is continued in the design for a Museum of Islamic Arts, Doha, Qatar (1997). The notion of a "museum" being an inherently eighteenth century Western concept is taken as being indicative of the cultural discrepancy between the original intent of the object and its contemporary identity as sanctified artifact. There being no strong precedent for any such museum, especially one found in the locale of the Arab world, we developed an original typology which was rooted in the Islamic predilection for repetitive patterns subverted by moments of difference. We were interested in developing a language that found a rhythmic parallel between the overall configuration of the building, its circulatory character, the topography and orientation of the site and the minutiae of detail located on coins, carpets and ceramics.

It transpired that there was a critical issue of scale. As such, we looked at the existing topographical situation of the site, which was close to the sea on one side, and on the other, marked the edge of the "city" of Doha. The Museum would somehow have to mediate between the grains of these two worlds, as well as the fierce climate and intense natural light which needed to be streamed and kept away from the artifacts.

The scheme is laid out as several fields of influence (institutional) which share a common roofscape. The gallery spaces are an extensive terracing of horizontal and sloped plates that house the spectrum of artifacts. Within this

13.05 Museum of Islamic Arts, Qatar: view of roofscape. © Zaha Hadid.

landscape one encounters a field of lightwells and treasuries which are set into the tectonic fabric like jewels.

The whole building can be seen as the capturing of single stretches of space between the tectonics of the terracing ground plates and a continuous, mirroring dune-like roofscape. This roof is seen almost to emerge from the arid sand and undulate over the internal spaces. The landscaping aspect is treated as an integral feature. Topiary paths and various soft ground surface treatments are proposed from the Corniche boundary to building edge in one continuous design. This area of land formally slopes and laps into the main lobby space.

Another aspect of the dialectic relationship between building and landscape is the treatment of the existing levels of the site, which serve to emphasize this relationship. In all, the scheme can be seen as a confluence of expansive dynamic forces which are generated by and act upon the given site, to produce something which is simultaneously monolithic and absent, a hybrid between natural and artificial form, constituent of a new rather than a given context.

URBAN CALLIGRAPHY

Seemingly against, but often corollary to the *Contouring* mentioned above, is a tendency towards the idea of the graft or the cursive line drawn on the plan and in

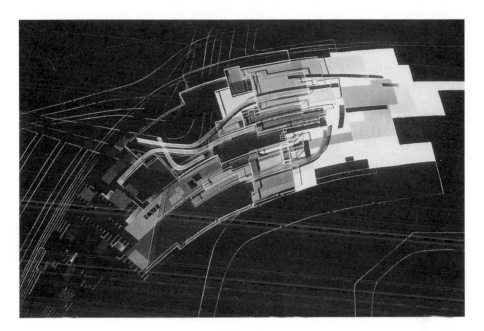

13.06 Museum of Islamic Arts, Qatar: plan. © Zaha Hadid.

space. It can be likened to "calligraphy", in that there is a similar fusion between the "gest", its graphic trace and capacity to embody and signify a "meaning" via an established code of language. This codification is a critical moment, one where the complexities and idiosyncrasies of a given program and the prevalent site conditions are crystallized into one or several "ideograms". Those are like chromasomatic origin points for the disposition of the project, and often, its quite uncanny final guise.

Like Dziga Vertov, in "Man with a Movie Camera", where he is seen to be quite literally bearing over the city he is filming, or Lucio Fontana with his slashes on canvases, the city is a dynamic fabric which can be marked upon. A dense, intangible diagram to be overlaid interrupted, exploited, exaggerated or simply written onto.

Elucidating upon the Museum of Islamic Arts, Doha, Qatar, this motif of gests and cuts organize a number of directional quantities amidst the open and expansive field space. Firstly, there are a number of cursive lines drawn over the plan, which delineate ramps taking the visitor from the lower level of the lobby into the gallery or educational spaces. Secondly, there are families of linear cuts amongst the terracing galleries that contain ramps between the individual floors and also let in natural light from above. They are like enormous vitrines, which pierce the skin of the roof. One's movement is choreography between these

13.07 Museum of Islamic Arts, Qatar: sketch. © Zaha Hadid.

light-filled ascents and darker field-like spaces where the exhibits are. This relates to the tradition of courtyards of Al-Finas, integral to Islamic architecture and city planning.

The design for an Exhibition Pavilion in Weil am-Rhein, Germany, called "Landesgartenschau 1999" takes this theme of metonymy between the gesture and landscape to a pared-down manifestation. Amidst the variegated plans for flora and fauna, the Pavilion is formulated as a "bundle" of lines that emerge, thicken and dissolve back into the landscape. In the convergence and separation of these vectors lies the interplay of exhibition spaces, cafés, offices and the sinuous corridors, ramps and stairways connecting each to the other.

The sinuous grafts that are etched onto the matrix of an existing quarry become routes of neither a specific origin nor destination. They instigate a moment of complication, choreographing space and movement to create instances of multileveled transparency and unexpected encounters.

There is a subtle panoply of velocities that these inhabited lines promote. To be caught in the building is to be made aware of the ephemerality of that moment in the field of vectors that interweave inside and outside, transparency and solidity, weight and lightness. It espouses the static, and instead creates a texture of the moving and the moved, as though transience was made concrete, and the still made fluid.

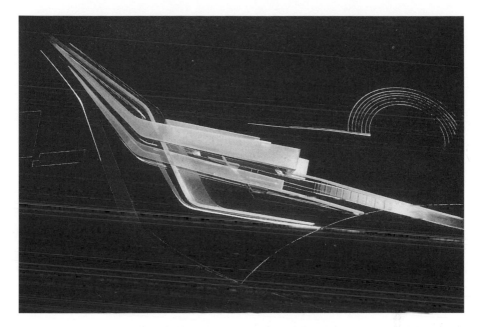

13.08 Landesgartenschau 1999, Weil Am Rhein: model of painting. © Zaha Hadid.

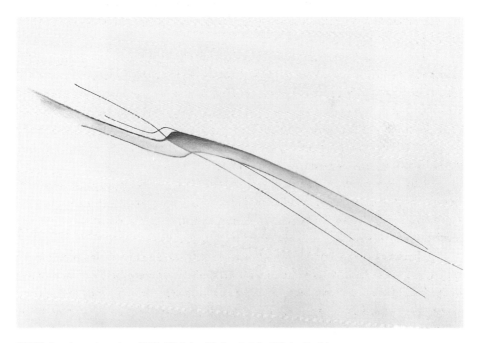

13.09 Landesgartenschau 1999, Weil Am Rhein: sketch. © Zaha Hadid.

A similar embodying of graphic lines occurs in the design for Addressing the Century: One hundred years of Art and Fashion, The Hayward Gallery, London (1998). Instead of negating the architectonic features of the gallery, we sought to exploit fully the sublime differences in the gallery spaces and reveal its primary structure.

By almost obsessively isolating patterns of movement found in the seams of dresses, or the weft of fabrics, and enlarging them to the level of the galleries, the Hayward is colonized by an alien presence which has close familial links to the objects that will be housed there. One accepts that the building has a logic of its own, and we were interested in installing a different order which almost ignored the visible characteristics of each individual gallery, but rather treated the entire building as a three-dimensional framework within which the garments and artworks could gain a new site-specific allusiveness. As such, each of the themes (from Futurism to Conceptualism) gives rise to its own specific plastic environment, whilst also being part of a meta-narrative which operates at the level of the whole ensemble. The graphic lines that initially appear as ruptures in plan only, emerge as landscapes that engulf the visitor and blur the boundaries between spectator and spectacle. The use of light and darkness, as well as shifting sightlines and viewpoints, is complicit in the resolution of the paradox of exhibiting objects that are normally in transition. The absence of a moving body complementing a garment is

13.10 Addressing the Century, Hayward Gallery, London: installation detail. © Zaha Hadid.

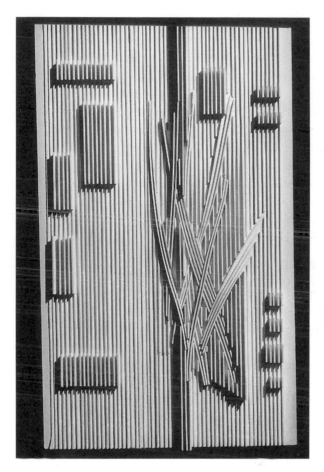

13.11 Illinois Institute of Technology, Chicago: site study. © Zaha Hadid.

alleviated by the dynamism of a gesture that manifests itself as catwalks and stages, settings for the *total theatre* of art and fashion.

Our design for a New Campus Center, Illinois Institute of Technology (1998), partly belongs to this family. Given the task to design the first new building on Mies van der Rohe's seminal campus site in 25 years, a number of pertinent issues arose. These ranged from the confrontation of "Modernity" in a "Post-Modern" age, to the future of Education Institutions. A more careful description of the genesis of the project will be given below, but to conclude this section, the ground level's articulation will be sketched out briefly.

Against the grid-like disposition of the other Miesian blocks on Campus, we focused on the slippages, both physical and visual, in Mies' incomplete game-board. We found that the most used routes were not necessarily the ones that were dictated by original paths, but often are the diagonals or curved lines between the official routes. The ground floor of the Campus Center is perforated by a number of these cuts, as entries, corridors, openings or windows, which are taken from the visual lining up of the other buildings on site. The main approach to the building is on the West Side of the site, transposing the incomplete space of the lawn in front of Crown Hall across State Street in a part-landscaped and part-graphic sweep on the ground. Through a play of graduating floor surfaces and cursive ramps, one is brought into a double height vestibule space, orientating the visitor to auditorium, cafeteria and retail. The emphasis on the overlaid diagonal and its transformation into tangential fields and hybridized formations manipulate the experience of the omnipresent rectilinear shift and impose a multitude of dissident readings onto the Miesian composition.

MAPPING INTERNAL COMPLEXITY

Oftentimes, within a single brief, one is confronted with a program that is large, diverse, extensive and complex in its breadth. It is, though, indicative of the way in which institutions are developing and, we believe, is an issue that will be met with increasing frequency in the future. Musea or educational facilities consist of a dense multi-textured program catering for both public and private consumption, and it is often the connective tissue between that we have explored, to challenge traditional institutional structures and hierarchies. The dissolving of information structures from their once corporeal base should begin to emerge in new configurations of social space that blur public and private articulations. It is as though, within a single building, there exists several micro-organisms which in themselves can be likened to a single entity. Interesting things happen when there is a tension between internal multiplicity and external unity. Like a series of chemical reactions occurring in a single glass vessel: the container maintains its composure, but allows for several kinds of fissures to take place within.

Our shortlisted design for the New Campus Center, Illinois Institute of Technology found its physiognomy through a kind of discourse with the various architectural, social and historical issues prompted by the brief and the context. Such was the profile of the problem posed that a conference was held at IIT in September 1997, to discuss the pertinent criteria the five competitors (including Koolhaas, Eisenman, Sejima/Nishizawa and Jahn) were to confront. Entitled "Beyond Mies", it involved lectures and seminars on issues of the legacy of Modernity, the significance of an "émigré" architecture in USA and post-modern readings of the "diagrammatic" Mies with its ensuing effects on recent architectural practice.

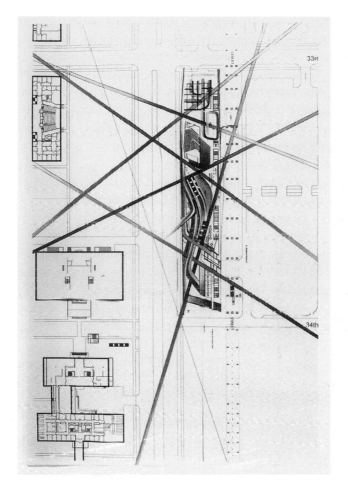

13.12 Illinois Institute of Technology, Chicago: plan. © Zaha Hadid.

We believed that, in recent times, a claim could be made that accelerating social changes at large has overtaken the once modernist utopianism of university campus design. These changes, in their essence, have begun to collapse the once discrete boundaries between education, research, residence and leisure. The New Campus Center was seen as an ideal opportunity to demonstrate these social morphologies in an equally forward setting that both recapitulates the new demands known to us and makes accommodation for further changes in user needs by adopting various typologies of hyper-flexibility. Various social groups have taken the modern thinking in standards and standard users (students) over by a heightened awareness of difference and multiple use patterns. The order of program breakdown and articulation of adjacencies is therefore less clear cut. In this way we have opted for a fluid organizational system which engenders multiple associations within the building, blurring the various areas of work and leisure.

The given Campus plan reveals itself to be less Cartesian and hermetic than it first seems. Each individual building on site, whilst operating as an object in a game-like condition, give rise to various readings in plan. The New Campus Center is an assemblage of multiple figures (ground plates, semi-enclosed spaces and volumes) which eschew a hermetic envelope and instead offer several open dialogues with existing routes, spaces and buildings on site, notably the Mies Historical district (including Crown Hall).

The original Campus Masterplan was based on a lateral distribution of program that promulgates movement over large distances. We were interested in taking this open dispersal and, as it were, fold it onto itself, registering multiple affiliations of the entire campus in a highly-compacted and layered volume. The Campus Center is seen, therefore, as a three-dimensional field of habitable circulation and interstitial spaces, contrasted by a collection of urban scale objects within, such as the auditorium. The indeterminate spaces between the programs are not seen simply as circulation, but become charged event spaces, where the "spillage" from one type of activity coalesces with another, giving rise to shifting affiliations of incident.

13.13 Illinois Institute of Technology, Chicago: view of folding campus. © Zaha Hadid.

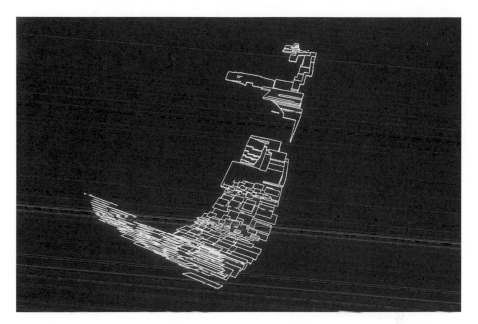

13.14 Boilerhouse Competition, V&A Museum, London: folding sequence. © Zaha Hadid.

The finalist design for the Extension to the Boilerhouse, V&A, London (1996), also operated in this manner. The V&A Museum is an urban block by virtue of addition and growth over the last 150 years. It is a rich patchwork of different buildings of contrasting periods strung together. Our response was a careful consideration of the multiplicity of programmatic needs and its relationship to the existing levels of the adjacent V&A proper. Every move made had to be justified with respect to the sensitivity of the V&A building. In this way, the internal mapping of the Extension was like an organism connected pliantly to its brethren.

In its most basic terms, the new building had to configure the following program in one so-called envelope: an *Orientation* space in the *Lobby* – here one could see the floor plane merging gradually to become the elevation, and how the horizontal planes of the floor would change from stops into benches, into low shelves, into louvers and finally into the facade plane running up the elevation. The *Virtual Reality Gallery* with VR objects would hang from the light-weight structure. In the main building, *the Gallery for Permanent Collection* begins the spiral wrapping around the *internal courtyard* as a series of planes, steps and ramps. The route ended in the *Public Café,* hung from steel trusses over the existing building. Sandwiched between the route was *the Temporary Exhibition Hall,* a rectangular volume inserted abruptly into the structural frame and designed as an independant container, capable of total blackout. Alternatively, the ground ramped down to the *shops,* into a sculptured volume containing a 250-seater *Auditorium* in the basement and an enlarged connection to the underground concourse.

The *facade* which wrapped around this agglomeration of program was a series of skins which serve specific functions, but which weaved or sometimes merged with each other to form either a floor, or a wall, or a window. The overall form of the facade was a skin that sometimes stretched taut and covered the volumes inside like a responsive mould, integrating inside and out. It was made of two skins, the outer a rain screen, the inner making use of weather-proofing glass and mechanically-operated blinds.

The building has been so exhaustively described to give a sense of the differentiated internal condition (suspended volumes, peels, cuts, transformations, all loosely structured around an ascending spiral) and the relative calm of the "skin" or "envelope", but also to highlight that there is a collapse in distance between inside and out, that the skin is also the ground surface, and that the furniture is also the elevation. The whole organism is "liquid". It has a gelatinous consistency with more solid parts of liquid (viscous) and other fluid liquid parts (more like water). Together, they perform an irregular fluid dynamic of movement and stasis, rendering its character as ever-changing, in constant flux.

The most recent example of the tendency to map complexity and contradiction in a monolithic entity is the winning design for the Contemporary Arts

13.15 Contemporary Arts Center, Cincinatti: bird's eye view. © Zaha Hadid.

Center, Cincinnati (1998–2002). The formulation of the gallery spaces, arguably the most critical factor in its make-up, will be described in full below. Here, it is relevant to mark out the conceptual framework for the entire building, which is an assemblage of strategies aimed at processing the various scales of information: between the movement of traffic, the repose of pedestrians, and the instantaneous moment of reflection in front/behind/underneath the work(s) of art.

The urban situatedness of the building in a fast-developing downtown area is manifest as an intimate participation with public space, such as the sidewalks and other public squares in the city. The Lobby is seen as a literal continuation of external space, and sweeps in, to become an articulated groundscape of cuts and lifts, an artificial public park. Considered a "free" zone for use by everyone, it also acts as a prelude to visiting the galleries.

The Lobby is split over the ground level and a lower lobby level, housing the Café and the Auditorium. The interaction between the two Lobby areas provide a continuous space of visual connectivity and public interaction. Towards the back of the building, the surface of the Lobby sweeps up to become the vertical wall enclosing the main circulation for the galleries. We call this the "Urban Carpet". This dynamic movement is a membrane between the outside of the building and its more inner, private spaces. A kind of memory skin, walked upon and walked through. The Galleries sit above the Lobby, in a strange equilibrium of mass and emptiness, con-

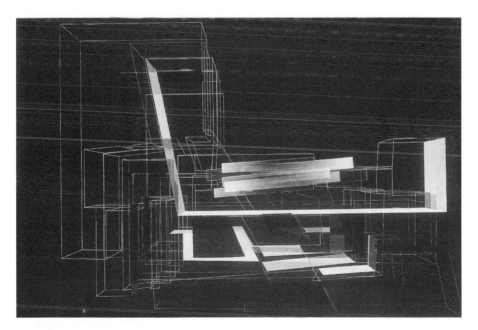

13.16 Contemporary Arts Center, Cincinatti: X-ray plan. © Zaha Hadid.

figurations of diversity anticipating the ever-changing belly of artwork. The South and East elevations testify to the accretive assemblage inside, as an activated collage of light and opacity, projection and emptiness, art and activity.

As such, the seemingly singular object is, in fact, composed of a number of unstable and always re-defining elements, agents of fissure and fusion, ruptures within that express themselves on the exterior, and events etched on the skin which transpire within. If anything, the Center will, at its most provocative, constantly invent and destroy its identity with the shifting of its content and users, whilst acting as a catalyst for the work inside, and the social interactions thereon.

JIGSAW AND PARTICLES

Another more specific strategy for the reconciling of a large program within a single envelope is through the densification and repetition of modular-like "particles". Whereas the previous category tends to be utilized for program where there is stricter explicit difference in program, the method of "particlisation" or making a "jigsaw" occurs when there is greater homogeneity in the program (often gallery space), but homogenous *space type* is not desired. Rather, it is through devising a formal pattern of self-similarity that effects of scaling, aggregating, intensifying and mutating occur. Not only does this take place in plan, but also in the sectional con-

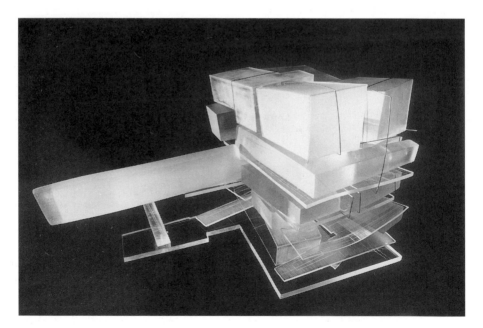

13.17 Boilerhouse Competition, V&A Museum, London: massing model. © Zaha Hadid.

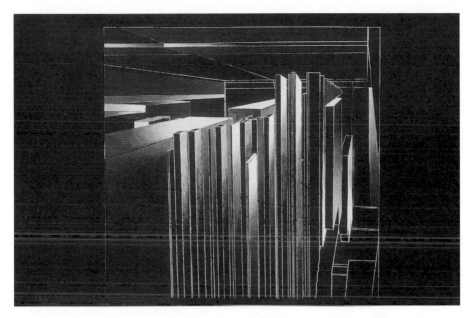

13.18 Boilerhouse Competition, V&A Museum, London: interior view. © Zaha Hadid.

dition, whereby the building culminates as a kind of clustered entity made up from versions of particle-like space and form.

Returning to the Extension for the Boilerhouse at the V&A, the notion of "pixellation" was instrumentalized. This manifested itself as the repetition of a modular-like element, be it a tile or a chair or a ramp, which simply took on the dimension and orientation of whatever was needed, wherever. Like the V&A itself: a massive collection of like and unlike objects which engender a topography of artifacts, the Extension embodied this very principle as a formal ruse. Additionally, the top three floors are interlocking volumes that house the Educational and Events Centre, Administration, and air handling plant. Like the volumes, the voids are not just linear, but interlock with each other.

The most recent application of the principle of subdividing a relatively homogeneous program into a spatially-diverse experience would be found in the gallery spaces of the Contemporary Arts Center, Cincinnati. If one were to read the aforementioned *Urban Carpet* as the upturned fabric of Cincinnati's plan itself; the galleries would become volumetric extrusions from that very texture. Like the urban space itself, they would comprise various sensations oscillating between openness and compression, enclosure and void.

What is extraordinary about the CAC mandate is the absence of a permanent collection in favour of various types of temporary exhibition. We see the

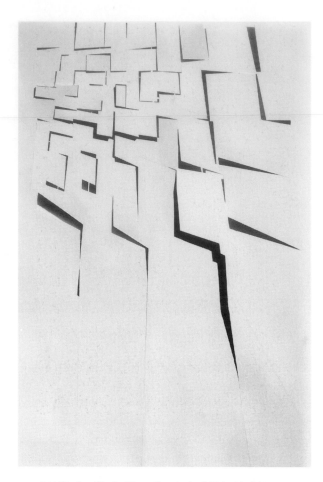

13.19 Contemporary Arts Center, Cincinatti: section study. © Zaha Hadid.

unpredictability in the possible medium on show as a unique asset. Utilizing the various shifts in perception, identity and social mores invented by recent art practice becomes critical towards the engendering of a new space for its perpetuation.

The increasing site specificity of art pieces makes the setting integral to the work wherein the space becomes critical of itself. There is also the tendency for an incredible divergence of scale, from urban scale objects to intimate experiences with video/film art. *Neutral space* is a wishful oxymoron. Individual memory and experience color all space. We propose therefore that the new CAC should reflect the divergence of contemporary art in its articulation of settings and spaces. Multiple perceptions and distant views free the sanctified object and, instead, create a more perplexing, richer phenomenal experience where the body is taken through a journey of compression, release, reflection, disorientation and epiphany.

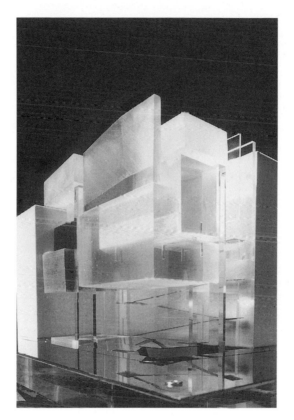

13.20 Contemporary Arts Center, Cincinatti: massing model. © Zaha Hadid.

This will be achieved through a three-dimensional jigsaw of solids and voids that interlocks a collection of gallery spaces. Slight shifts and ruptures within and in-between the individual elements of the jigsaw break open gaps and crevices which in turn create vertical, horizontal and diagonal transparency, visually tying together gallery spaces and opening them to the outside at their fringes. On each floor level the visitors' *promenade* weaves the galleries back into the *Urban Carpet* where the multifaceted space of the exhibition areas transforms into the vertiginously compressed verticality of the main circulation area.

Coda

Although it may appear that there is a systemic and academic process at work, this is exaggerated in the form of an essay. The reality of the work process is heuristic and aleatoric, finding resonances with work done many years before. To this extent, it is an ongoing thought process which will never reach a point of resolution since it knows there is no such place.

Showing

Chapter 14

Hombroich
Oliver Kruse

The Hombroich foundation in Germany signifies a complex initiative. The privately-founded Museum Insel is embedded in a carefully-restored landscape in the heart of Hombroich. In 1994 the museum managed to acquire an ex-NATO base, a rocket station in the immediate neighbourhood. The site was renovated between 1994 and 1995. In distinction to the Museum Insel, a place where works of art are shown to a public, the rocket station is now a place where visual artists, poets, composers, musicians and scientists work. It can be seen as a cultural laboratory where the idea of bringing together different interests in order to create an atmosphere of mutual dialogue and stimulation is the underlying spirit.

Hombroich is the historic name of the site. *Broich*, the ending of the word, means the moor and marshland in this case along the small river Erft located

14.01 Museum Insel Hombroich, tower, architecture by Erwin Heerich.

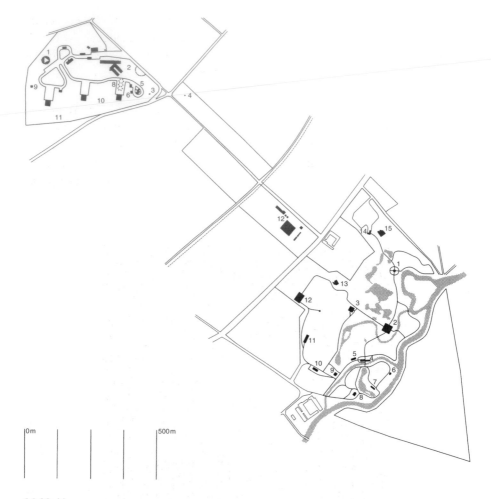

14.02 Map.

between Cologne and Düsseldorf. The culturally-rich area is of historic significance dating back to Roman times. In the early nineteenth century an industrialist bought the former moorland and turned the surrounding area into a landscape garden following an English model. In changing the natural flow of the river, he established the isle of Hombroich where he built a country house.

When Karl Heinrich Müller, the founder of the initiative, came across the site in 1982, the old landscape park with its remarkable variety of old and exotic trees and little hidden gardens had turned into a jungle. Müller, a patron of the arts, had been looking for a place that could house his art collection. The sculptor Erwin Heerich and Müller wanted to consciously break with most aspects of contemporary

14.03 Museum Insel Hombroich, Long Gallery, finished 1985, architecture by Erwin Heerich.

14.04 Museum Insel Hombroich, Round Gallery, architecture by Erwin Heerich.

14.05 Museum Insel Hombroich, tadeusz house, in foreground a work by Giacometti, architecture by Erwin Heerich.

museum architecture. Heerich represents a sculptors' approach to architecture and his buildings are walk-in sculptures. His idea was to build a sequence of small and larger galleries imbedded in the park. According to the old flow of the river, a lake-land that brings the landscape back to a pre-Roman state was dug out. Ninety old willow trees have been planted along the lakes that are now home to numerous frogs, songbirds, water birds, fish, dragonflies and mayflies that had completely disappeared in the area. This is a romantic place where the circle of regeneration and degeneration is emphasised by a minimal amount of human intervention.

From 1985 to 1993, 11 walk-in sculptures by Erwin Heerich were erected – often by only a few workers that carefully inserted the structures into the framework of river, lakes and huge trees. Some buildings are, and will remain, empty, functioning only as walk-in sculptures. But the two historic buildings, together with most of Erwin Heerich's buildings, provide an area of 5500 m² of exhibition space. The museum's collection of historic and modern art from different cultures and periods is displayed without any classification of style or era. Different characters and epochs are juxtaposed. There are no labels, titles of works or information indicating the names of artists or periods – thus allowing the exhibits to speak for themselves.

14.06 Museum Insel Hombroich, house of 12 rooms, Architecture by Erwin Heerich.

The pavilions demonstrate how simple but essential sculptural decisions lead to intense spatial effects. The deliberate use of building materials carries through the whole museum. Thick heavy walls, outside of brick, are inside smoothly plastered and painted white. Opalescent glass roofs and white marble floors create a clear, intense, crisp white light. There is no additional electric lighting, no climate control and no other atmospherically-disturbing technical device except for an invisible floor-heating system that keeps the space from freezing in winter. The geometrically-composed buildings are clad with brick material that comes from demolished old houses and that communicate well with the environment and the traditional building materials used in the area. Also, the buildings seek the exploration of acoustic phenomenon as each little noise one makes will result in a spectacularly long fading tone.

Some of the buildings are today nearly invisible, being surrounded by dense beech hedges and bushes. When crossing a gateway through a hedge, one finds oneself in a long passageway, determined by the suddenly appearing brick wall of the building at one side, the hedge on the other, gravel below and sky above. The sequence of passing through green walls, a brick wall and then following an inner path to the unknown creates a hermetic quality. Being more complex structures, the larger galleries can only be perceived step by step, composed of a sequence of meandering rooms. If the buildings were empty, the repetitive sequence of rooms would cause the orientation to be completely disturbed. As exhibits become the points of orientation in an environment, where spatial elements are constantly recurring, they seem to have a strength of presence that one rarely experiences. Exhibition architecture and the exhibited works of art seem to intensify one another.

As opposed to most newly-built museums, where mainly cultural politicians, art historians, curators and architects are involved in the planning, the process and growth of the Insel Hombroich was mainly determined by artists. The uncompromising clarity and directness in which the collection is displayed is manifestly a result of this. It feels most agreeable to see the works displayed in a light intensity chosen by criteria of visual artists – and that consciously sacrifices the various technical standards and restrictions that insurers on the one hand, and restorers on the other, would dictate. In a contemporary context, it is sad to find that once again such pathbreaking decisions are left to artists.

The idea of the museum embedded in nature is, however, not new. The approach of the Kroeller Moeller Museum in Otterloo in the Netherlands as well as the Louisiana Museum in Hummelbaek, Denmark, were in many ways an inspiration for the Insel. But in the clarity of expression Hombroich is more radical and goes beyond ideas of its mentors and guides. Also the idea of expanding the museum by

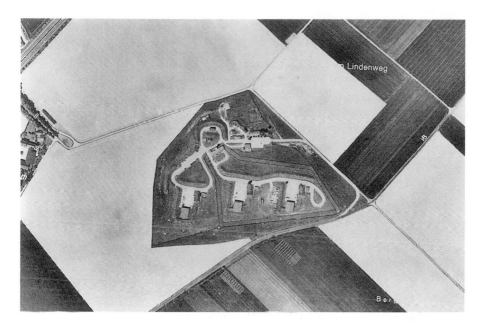

14.07 Raketenstation Hombroich, aerial view, 1992.

the newly-acquired rocket station where people work in a cultural laboratory points in a new direction.

Located about one mile across the fields from the Insel, the "Raketenstation" is a culminating point from where one can overlook 50 m² of the surrounding area. The former Nato site was designed to launch missiles during the Cold War. The missile-storage buildings, personal shelters and missile-assemblage buildings were left by the American technicians and Belgian guard troops about two years before the museum was to take over the plant in 1994. When we entered the place for the first time, it was surrounded by several fences, barbed wire and lamp posts. The buildings were empty and vandalised. The atmosphere was cold and threatening – it was hard to believe that it could become part of the romantic river island in the neighbourhood.

Our basic aim in the renovation of the military structures was to transform the hostility into a calm expression of neutrality. We didn't want to cover up the fact that it was an army site, and kept that general layout as a reminder. The numerous barracks, hangars and halls where turned into functional and simple spaces that were to serve as studios and workspaces equipped with running water, heating and good natural lighting. All the buildings were clad with camouflage screens of

14.08 Raketenstation Hombroich, studio, Oliver Kruse and Katsuhito Nishikawa 1994.

14.09 Raketenstation Hombroich, studio, Oliver Kruse and Katsuhito Nishikawa, 1994.

14.10 Raketenstation Hombroich, one-man house, guest house for the rocket station by Oliver Kruse and Katsuhito Nishikawa, 1995.

14.11 Raketenstation Hombroich, former watch tower, 1996.

asbestos cement. We removed this material and replaced it with galvanised steel throughout the whole rocket station in order to keep the structure that was already there unified as it was before.

Soon after the renovation of the rocket station was completed, about eight visual artists were invited to work in the new studio spaces, as well as a composer, a poet and a group of scientists – to create a wider spectrum of interdisciplinary activity than the typical "artist in residence" model. The people that were given spaces were chosen unbureaucratically – since many of them had been engaged in various activities of the Museum Insel before. Opposed to a typical residency programme, the people here have been offered the use of the facilities for at least 5–10 years.

The rocket station is now due to grow further. A number of artists and architects have been invited to develop structures that could house future activities. Erwin Heerich is currently erecting a pavilion that will house a large ceramic relief work of the artist Lucio Fontana. The Austrian–American architect Raymond Abraham will be commissioned to build a house for musicians and composers. Tadao Ando has designed a museum for a private collection of modern art, comprising of a large exhibition space under the earth. The Hermansdorf producers of organic foods have been encouraged to start a branch in between Insel and Raketenstation. A farm house and stables have been planned where agricultural products would be produced and sold on a large scale.

It would be diversionary to describe all these activities in detail. However, it is important that they are listed here. As far as the development of the future museum is concerned, the Hombroich foundation can be seen as a pilot scheme that does not end with visual arts but that makes the museum a place of interdisciplinary practices. The development of contemporary art demonstrates that the artistic media that can be shown in the museum can not be limited. Therefore it is important that the Raketenstation and Insel Hombroich are in one foundation – as contemporary arts practice often demonstrates that the process of making art is often more interesting than the discussion of the final result.

14.12 Raketenstation Hombroich, former missile storages, 1996.

Chapter 15

Dear Peter
Richard Wentworth

Dear Peter

The world is made of light. Thousands of paintings and photographs emphasise and celebrate it.
Light falls, irrespective of the material it meets.

Light reveals the world and the ways we try to regulate it.

Do people seek light and shade for different reasons? Is it different for different people?

If the world is made of light, what is the ground made of? What impression do we make on it?
Should we leave one behind?

Paved with gold? Made of end grain timber, certainly.

Are we archaeologists? How do we recognise the material we encounter?
Is every one a sign, or only some?

When we say "landscape", what do we mean? Can it be too beautiful? (Safe to say this looks northward in the northern hemisphere?)

Can indoors move outdoors, and vice versa?

Can warnings be decorative? Can decoration be a warning? Why is paint different from something made of itself? Is wet different from dry?

How do light and shade change what we think? Can a warning be precious? Granite punctuated with marble. Provincial town, where people know their masonry.

What is a palimpsest? Is this one? Dug, rolled, scraped, painted.

Is decoration measurement? Is measurement decoration? Light measured by shade?

It depends on your point of view, the time of day, the time of year.

Yours Richard

Changing

Chapter 16

Autopoetic architecture: the Open City, Ritoque, Chile
Ann M. Pendleton-Jullian

Having been raised in the United States, in suburban North America, and having studied at the schools one is supposed to study at to position oneself as an architect, I was adequately prepared for Europe. As I discovered different parts of Europe, it all seemed somewhat familiar although there were, of course, still many surprises. Ironically, however, nothing had prepared me for South America. I say ironically because we are after all connected – not truly two separate continents. And nothing in my architectural education or experience had prepared me for Ritoque, Chile.

What I find most important about the Open City in Ritoque is not so much what it gave me through what it is, which I will attempt to discuss here, but rather the questions raised for me about architecture by Ritoque. These questions have left a profound impression on me as they begin to inform my own way of working. So, I do come to the work very much as a practicing architect, not as a theoretician or historian of architecture. I have no pretensions in that direction and for that reason I will approach the Open City first through its physical manifestation and only then through its historical development and the questions it raises for the general discourse of architecture.

Chile extends from 17 degrees below the equator to the South Pole, from the deserts in the north, to the fjords and glaciers in the south. Never more than 200 miles across at its widest, it is literally a seam between the mountains in the east, where the sun rises, and the Pacific Ocean in the west where the sun sets. When the seam narrows to 20 or 30 miles across you can imagine the drama as the mountains fall into the sea. But in addition to this grand landscape, it is also a country of tremendous intimacy as the topography folds around one, forming tremendously articulated vistas. About a third of the way down the country is the Central Valley and the capital city of Santiago. Directly west, on the coast, is the port city of Valparaíso. Travelling 20 miles or so northward along the coast from Valparaíso, one reaches the mouth of the Aconcagua River, one of the major rivers of Chile which crosses the country bringing the snow waters down from the mountains to the sea.

It is at the mouth of the Aconcagua River, at the intersection of river and ocean, among the dunes, that one comes across a group of buildings and structures in different states of being constructed and deconstructed, *literally* deconstructed. This is the Open City of Amereida, which was conceived and built by the Faculty of Architecture of the Catholic University of Valparaíso – a group of architects, poets, artists and engineers.

The site is spacious and diverse. It extends from the rolling and moving dunes at the sea's edge up into a highland plateau that is mostly covered in grasses. When one enters the Open City the first thing one sees from the road is a building whose gable end rises up out of the sand in an animalistic pose. This is the first clue I had of the existence of the Open City as it is rather unusual within the context of the built and natural landscape around it. I have been involved with the Open City on and off over the past seven years as a fly-on-the-wall more than

16.01 Hospedería de la Entrada seen from the coastal highway.

an active participant – as an observer and not as one indoctrinated into the workings of the school and City.

The building you see rising out of the sand is called the Hospedería de la
Entrada (the Entry Hospedería) – all of the structures have names; this is very
important – and this is one of the first house-like buildings, called "hospedería",
that was built. As one moves around the building on the oblique, the collapsed
space of the apparent gable end telescopes, revealing a five-bay wood structure
whose enclosed spaces step up from the sand, releasing three staircases that
descend from the house to touch the ground. Two move laterally outward, anchor-
ing the house into the site, while the third spirals straight downward to attach to a
cut in the ground through which a footpath moves on its way to the sea. A bowl is
carved into the sand on the north side of the path forming a natural amphitheater.
The path that connects the amphitheater to the highway and sea defines the
course of the house, while the roof planes orient themselves toward the sun rising
off the upper plateau. They simultaneously herald the rising sun and shelter the
interior spaces from the southwesterly winds. The house was born of a poetic act,
as all the structures are born of poetic acts. It was a meeting on the site in this
hollow of land that the house now hovers over. They decided through poetry that
this was a place for construction. They decided that the site was about occupying
the dunes, about the transparency of the light over the sand, about the footpath
that went from the road to the sea, about the sun's movement off the plateau,
about the maritime winds, and, very significantly, about the act of meeting in
community. From that meeting they developed a strategy which resulted in a series
of five bays which form the skeleton of the house. Within those five bays the house
was built piece-by-piece, according to the needs of the inhabitants. The last bay
has still not been filled in.

In this building there are no windows that look to the sea. This is a rather
strong position of most of the constructions in the Open City because of how they
perceive their relationship to the site. The site is not something to be seen through
the commodification of natural amenities such as view, but through a more profound
understanding of its rhythms and phenomena. The denial of the view allows them to
replace the actual image of the ocean with a memory of the ocean, with the sounds
and light of the sea, with narratives or stories about going out to sea. It is about the
ocean as storyteller, peacemaker, enemy, foil, ocean as beginning and end.

This house was built in a series of different moments, as many of the buildings at the Open City are. Often built in stages and added to as needed, different
members of the community can operate on any one of the buildings provided it is
negotiated with the community. Everything in the Open City is held in common by
the community.

It is important, here, to talk about the concept of the hospedería, which is more than a house. The word translates to mean "inn" and comes from "huesped" meaning guest. Although the family or inhabitants living in each hospedería regard the place as their home and are, in most cases, the ones responsible for initiating the construction, its renovations and additions, they do not own the structure or site. The inhabitants' role is that of caretaker. This means that the hospederías are theoretically open to all those who may come, receiving food and/or lodging in exchange for sharing their experiences. Each hospedería serves a civic purpose as well, be that gatekeeper, or banquet hall or meeting ground, et cetera. The entry hospedería is a house with traditional spaces for sleeping, eating, socializing and working, but it also serves the city by sheltering the hollowed-out communal amphitheater below it from the winds and by standing guard at the entrance to the Open City.

At ground level, adjacent to the hospedería, is a series of spaces that serve as informal reception areas for entry and departure. Here one finds a series of brick and concrete pivoting gate panels and a field of hollow pipes that seem to be participating in some pagan ritual: a walking wind organ that converts the currents of air moving across the dunes into sound, transposing wind into tone that varies with direction and velocity.

16.02 Entry plaza with walking wind pipes.

16.03 Hospedería de los Diseños north face.

A second hospedería near that of the entry is the Hospedería de los Diseños of the designers/architects. This was conceptually begun as a simple volume laid on the sand and split into two by an existing passagoway through which one now enters the house. The passageway bisects the volume into two halves, one of which faces the light and the sea and is bleached white; the other half, whose shadowed southern face gives to the upper dunes, is stained black. Light is not about random illumination but about its absolute qualities of presence and absence – light and shadow.

This hospedería is about the qualification and quantification of the phenomena associated with light and sand. The footpath turns to brick as it enters the house and the blowing of the wind washes the sand into and out of the house revealing more or less of the brick path in a mimetic relationship to the waves on the sand at the shore. Continually swept out and reappearing uninvited, it becomes rather like a perpetual guest or the neighbor's dog you cannot get rid of. It becomes a member of the household that has an active participation in the gestures of the family.

Bisected into two halves by the path – into the lit half and the shaded half – the two volumes of the house are fused back together by a volume of light which is formally manifested in a wood wall that resonates the patterns of light entering. In

16.04 Hospedería de los Diseños entry path.

this way, the sand is one active participant of the house along one set of co-ordi-nates, and the light is another, along a second set of co-ordinates. Reattached to the body of the house by the light shaft, the major interior space is focused down into the sand, not out to the sea – monitoring the movement of the dunes, rather than open to the constancy of the sea. On the exterior of the hospedería, brick mediates between sand and wood registering the migration of the sand – its rising and falling – not dissimilar to the way in which the beach registers the tidal move-ment of the sea.

Two workshop buildings sit adjacent to each other among the dunes oppos-ite the Hospedería de los Diseños. In the first one, space was discovered between a plane which rises up continuing the swell of the dune and the fall of the sand leeward to a lower ground level. The upper surface of the plane is set with paving stones to create an informal plaza and outdoor discussion space. It extends toward

16.05 Workshop in the dune from north.

16.06 Workshop between two sculpture courts.

16.07 Music Room and exterior plaza.

the city of Valparaíso standing in as foreground and reminding one of the relative understanding of "ground plane" with regard to the position of the eye. One enters downward through the dune to a simple space of wood columns and trusses that displays the simplicity with which one can discover and construct space in the primitive gesture of delaminating the surface of the ground.

A second workshop is a simple rectangular box placed on a precise east–west axis on the site. The placement allows the rectangle to form two courts, one on the shaded southern side of the box and the other on the sunny southern side. The roof of the workshop is translucent plastic – in essence there is no roof, only the presence of ambient light. Two large doors centered on the longer sides of the building and a truss allow the sculptors who use this workshop to move their pieces between different and precise conditions of light. They can work in either strong natural light, muted ambient light or in shadow as they wish. Succinctly, the building is a filter that separates out these three conditions from the mixed light on the site.

Out in the dunes of the Open City, in a sheltered hollow, is the Music Room. The open space adjacent to the building is where the construction on this specific site was begun. I believe it was a wedding of one of the founders' daughters that

16.08 Music Room.

initiated the space. This hollow in the dunes was picked because it creates a space below the line of the dunes in which the sea is only present through sound and light – not visually. As the event unfolded into a party, the perimeter of the gathering was marked and later formalized into a plaza by clearing away the indigenous plants and formalizing the edges. This plaza set the size and form of the building to be built later. The Music Room itself is a simple rectangular box – the space of the original gathering displaced to the side and built – whose corners are broken into for entry and services.

The most interesting piece of this construction is a hole down through the center of it made of four scavenged triple-hung windows. It is a volume of natural light and sound approximately five feet square. This volume of light funnels the atmospheric conditions of the exterior, which change with the time of day, year and weather, into the interior of the building. When the windows are open, the sound of the sea enters the box resonating through the interior just as a tone moves through a sounding box.

This is a pavilion designed for modern music. Yet, due to the placement of the central light volume, the musicians cannot occupy the center of the room and are, instead, dislodged to the side. To compensate for and make use of the

16.09 Casa de los Nombres.

off-centering of the music, the ceiling of the space folds into a series of acoustical plates and the interior walls are built of panels which move out from the wall and turn to make use of their acoustically absorptive or reflective faces. The musician can enter the box and literally tune the space.

The displacement of the musician by light and the conversion of the entire room into a sounding box create an experience of the harmonies and dissonances of the properties and phenomena associated with light and sound. Within the box, one is enveloped by the two as presences in the space whether music is being played or not. When players are absent, music is made with the voice and the light of the sea. An understanding of the sea that you cannot see, as sound, rhythm, cadence and light has been brought to the foreground. And it begins to be a building that recreates, in an augmented way, what was happening in the natural hollow to begin with.

From the Music Room, a bamboo road heads off into the high sand dunes to end at the top of a large dune that commands a view of the entire coastal plane and Pacific below. This is the site of the Casa de los Nombres (The House of Names) which is the only structure built, to date, in the raw dunes that are completely exposed to the forces of the wind, the consequent movement of the sand,

16.10 Casa de los Nombres.

16.11 Casa de los Nombres.

the unshaded passage of the sun and the clarity of the night sky. This is a building that was built during my visits there and some students of ours helped construct the road you see on the left. The Casa de los Nombres was built as an exhibition hall and meeting room. The idea was very simple. They knew the dune would move and therefore instead of building on top they decided to build under the dune assuming that the construction would have a tendency to stabilize the sand.

Discussed, elaborated and logistically planned over two years, it was built in eight weeks during which 400 people worked continuously. To create the room, its area was first mapped onto the surface of the dune not by posts and cord but by the placement of bodies within the site during a poetic act in which a relationship was made between the reading of the lines of a poem and the length of travel of the reader. There were 29 lines, 29 people and, therefore, 29 names in the "casa de los nombres". After mapping the points, a series of 29 concrete pillars, 26 feet high were driven into the sand at each location until their tops were level with the convex surface of the dune. The sand was excavated to create a concave bowl for the volume of the room. Once the pillars were stabilized, wood and cable truss members were set into place and a translucent covering of industrial fiberglass cloth was laid over the structure.

While the pillars physically map the surface of the dune as it was at the moment of its excavation – for the dunes are always moving – the roof recreates, represents and rephrases the dune's formal and physical phenomena. The original surface of the dune is translated into a covering, not a roof, that is light, airy and translucent. With the wind, the sand moves over the surface of the new dune and recedes, and voices seem to emanate from the earth itself. From elsewhere on the site, it presents itself as an amplified segment of the continuous structure and profile of the dunes, revealing the essential qualities of the sands through imme-diate quotation. As the fluid and primordial state of the land, of the mountains that can be seen in the distance, the dunes are always moving and reforming. The Casa de los Nombres is a meditation on this as it oscillates between its reference to the mountains or the dunes and to the precise moment in time it physically captures within the continuum of the dunes' transformation.

The leeward side of the dune was the side that was left open under the assumption that the sand and the wind would continue their expected migra-tions. After being built, however, it was discovered that the winds are not as con-sistent as they seemed and that the new structure had altered the micro-climate enough that the sand changed course somewhat, resulting in sand that enters in unpredictable ways. For them, however, this is not truly a problem. There are people within the community who would like to rebuild it in a more permanent manner – to turn it into a "real" building. But the majority of the people who have been there longer are willing to let it do what it will do. If it disappears, it does. It has not yet.

As you move through the site of the Open City, two impressions form. A first impression is that the site is land and space in one of its most transparent, ephemeral, and mutable states. A second impression is that because of, or in deference to, these qualities, the constructions on the site of the Open City are light. They attain a status of lightness. Consequently, there is an apparent lightness of physical impression in the site.

By lightness I mean several precise things. Firstly, lightness because the way in which the constructions touch the ground does not demarcate territory of building through strong physical impact and authoritarian footprints but, instead, lets the land initiate the configuration of territory and space in both plan and section. Because of the movement of the sand by the wind and movement of the ground (earthquakes), building weights and volumes are supported by many points of contact distributed according to structural and spatial needs and intents. Volumes lifted off the ground allow the natural migration of the sand to continue, whereas those buildings that do make physical contact with the ground, whether it be shallow or profound physical contact, allow the physical forces of the site into their spaces. One gets the impression that if all the constructions were removed from the land, the land would not hold their memory.

Lightness, also, because the materiality of the constructions at the Open City are related to a type of construction that is artisanal, which remains attached to the physical process of building at the scale of the artisan and not the machine. It therefore reveals the hands of the builders and is a representation of human occupation of the site and not the mechanical domination and reconfiguration of the site. One senses the presence of raw nature and not manipulated landscape – of footsteps and not tyre tracks.

Beyond lightness of materiality and lightness of step, the buildings of the Open City convey what I would call a "status" of lightness. Status of lightness because there are no apparent imposed formal ordering devices that regulate the development of the constructions. Instead, each construction is attached to the space of the site through ideation and ideaphoria that are manifested in spatial strategies which take on spatial form and relationships. However, the forms and formal ordering devices do not come first and are not fixed but can transform as specifics and tactics are developed. Because form and formal relationships of space are rendered through this mental activity and not through the superimposition of preconceived formal devices, physical centers and boundaries do not exist in any conventional way. Centers of gravity of the constructions remain unpunctual and difficult to locate because they are never formalized and because they migrate as structures are added to or transformed – they migrate because they are a resultant, not a determinant, of construction activity. Often edges of constructions are even more illusive than their centers, just as walls or fences have never defined the edges of the city.

And "status" of lightness, also, because not only are physical centers and edges illusive but because there is a tendency for meaning to migrate and transform within single buildings and within the city as it has grown and matured over time. It is both a formal and conceptual lightness. You can look at some of the buildings such as the Entry Hospedería and discern a basic concept or strategy inside which other things have begun to occur. But with other buildings you cannot. There is one construction that started as two different constructions on two different but adjacent sites. One decided that it wanted to grow in one direction and the other decided it wanted to grow as well. The first moved up over the second and the second moved under and around the first and they negotiated the connection to incorporate a third unit in the middle. This same set of constructions

16.12

began to leak over time and so a roof was draped over it. It is very hard in this building to say that it is about one thing or another yet each moment is about something very precise, related to the sea or the sand or the sky or memory.

The lightness of physical impression on the site as well as the attitude toward the building process, the materiality, and the ad hoc application of these aspects, creates a type of work that has a striking similarity to the spontaneous and aggregative works of necessity found in the cities and countryside of Chile – works that are usually characterized by the word "vernacular". They are both about constructing space with materials on hand and for the purpose at hand. They are ad hoc in a very precise way. Yet there is a tremendous difference between the two. What separates the work of the Open City from the vernacular is a mental as well as physical link to the process and to the site. Whereas the vernacular demonstrates a way of *building*, the work of the Open City results in objects that demonstrate a way of *doing*. The vernacular relies on construction to make space that either conforms to, or mitigates, the difficulties of the natural context with regard to needs for interior space. It relies on a certain intuitive process, but the editing of this process is regulated by the logistics of getting the thing built. The work at the Open City relies on a more self-conscious way of acting and thinking that sponsors an intuitive process informed by poetic concerns. In this process the intuitive is edited by the process itself or by the unfolding of the intention into an enigmatic logic. This way of acting has resulted in the informal development of a highly-mutable thematic base that underlies the work.

The Open City was founded in 1970, but the experience from which it emerged dates back to 1950 when the Chilean architect Alberto Cruz Covarrubias first met Godofredo Iommi, an Argentinean poet. Both men were 33-years-old at the time. The meeting was significant because it established the beginning of a long and profound dialogue between poetry and architecture – between word and space – and set the foundation for a pedagogical program of research based on this relationship.

Together they conceived of the idea of effecting a great switch, by removing architecture from its doctrine, buried in mathematics and formalisms, and re-centering it in the poetic word. Concurrently and conveniently, in 1952, the Jesuit order took over the Catholic University of Valparaíso and the new rector decided to initiate a complete renovation of the school. He offered a post to Alberto Cruz whose reputation for innovation, as a professor at the Catholic University of Santiago, ensured change. Knowing that a transformation of consequence could only be achieved by a comprehensive influence produced by a group of people dedicated to this task, and not just one individual, Cruz accepted, stipulating that he bring a group of young architects, painters, poets and engineers who were known for their

16.13 Banquet Hospedería.

open defiance of the conventional academic canon. They began working together on an active program of research that engaged all aspects of living and working.

The pedagogic program the Institute presented was very simple – to plant within the context of architecture the experience of working in a group and the proposition of employing the poetic use of "word" as the foundation for an architectural polemic. And it insisted that the program of research engage the modern context not directly through modern architectural precedent or the positivist underpinnings associated with these precedents but through poetry, which engaged modern culture in a transformative dialogue. The founders of the Institute believed art that is true transcends its own materiality. True architecture, true sculpture, true poetry derives its sense from its ability to reveal the invisible of itself – interior truth not physical reality. Modern poetry sponsored and questioned the relationship of these truths and values to the assumptions and values prescribed by the structures of modern culture.

16.14 Storeroom in the Valle del Elqui, Chile.

The central poetic preoccupation of the group, which was considered its "unconventional" approach, was the relationship of poetry to architecture, sculpture and painting. It was to be a direct relationship, without mediating elements and one, which stated, and required, the bond of action to word. It was not poetry as a bias or sentiment but rather poetry as a way of acting and of doing creatively. The poetry around which the group united was that of the Modern French poets and of the Surrealists: Baudelaire, Mallarmè, Rimbaud, Verlaine, Lautréamont, Breton. This poetry involved a passionate quest in which poetry, no longer a commodity, transformed itself into poetic activity that aimed at recuperating the mind's original powers. The poet was an alchemist who employed the imagination to transform reality both mentally and physically, who embraced the mystery and adventure of creative activity as reality was opened up to a different reading, a different understanding, a different reality, ignited by the power of words to embrace multiplicity and plurality within the unifying body of poetic language.

The influence of the Surrealists and Modern French poets on the founding and subsequent development of the pedagogical program and work at the Catholic University of Valparaíso's new school of architecture was an influence that I do not think one can emphasize enough. It was not poetry as a bias, sentiment or inspiration. It was a profound structural relationship that existed at several depths:

methodologically, theoretically and philosophically. Poetic acts, "travesías" (poetic voyages or crossings), card games, unprogrammed wanderings ("derives") and other methodologies engaged in by the members of the Institute derive their structure from the methods of Breton and the poets of the Modern French movement. Not unlike Breton's "psychic dictation" or the Surrealist performance-like "acts", they are used deliberately to release the imagination from a programmatic and physical reality in order to relate architectural proposition to the poetics of space, context and making.

The propositioning of space, form and tectonics through language and word, methodologically linked to the making of poetry as influenced by the Surrealists, is part of a larger program of the Institute in which poetry superimposes itself on traditional architectural discourse. More significantly, at the level of creative activity, it replaces this traditional discourse. Additionally, because there is such a strong emphasis on creative activity as the basis for life, poetry virtually takes over as the motivating force of life. This was the intention in the founding of the Institute and it is consciously tied to the theoretical foundation of the Modern French poets where men and women were to be "transformed into living poems". The community of the school began to operate so consistently in this manner that, in a sense, it became like the communities dreamed of by Blake or Novalis – utopian communities of men and women as poets.

But beyond methodologies and theoretical intentions, the larger program of the Institute is also influenced by the metaphysics of the Modern French poetic movement. The critical questions that were posed by the German Romantics and translated by the French poets become redirected in their work. The work of the Institute redirects the question of the European "modern" man's relationship to his historical and cultural sites specifically onto Latin American man and his relationship to his historical and cultural sites. The condition the Modern European poets faced was the world as a place in which new technologies and systems of knowledge, as well as a shift in the power base from church and state to industry, had distanced modern men and women from themselves, from others, from reality. The Latin American condition is not as critically related to technology, knowledge systems and industry but, instead, to the search for an authentic identity with regard to the world – a replacement for the identity given to Latin Americans by European self-interests. The question, the issue, the desire remains the same – meaning within the world, meaning grounded in man and meaning accessed through poetic activity – but the Latin American intellectual site created by the program of the Institute refocuses the imagination which then operates through the inter-relationship of space and poetry.

The action and morality that was demanded by the founding attitude of the faculty of architecture – the reconnecting of goals and ways, of word and act – led

16.15 Valparaíso.

to a very different way of working and teaching at the Catholic University of Valparaíso. It was a way of working that removed the students from the drawing boards and lecture halls and bound them to the city as laboratory. Alberto Cruz emphasized that "the architects are those that in life know how to read, know how to build the countenance which the space holds". To understand architecture as the container or skin of the "countenance" of space required divesting space of its superficial relationship to function in order to discover its more intimate relationship with the social and physical phenomena it engages. For this discovery it was necessary to go into the city, to travel through it, to read it – to see how the spaces grand and small, all the nooks and crannies of the city, engage and hold these acts of life – how they accommodate, accumulate and articulate the gestures of city life.

The city in which the students of the Institute work to research the "countenanoo of the space", and which influences much of the subsequent design work including the work at the Open City, is the city of Valparaíco. Valparaíso is a city with a very strong spatial presence as the result of how it occupies a site whose topography is emphatic and an unmitigated challenge to the right-angle posture of human occupation of space. A port city of extraordinary beauty and structural and gestural complexity, it is more like two distinct cities than a single urban organism because of the natural forms of the coastal topography – a flatland that is overlaid by a series of steep finger-like hills to form a kind of wrinkled amphitheatre. The "downtown" is determined by an imported formal program and classical principles of grid, axis, plaza, court, periphery, et cetera, with color and informality provided by the human traffic. In contrast, the "uptown" responds to prosaic needs for making space on earthquake-prone sixty-degree slopes while, inadvertently, engaging the poetics of sea, sun and horizon. The "uptown" is apparent disorder with the topography determining location, orientation, geometry and structure of building. The buildings twist and turn to conform to the slopes. The oblique, diagonal and non-rectilinear rule in plan and in section. Roofs become terraces and new ground. Retaining walls become buildings and buildings become earth. Left-over fragments of space are built into strange-shaped buildings or configured as tall voids through which one moves up to the sky or down to the sea. The sky and sea become space, and everywhere are reminders of the inhabitants' tenuous hold on the horizontal. It is not a city where formalisms are relevant but instead one which is structured by the simple act of finding a way to position yourself on this terrain and occupying and navigating that site urbanistically. The structure that emerges creates a poetry of the prosaic.

Prior to 1965, the action that was demanded by the founding attitudes of the Catholic University of Valparaíso translated into poetic activity that focused its research on the city and surroundings of Valparaíso. This research transformed the first architectural studios significantly yet, at the same time, there was still a certain separateness between the activity of the studios and the activity of the poetry classes. The first studios, while emphasizing work that arose as a consequence of research into the life of the city – research that was initiated and set in motion by poetry – and at the same time integrating text poetically formed and motivated into the architectural process, still maintained a traditional autonomy relative to the work that was being done by other members of the Institute in the poetry classes. The poetry classes, perhaps the more radical of the two initially-parallel activities, transgressed more significantly into the realm of architecture through the use and subsequent development of the Surrealist inspired "poetic act" or "phalène". The phalène developed out of a series of seminars given by Godofredo Iommi on modern poetry and art. Because modern poetry was not intended as an elitist preoccupation, and it was to be of and for life, the students were incited to take poetry out of the classroom and into the city. They recited poems in the streets, on the buses, in the hills, on the beach. No longer spectators, they entered the life of the city as participants and they engaged poetry as participants. These original group recitations developed into the phalène, which became a way to make poetry as well, in an impromptu way, on the site. In this manner the possibility of linking poetry to place and space was introduced – to the place in which it occurred and to the space that the act of meeting itself configured. It was very much a proposition about space although it was still not a proposition about constructing space through an integrated effort of architecture and poetry.

In 1965, the foundation for a more significant inter-relationship between architecture and poetry, as well as a more profound research into the meaning of their Latin American identity, was begun with the writing of the "Amereida" by Iommi. The "Amereida" is an epic poem that poses and debates a critical set of questions about the Latin American heritage. It translates a closed history, as written, into history as poetic memory open to rediscovery. It is this memory that the architects, artists and poets of the Catholic University engage in order to create. The poem has proved to be a manifesto of great importance to the work of the school and it serves as an informal charter as well for the Open City in Ritoque, also named Amereida. And very importantly, it introduces the "travesía" – a manner in which to begin a proposition about constructing space through an integrated effort of architecture and poetry. The Amereida, whose name comes from a joining of America and Eneida (the "Aeneid" – the poet Virgil's great mythological foundation epic of Rome), is a poem of longing and, more importantly, a poem of action in that it proposes the discovery of an authentic Latin American status specifically through poetic action.

The poem begins by reframing the question of Columbus' discovery. It begins with the question "was not the finding alien to the discoveries?" Contained within the space generated by that primary question is an implication of the contradiction that lies at the heart of the Latin American condition – the difference between motives and events. And between what the continent was and what the European clergy and scientists invented it to be in order to be able to assimilate it into their intellectual systems. Columbus, on his way to the Indies, was not looking for Latin America. Totally unexpected, it could not have been a discovery or a finding. In the poem, the perception of the continent presenting itself to the "discoverers" as a gift is stated in conjunction with the observation that, because the continent was perceived by the Spanish and Portuguese as an obstacle in the path of a western route to the Indies and the promised wealth of that enterprise, it was encountered, not accepted. The poem continues, stating that because it was this enterprise that forced the encounter and the conquering and settling of America by the Europeans, their eyes, veiled by other objectives, were unable to see the gift before them. Thus, in essence, the continent remained undiscovered. Instead of accepting the gift and the responsibility of unveiling – revealing the meaning – of that gift, which is implicit in the acceptance, an invented and imported reality was created. The "Amereida" sets itself up to accept the responsibility of the unveiling.

The conquerors and settlers built their cities at the edges of the continent in close proximity to the sea for trade, in an urban vision eminently Spanish. This is drawn in the "Amereida" on a first map.

Out of this first map is born the thesis of "the interior sea" – the undiscovered and unconquered lands of the continent, neither accepted nor forgotten, but absent when one inquires about the Latin American destiny. And this "interior sea" dares one to lift its veil through "travesía". The word "travesía" translates to mean voyage or crossing, but specifically in nautical terms. When crossing the Atlantic Ocean, the navigator lifts his face to the stars and is guided by the constellations. In the Northern Hemisphere these constellations move around the pole star. The Southern Cross guides and guards the travelers of the Southern Hemisphere. Therefore, the poem "Amereida" lowers the Southern Cross from the sky and places it over the South American continent to guide travesías – or voyages of discovery – through the interior sea.

The travesía uses the sky as its eyes and the reversing of the cross on the landscape as its map. As it was from the north to the south that the Spanish conquered America, so it is from the south to the north, guided by the imposition of the Southern Cross on the continent, that the interior sea was to be discovered, the countries separated by the interior sea rejoined and their common heritage pursued. The first travesía occurred in August and September of 1965 with a group of ten faculty members of the school. They advertised in the London *Times* for poets, architects and artists to join them. It was an arduous trip that began in Punta Arenas in the south and had as its goal Santa Cruz in Bolivia – where the axis of the Southern Cross laid over the continent intersected. Although the goal of Santa Cruz was intended from the outset, the travesía itself was structureless. Not unlike the Surrealist wanderings, but on a much larger scale, it allowed chance and the spontaneous to intervene. Intermediate directions and goals were improvised by members of the group, changed or redirected by others. Often the weather and travel conditions were extremely inhospitable and the last 50 kilometres of the trip were abandoned completely because the road into Santa Cruz was blocked by Che Guevara's men. The journey was made up of numerous poetic acts improvised on sites along the route and each poetic act, beyond reciting and making poetry, initiated the construction of a physical mark, inscription or offering on the site.

Specifically from the proposition of travesía – of creating something on the site, of the site, in a poetic way – one finds in the poem "Amereida" the articulation

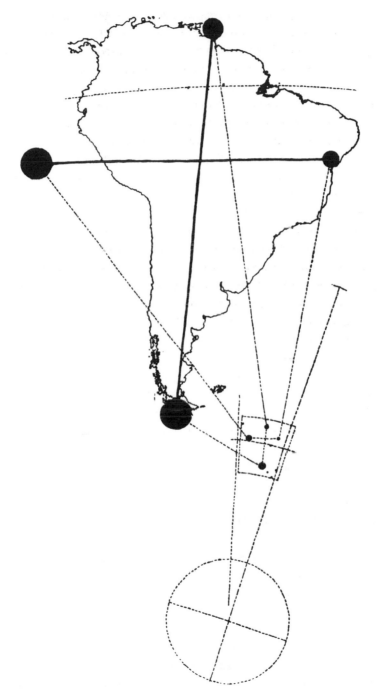

16.16 Map from the Amereida.

of several inter-related ideas that provoke the conception of the Open City Amereida in Ritoque. These ideas include concepts of imaginary cities, or a single imaginary city, thoughts about the tradition of agora as the intersection of public man and natural site, thoughts about the laws of nature as traditionally related to the process of building in the "innocence of an archaism", and speculations about building on an earth in which the "act of building is light" – of little consequence. In its specificity, the "Amereida" can be seen as a charter for the Open City. However, unlike traditional charters, it does not lay down structures and laws but, instead, establishes the foundation for a way of acting. It is the concept of travesía invented by the "Amereida" that bridges theoretical speculation relative to this way of acting, and concrete action necessary to the making of the Open City.

Since the first travesía – the Amereida Travesía – the concept of travesía has proven to be of immense value to the research of the institute. So much so that they have become part of the pedagogical program in which the third trimester of each year is reserved for research in travesía with students and professors. As an extension and prolongation of the original journey of discovery, the travesías that have occurred since have proven to serve two purposes. First, to discover the

16.17 Travesía in the ghost port town of Pisagua.

power and value of the natural continent in relationship to a concept of history in which the Latin American heritage is considered as a gift and, second, to inform the way of doing/making through discovery. Like the wanderings of the Surrealist poets, the travesías probe the boundaries between rationalized experience and intuitive discovery, provoking the interpretation of the space of the site through words and language and then, through words and language, making a proposition about the construction of space within the site. In this manner, travesía unites the process of interpretation and transformation.

In essence, the work at the Open City has been done in travesía. Like the first travesía, there are certain parameters that loosely structure the improvisational making and marking of space in an extended natural site. Also, like the first travesía, there is an element of wandering attached to a crossing or voyage. However, whereas the wandering of the first travesía was attached to a theoretically-constructed geometric projection that extended half the continent and occurred over several months, at the Open City the wandering is across and through the territory defined by the boundaries of the site. It is a journey and a mental crossing – a crossing in understanding – that constantly folds back on itself and has been occurring for over 25 years. At the Open City the original idea of voyage as something projected, from one point in place and time to another point in place and time, is replaced by a concept of voyage, or crossing, that occurs again and again across the site along different trajectories with different characteristics.

Although the Institute for Architecture at the Catholic University of Valparaíso was founded in 1952, it was not until March 1970 that the Open City was begun: 18 years of experimentation and vigil in which the founding attitudes related to the centering of architecture in the poetic use of words were at work. It is through travesía that much of the teaching and experimentation is now focused, and it is through the idea/attitude/method of travesía that the Open City has achieved material significance. Travesía as poetic acts are used to discover sites of construction and they are used to discover strategies for the making of space. Depending upon the complexity of the proposed project or the length of its construction time, these may or may not occur simultaneously, or there may be a series of poetic acts that occur at different stages of the conception and design of the project.

Here you see the Palace of Dawn and Dusk (El Palacio del Alba y del Ocaso) – a major place of congregation with spatial relationships to the sunrise and sunset. It was intended to be a much taller-roofed building whose unbuttressed brick walls were built in bowed segments to provide lateral stability. However, when the walls were built to approximately five-and-a-half feet in height, the poet Godofredo Iommi appeared on the site and declared that the palace was finished. As it stands, it is a series of spaces roofed by the sky and defined by the

16.18 Palacio del Alba y del Ocaso.

rhythmic brick walls upon which the sun acts to dematerialize and re-materialize the surface, its mass and volumes. Exposed to the elements, the floor of the palace is marked with water channels and surface elements that channel and fracture the rainfall. The height of the walls, as built, creates a strong horizontal line parallel to the horizon and just above eye height. An experience is thus created in which the horizon line demarcating the boundary between sea and sky weaves through the openings between the walls of the palace, merging the space of the palace with that of the sea and sky. Because the palace and its significance were defined by the moment when the founding poet declared the palace done, the physical object contains within it that gesture and the memory of the moment of its appearance, of its coming to be, and it contains the significance and purity of the architectural intention materialized in that gesture. It is a building about time in many aspects: time frozen in the instant of the architectural proposition; the continuum of time and the cycles of time as witnessed in the phenomena of the sky; the separation of time into its two faces of night and day, specifically highlighting the moments of trans- ition at dawn and dusk. And it is a building about the vastness of the sky whether crossed by the sun or by the figures of the stars. These are materialized in the simple gesture of stopping and reforming one's original premise – the conviction, the ability to be convicted to the poetic act.

Another civic project at the Open City is the cemetery which was begun when two children of the founders died, one by fire and the other by water. Two tombs were built – one as a brick dome embedded in the ground and the other as a brick dome spiraling up to the sky. These tombs are connected by a path – the first mark on the site – that begins at the crest of one hill of the gently sloped ravine in which the cemetery is found, moves down into the void and up the other side, dividing the ravine into different territories for burial. The ravine, itself, establishes the first and largest scale of entombment, metaphorically, and its topography is gently manipulated to find other pockets for burial and contemplation. The ravine also encloses an outdoor chapel and a cenotaph which is a lightning-bolt-shaped cut in the ground formed by two brick walls held little more than two feet apart by steel rods. The cut begins at the bottom of the ravine slope and moves horizontally into the slope that ascends around it. Following it, one finds oneself surrounded by a tall room in the hill that is roofed by the sky.

16.19 The cemetery.

These last two projects were intended as, and clearly are, civic projects. There are several others as well. But without the urban imprint of a city plan, without the physical aspect of city – roads, streets, density, fabric – and without the inclusive accommodation of all aspects of daily communal life – there are no schools or churches, commerce does not exist and daily articles of consumption are brought from the outside – one has to wonder what it is that makes the Open City of Amereida a city. *Is it* a city? Or, given its relationship to the pedagogical agenda of the Institute for Architecture, which insists on the transformation of study into creative research – the merging of life and art so that life becomes a laboratory for the imagination – is the Open City a laboratory: a laboratory of urban settlement? In the sand, in what was originally zoned as coastal park, there is something occurring that is not recreational in intent but instead is about civic work. It certainly could be considered a laboratory in that the work is research oriented – not dependent on clients and commissions. But it also has a physical consequence and communal framework that transgress the boundary between research and practice. From either position, as city or as laboratory, what is significant is that the Open City poses fundamental questions as to what constitutes "city" and urbanism.

Certainly no city has appeared overnight with all of its physical characteristics intact. However, it is possible to affirm that a city has its character predetermined from the moment of its founding. In Latin America, this idea is especially relevant as the cities of the Spanish conquest and settlement were conceived intact. It was a vision of city ordered and structured for settlement. Just as Latin America, itself, was an invention and a coming to terms with the piece of land that interrupted Columbus' westward route to the Indies, which necessitated a significant revision of the existing Latin world concept, the Spanish and Portuguese cities founded in the New World were also inventions. They were not formed from morphological growth. They were new, begun from nothing but the idea of settlement and settlement for Spain. They represented Spain and the model, itself, defined by the Law of the Indies, became a significant symbol. In Ritoque, at the Open City, the project of building a city is very much attached to this attitude that a city is inherent in its founding because the founding sets in motion the city's destiny. Unlike the Spanish model, however, the destiny is not one formally predetermined, intact with all of its infrastructure and building types in place, but is instead open.

The symbolic act of founding the Spanish Colonial city was accompanied by drawings, or traces of the city and the assignment of territories to the colonists, remaining literally and graphically described in documents of vital political, administrative and urbanistic importance. In the tradition of these Spanish American cities, the Open City was founded as a city around specific foundational acts – it

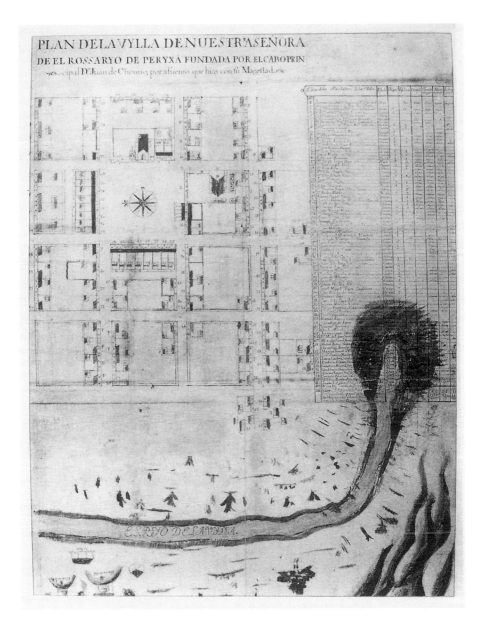

16.20 Foundational map for the city of Nuestra Señora del Rosario de Perixá, Venezuela.

occurred in a similar self-conscious and ritualistic manner – and the poem "Amereida" serves as the charter of that founding, the document or trace of the city. The intention of city appears in its naming. The act of founding of the Spanish American cities conferred the status of city to the most embryonic settlements whose purpose were, very specifically, settlement for Spain at any cost. At the Open City, the purpose is, metaphorically, settlement for poetry with loyalty toward America.

As a corollary to the concept of founding, within the context of this discussion, is the notion of the destiny of the city and its attachment to the forming of city. The founders of the Open City believe and state that the "role of the urbanist is to discover the destiny of the city and position it in space so that the city and its inhabitants live their destiny". Destiny is not something to be imposed upon the city but allowed to unfold through time and space. It is, however, present within the city from its very founding. Like a mirage, it is a mental image of city that is projected out of the physical and cultural context in which the city is sited. The destiny must be discovered, not imposed or invented, and then set in motion in space. It is an implication of working from the inside out and not from the outside in.

16.21 Jardin de Bo.

16.22 The Plaza José Vial Armstrong in Valparaíso dedicated to the memory of one of the school's founders.

Because the destiny is a mirage, an implication of the city formed, and because it is attached to the city from the very beginning, it is something that implies that the city is city from the moment of its founding – from the moment the intention is focused – and that its character is initiated at that first moment. How long it takes to establish conventional urban density or build that character is an exterior issue.

The Renaissance architect Leon Battista Alberti claimed that the city has two meanings: a grouping of edifices in a certain pattern and a meeting of men. The Open City is composed of a grouping of edifices, although not in any discernible pattern. It was founded as a city and there exists a precise intention to construct a communal field of activity based upon a certain way of acting. This field of activity is outlined in a charter, the "Amereida" and all issues important to it are debated in public forums. The physical environment of the city is a consequence of this field of activity, not the reverse.

For the builders of the Open City, the keys to urbanism are its men and women – for it is men and women who are capable of poetic activity – and the collective energy of community. It is not a theoretical urbanism, but one of action completely removed from the drawing board and transferred into the hands of the individuals working in community. It is not surprising, then, that the first structures to be built were not churches or markets – power functions – but hospederías and agoras. The house is the place that unfolds around the activities and gestures of the individual and in which ones spends the most meaningful parts of the day. It is the place of renewal. And the hospedería, which is more than house, is, additionally, a place of meeting and exchange among members of the community. It serves both the individual and the group whereas the agora is, specifically, the place that unfolds around the gestures of the community.

The way in which the Open City sets up the discussion about city making, as well as its philosophical base and way of acting certainly has utopian propensity. In its repudiation of contemporary values associated with the production of architecture and its emphasis on a new course of action in which these contemporary values are transformed or turned completely upside down, it implies a utopian drive. Despite this propensity however, the Open City is not a model for social, or even architectural, reform because it generates more problems than solutions. More a laboratory than a demonstration, it does not pretend that its discoveries are applicable outside of itself. With regard to the laboratory, it is not the proof that is important – because art does not advance as science does by proofs and errors – but by the process of discovery. This process is not fueled by reason but ignited by a poetic impulse that connects the field of inquiry to another level of understanding. In this sense, the utopian drive of the Open City is much closer to the "eupsychia" fabricated by Rousseau – an optimum state of consciousness in a society whose material structures tend to fade into the background.

Although the utopian propensity exists at the Open City, there are three key issues that separate it from utopian status. Firstly, is the issue of immutability. Utopia projects a model for an ideal society that is considered so perfect, and so in tune, with the basic human condition that it is, itself, a-historical and a-cultural, transcending particularities and peculiarities of any given place or period. It proposes a changeless society with immutable institutions that would never need to be changed because they are so "right". This is hardly the goal or reality at the Open City. If anything, mutability is one of the laws in Ritoque. Each project tries to be loyal to the muse of invention and no work is ever considered complete and finished, or sacred to the exclusion of transformation.

Secondly, is the issue of generality and universality. The ideal condition has a measure of generality or it becomes merely a romantic and narcissistic yearning. The work of the Open City does not propose an application of its specific combination of working and living through poetry on any level of universality and it does not even suggest, or require, its own continuity. Thirdly, is the issue of nostalgia.

16.23 One of the stones from the Plaza José Vial Armstrong.

The concept of Utopia was born out of two very ancient beliefs that have molded it and nurtured it: the Judaeo-Christian belief in a paradise that was created with the world in the form of the Garden of Eden and the Hellenic myth of an ideal city built by men for men without the aid or approval of the gods. Nostalgia for a return or re-appropriation of this heaven on earth is one of the key corollaries to utopian thought. The attitude and work of the Open City rejects completely this nostalgic mode. The poem "Amereida" denounces the European nostalgic drive that was a component of the conquering, enslavement and destruction of the Native American populations and the continent that it intellectually ennobled as a manifestation of the primitive Garden of Eden. Instead of a nostalgic relationship to its physical and historical context, the work of the Valparaíso architecture school deals with its context as an essential reality. It is not abstract or intellectual, both prerequisites for nostalgia.

Utopia, as well as a set of conditions, is a philosophical stance. U-topia – no-place – implies a state of existence so perfect that it cannot exist in an imperfect mundane world. It is by nature a goal, a philosophic model that mundane reality attempts to mimic. It is no-place, in reality, which as a model, however, is capable of creating place within reality. In their essay "La Cuidad Abierta: De la Utopía al Espejismo", Alberto Cruz and Godofredo Iommi maintain that the Open City, instead of being Utopia – no-place, "no-lugar" – is "sin-lugar", without place, meaning: a place that does exist within the reality of the mundane but has the quality of being different or less than what we expect of reality in the physical world. In other words, it is a place with a mundane physical existence whose defining characteristic is to not have the density (*espesor*) of the real world – like a mirage (*espejismo*). A mirage does not have density. It is nothing more than pure appearance or apparition. It is a real presence with a less-than-real dimension, like the mirage in the desert that makes the oasis visible. The oasis does exist somewhere else in the desert. It is not invented. The mirage marks this other place in the space.

The Open City then, as an attempt to construct the mirage, is not Utopia, but city in pure form as Iommi and Cruz contend:

> A work for the pure apparition – is it not truly "poiesis"? If opened up in the apparition is all of its manifestations, its being, mere apparitions, appearances, mirages.

Perhaps poetry, in fact, reduces this dimension to which we are alluding (time); perhaps it assumes the suspension of all disbelief, as Coleridge claimed, and expresses itself from its belief in all work. From this being possible, the possibility of a concrete and real task unfolds, of a complex of poetic works whose manifestation is only to appear. Would not this complex of works be "city"?

City as mirage which is city precisely at that moment in which it appears to mark its destiny in the space.

Chapter 17

@morphous mutations

François Roche

> I had to admit defeat. Something wanted it that way. I, too, was just an instrument. The world was nothing more than an infinite interweave of instruments. The respite had only lasted for as long as the mirage that it was. *Les Racines du Mal*, Maurice G. Dantec, Série Noire, 1995

SITUATION

Sites and territories nurture identities, preconditions and affects that architecture and urbanism have continuously restrained and eradicated. The architectural object, having claimed authority for four centuries[1] has the power of unparalleled destruction of modernity to maturity. But in so doing it signs its own limits and end.

The numerous "aesthetic orthodoxies" born in the antechamber of reason and the wastedumps of ideology have now not only become unworkable but are also criminal in their discrepancy with society.

Judging each operation on the validity of hypotheses within an enormous assortment of ever-increasing facts and artefacts is not an easy task. Signs and referents are not pre-given, like a symbolic reference, but have to be discovered in real time, on the "real site".

If architecture did not know or could not substitute for the modern culture of breaking in a culture of place, more attentive to what it was bulldozing, it was because the verse was already in the fruit. In short, a genetic error . . . The horizons of the world of perception, of corporeality and of place have only too rarely been the mediums of a production.

Territorialising[2] architecture does not mean cloaking it in the rags of a new fashion or style, which would be just as out of such and separate from the styles and fashions already consumed. Territorialising architecture in order that the place gains a social, cultural and aesthetic[3] link means inserting it back into what it might have been on the verge of destroying, and extracting the substance of the construction from the landscape (whether urban or otherwise), whether a physical, corporeal substance within it, or climates, materials, perceptions and affects.

This is not historical regression, nor modern projection, but an attitude that affirms itself by what it doesn't belong to, outlined against a razor's edge, in

17.01 La route de Soweto, le Bush. Afrique du Sud, Création d'un Musée-Mémorial, intégrant les archives du Township, commande de AICA à Johannesburg et FRAC Réunion, 1997.

permanent equilibrium. It is a process that is renewed at each new place, allowing for an *in situ* attitude rather than just another aesthetic code. From that, a radical displacement of our function can be born.

To identify that which characterises a place is already to interpret it and to put forward a way of operating on it. But linking being to its ecosystem can only save linking the body to the body of architecture. This process of reactive mimesis

17.02 La route de Soweto, le Bush. Afrique du Sud, Création d'un Musée-Mémorial, intégrant les archives du Township, commande de AICA à Johannesburg et FRAC Réunion, 1997.

is not a simulation of the "exquisite corpse" game, a visual avatar, disappearing and camouflaging itself with an ecological alibi. Its ability to take hold of a territory without subjugating it depends on the unclear identity that develops within it, on the transformation it operates, on the gap of its implementation, on the ambiguity of the network of extraction/transformation that the materials have come from. This antidote to the separated,[4] autonomous body, this "live" production process, could not operate were it not nourished by these active materials: "there are the images of materials . . . sight names them and the hand knows them."[5]

In order that these "barren" propositions do not add, subtract but rather extract, and in order that the object of architecture can spur on the real, like a contorted alterity of the territory in abeyance, we should, perhaps, shift the origins of architectural referents into a precondition that states "there is".

We had spent several years looking for the instrument that would enable us to explore the minimal act, somewhere between the not-much and the just-enough, where the territorial change stemming from architecture would be steeped in prior geographies, where the development can work its way in, and embed itself in what it was supposed to dominate, to exacerbate issues of mutation and identity. We were after an instrument that would enable us to introduce strategies of hybridization and mimesis in the "here and now" of each particular situation. In view of the many different manipulations of history, involving morality and heritage alike, geography and cartography – and not the tracing, as Deleuze and Guattari[6] remind us – have always seemed more operational to us. But to contrast the already existing site with its future, in an encounter between the image of the exposed context and the image (in photomontage) that embraces the architectural project, like the demonstration of a processing economy, was not enough for us. We were missing the grasp of the process, in the breakdown of successive hypotheses. Despite formulating hybridization scenarios, the medium was lacking. The mutations not only never appeared in the movement that had given rise to them, but, even more so, the documents, in the final analysis, could, by virtue of their isolation, be re-interpreted as decontextualized artefacts.

The processes of distortion, originating from morphing, stem from this dearth and open up a field of possibilities. Over and above a fascination with the technological tool, and with the contrived metamorphosis that it creates, we are exercised by its revelatory and operational function. The more "deceptive" the morphed movement seems, the more inert in its transformation, the more the urban and architectural project seems to be dominated by the prior situation. The more the morphing can be read in its artifice, the more the projection seems, this time around, to be deterritoralized. Unlike an instrument of representation, morphing thus reveals the degree to which the hypotheses are decontextualized, and in an

17.03 Venise, Acqua Alta. Magazzini Frigoriferi at San Basilio, Venise. avec Ammar Eloueini, Centre Culturel et Pédagogique (École d'Architecture de Venise), 1998.

17.04 La route du Maïdo, la Clairière. Ile de la Réunion, Création de la Villa Malraux, FRAC Réunion, une Villa Médicis de l'Océan Indien, 1997.

on-going back-and-forth between deduction and induction, a re-reading of the successive phases will validate or invalidate the relevance of the choices, in a making that requires less strategy.[7]

It is no longer a matter of contrasting the project with its context, like two distinct hypotheses, but of linking them together by the actual transformation process. The project is no longer the issue of an abstract projection, but of a distortion of the real. The blank page and the empty screen cannot be. This software calls for a body, a generic physical matrix.

The skin[8] of the photographic, cartographic image is transformed and metamorphosed in one and the same envelope, in one and the same; it undergoes manipulations akin to folding, extrusion and scarification. And the pixels, fractal fragments of the real, are put back together again in a series of genetic mutations. The context is no longer idealized, conceptualized or historicized, it is rather an underlayer of its own transformation. This is a political difference. The virtual instrument paradoxically becomes a principle of reality.

A few words of explanation: morphing lies at the root of a software which makes it possible to merge image A with image B by means of a topological shift of salient dots. With the "Warp" technique, which is a variant of this process, it is possible to produce this alteration, but without being aware of the resulting B. Image A can thus be easily manipulated, and distorted, when it comes into contact with a programme and a scenario, but it cannot sidestep its own matter, its own physicality, by resisting it. And it is this amorphism that is involved here.

Presenting the conditions of a hybridization and a transformation that are paradoxically static and which, by virtue of the mobility/immobility that they create, reveals at best the various issues of prior identity and geography. It is tantamount to producing a critical state both on the "territorial development" processes but also on the use and misuse of technologies. Doing nothing is to raise questions and problems, alike. Doing things on the map, by way of this concept of "@morphous Mutations", is like trying to do things from the negative angle, without the preformatted and accepted skills. The model already in place obliges us to switch our skill towards other arenas (social mechanisms, political economics, territorial challenges). This process thus opens up areas of investigation likely to extricate us from the diktat of modern projection (medium and alibi of twentieth century architecture), which has muddled the programme with the declaration of functions.

To make the architectural object ambiguous, and to force it out of the real, is to question our own perception.[9] Nothing seems more pertinent to me than an architecture that straddles such ambiguities. The binary structures of the predominant thinking about heritage/modernity and servility/domination have, happily, imploded. The transformations of the body and its sexuality, using silicone and collagen, as a

17.05 Saint-Sauveur, la Lisière. Forêt de Compiègne, Maison d'été pour un Horticulteur, commande privée, 1994.

diametric opposite of the *Metropolis* Cyber-Robot, are the lead-in to this. The contemporary prosthesis is made of flesh, and the functional outgrowth made of artificial skin is re-formed. The body is not denied, but exacerbated and hypertrophied.

Technology thus enables us, by way of this concept of "@morphous Mutations", to involve processes and write scripts which reactivate the concept of "localism", not to serve up dishes again that have got cold, and museified models, but a thrilling localism, made up of contradictions[10] and respect, and reactive membranes, in an elastic topography.

Identifying what characterizes a place by these new tools is already tantamount to putting forward a new operational method. So there's not much point in doing a whole lot more.

Notes

1   Brunelleschi's perspectival geometry is responsible for this, in the rationalization of instruments of production and the domination of architecture on the site. The rule of visual representation is thus substituted for corporeal perceptions.

2   See the notion developed by Félix Guattari in his *Schizophrénie Analytique* on ecosophy, that architecture has "imploded" and is condemned to being pulled and torn in every direction.

3   In sense attributed to it by M. Maffésoli, *Du Temps des tribus*, 1988, "History can promote a morale (a politics), the space will favour an aesthetic and exude an ethics."

4   See Augustin Berque's *La Théorie du paysage en France*.

5   Gaston Bachelard, *L'Eau et les rêves*, 1942.

6   "The rhizome is quite different, map and not tracing ... If there is a contrast between map and tracing, it is because the map in its entirety is oriented towards an experiment to do with reality. The map does not reproduce a subconscious that is closed in on itself, it constructs it." Gilles Deleuze, Félix Guattari, *Mille Plateaux* (Les Éditions de Minuit, Collection Critique 1980).

7   "Making with to do less", R, DSV & Sie. P., *L'Ombre du Caméléon*, IFA/Karédas, 1994.

8   "These tear the body within and seek a hole to escape through, it throws its hands on to the body and they vibrate under the fingers; it pushes them towards the joints, towards the cavities of the belly and throat, it crushes them there, its fist digging into the skin, which, bespattered with blood beneath, turns cold." Pierre Guyotat, *Tombeau pour cinq cent mille soldats* (L'imaginaire, Gallimard 1967).

9   L'Hiver de l'Amour/The Winter of Love, Musée d'Art Moderne de la Ville de Paris, Paysage/Landscape n°2, R, DSV & Sie. P. An installation on the stairs. The fitted carpet was laid, the height of the steps slightly altered, and the carpet relaid. A study to do with the dissociation of the senses, between what was perceived (the treads) and felt (a moving topography), March 1994.

10   "How to live by following – not without fascination – the bulldozer's passage in the Amazonian forest and campaigning for its protection ... while remaining on the razor's edge. It is with this terribly human dimension that we must work. An admittedly schizophrenic attitude, but one which preserves us from the snares of the clear conscience, environmental activism and destructive forms of extremism." Lecture at the Pavillion de l'Arsenal, F. Roche, 1997, Mini-PA.

Prospecting

Chapter 18

Imagining E-Topia
William J. Mitchell

In a world without action at a distance, the parts of functioning systems end up being jammed closely together. The blade of a knife has to be connected to its handle. The engine, power train, wheels, and steering mechanism of an automobile are tied together by mechanical linkages, and you cannot imagine them being distributed over, say, a city block. The electronic components on a silicon chip are packed together as densely as possible since electrons flow among them, and the shorter the distances the faster the chip runs. And cities are dense, too, since many human transactions have traditionally required face-to-face contact.

Under these conditions, adjacency is a scarce resource. Many things need to be adjacent to one another, but they all occupy finite amounts of space, so they will not all fit – not easily, anyway. As a result, designers of all kinds spend a lot of their time prioritizing adjacency requirements and working out clever schemes for satisfying as many of them as possible. A modern automobile, for example, is a miracle of tight packing.

But our emerging world of telecommunicating smart artifacts and relocatable software is fundamentally different, since many functional connections are established by flows of digital information that do not depend upon adjacency. These information flows often substitute for mechanical linkages, metal-to-metal electrical contacts, materials transfers, line-of-sight visual links, or other adjacency-dependent types of functional connections. Thus designers can now consider distributing functions over physical devices in new ways, and they have considerable freedom to scatter the separate physical devices in space.

DIGITAL INFORMATION AS SOLVENT

Consider, for example, the components of a digital photographic system – let us say a lens, a viewfinder, an image capture device, an image memory, a display screen, image processing software, and a printer. You could package all these elements in one stand-alone unit, but it would be complex and bulky. Another strategy – one commonly followed in early digital cameras – is to put the lens, viewfinder, image capture device and memory into a hand-held camera, assign the display and image processing functions to a desktop personal computer, and utilize the printing capabilities available somewhere in the network to which the computer is connected. And there are yet other possibilities. Some digital cameras integrate the display and image processing software into the hand-held unit. Some eliminate the traditional viewfinder and let the display screen perform its function. And the most stripped-down digital cameras consist of nothing but a lens, image capture device, and wireless transmitter to an image storage device located somewhere else.

In general, when information flows substitute for direct connection, some traditional adjacency requirements simply disappear, some physical components become virtual, and as a result, systems can fragment and recombine. Thus, in old-fashioned film-based photographic systems, lens, image capture, and image storage devices were located in the hand-held camera, while image processing and printing functions were assigned to the darkroom; now, with digital photography, the darkroom just disappears, cameras can take a wider variety of forms as we have seen, and some of the functions are typically reassigned to the personal computer.

Do not jump to the conclusion, though, that any function can now be performed anywhere you like! On the contrary, those adjacency requirements that still remain under the new conditions emerge as the generators of new types of physical clusters. In a camera, for example, the spatial relationship of the lens and the image capture device is closely determined by the laws of optics, and it remains constant when a CCD array is substituted for photographic film. Thus, some of the first digital cameras were produced simply by replacing the film back with a CCD back. Then, as digital camera designs evolved, and began to take radical new forms, the lens-to-image-plane relationship was one thing that remained constant. On the other hand, substitution of a display screen for a traditional viewfinder freed up the relationship of the lens to the photographer's eye, and thus the shapes that camera bodies could take.

In general, then, digital telecommunication has created a condition of recombinant architecture for everything from small consumer products to great cities. And as we shall see, this recombination is particularly dramatic at an urban scale.

CONSTRUCTING THE NEW SPATIAL TECHNOLOGY

How did we get to this point? How did the necessary technology get constructed? There are many strands to the tale, but it will serve for our purposes to identify a few key stages.

The story began in the 1960s, with the development of packet-switching technology for computer networks. This provided an effective way to manage the flows of digital information among computational devices in large, complex, geographically-distributed networks. Eventually, it gave us the Arpanet, the Internet, the World Wide Web, electronic mail, and the beginnings of electronic commerce.

Next, during the 1980s and 1990s, there was a transformation in thinking about computer software. Object-oriented programming languages like C++ allowed software to be broken down into modular, reusable fragments that could easily be recombined into new structures as new needs arose. Soon after, the Java language provided a practical way to move such fragments around freely within computer networks. Thus it became easy for computational devices to download not only electronic mail and data files, but also executable code. As a result, their functions became much more fungible – deriving not only from repertoires of locally-installed software, but also from the capacity to access the globally distributed resources of the Internet.

Then, as processors and memory devices became smaller, cheaper and more robust, they began to migrate from desktop computers to vehicles, appliances, wearable devices, and other everyday objects. Increasingly, machine intelligence was embedded everywhere.

And finally, technology was developed for quickly and automatically integrating these smart devices into networks. In many contexts, wireless telecommunication links began to substitute for cables and jacks. And software technologies such as Linda, Jini, JavaSpaces, and TSpaces began to manage, transparently, the otherwise daunting complexities of interconnecting disparate machines.

As the end of the 1990s approached, we were seeing the emergence of a world in which almost any artifact might have embedded intelligence, memory, and telecommunications capability, and the capacity to function as a component of a globally distributed system of hardware and software resources.

THE TRANSFORMATION OF BOOKSTORES

What does this mean for architecture and urban design? Let us consider a few telling examples.

If I wanted to open a bookstore tomorrow, I could consider two radically different models. I could create a bricks-and-mortar facility like Shakespeare's in Paris, Blackwell's in Oxford, Cody's in Berkeley, or the Gotham Book Mart in New York. Alternatively, I could create an online system like Amazon.com.

For the bricks-and-mortar version, I would need a prominent urban location, and a sign out front to identify the store's function and attract the customers. I would stock it with books displayed on shelves, arranged so that the customers could browse. I would provide a counter near the exit to serve as the point of sale, and I would hire some staff to provide help and advice as required. All this would be packed into one tight architectural package.

For the online version, I would need a Web site that was sufficiently prominent in cyberspace — that is, easily reached from popular Web portals such as Yahoo. The site would need an identifying banner at the top of the front page rather than a sign over the door. I would provide an online catalogue for remote browsing, and store the physical books at a large, central warehouse located near a transportation hub. (This, incidentally, would allow me to keep many more titles in stock than the largest of physical bookstores — since I would not have to keep them on hand in restricted, high-rent urban space.) Instead of a counter and cash register for the sale transaction, I would provide an online order form with the capacity for secure transmission of credit card information. I would provide online access to reviews, expert recommendations, and collaborative filters in place of advice from sales staff. And I would use a package express service to get purchased books rapidly and reliably to the doors of customers.

Clearly the online version has a very different spatial organization from the more traditional one. It centralizes book storage. It allows back-office administrative functions to be performed at any locations, worldwide, that have network connections and competitively-priced skilled labor. It decentralizes browsing and sale transactions to homes and offices. Within this transformed structure, it creates new transportation demands and patterns. Overall, it is a geographically distributed system involving physical sites, transportation links, and telecommunication links.

Who will win in the developing competition between traditional and online bookstores? There isn't a simple answer. Online stores will press their advantages of convenience, speed, reliability, and much larger selections that traditional stores can offer. And they will serve areas that are beyond the reach of traditional stores. But old-time bookstores will fight back by emphasizing those aspects of their service that depend on face-to-face contact or are enhanced by it. They will put in cafes, create pleasant places to hang out in a literary atmosphere, promote readings and book-signings, and try to become settings for valued social relationships.

Probably there is room for both, and for a variety of yet-unexplored combinations. My guess is that the net result will be a pattern in which online bookstores play a very major role, while the functions of the remaining traditional bookstores will, in response, be transformed in subtle but important ways.

REVOLUTION IN RETAILING

Other retail sectors are experiencing similar changes. High Streets and shopping malls are beginning to feel the effects.

Online grocery stores are growing in popularity, for example. Like online bookstores, these present catalogues to Web surfers. But, because grocery purchases are repetitive, they also maintain personal shopping lists that can simply be edited each week – a great time-saver. (In the not-too-distant future, smart cupboards and refrigerators that automatically keep track of their contents, and smart laundries and dishwashers that order their own supplies, will automate this task even further.) Since groceries – unlike books – are bulky and perishable, the distribution warehouses need to be located in regional service areas rather than at national transportation hubs. Fleets of specialized delivery vans make more sense than general package delivery services. And the deliveries cannot just be dropped in a mailbox; they either require sophisticated scheduling or secure, refrigerated receptacles at homes.

As with bookstores, some traditional food stores are finding ways to fight back by making the most of the particular virtues of face-to-face. They are emphasizing the sensual pleasures of food shopping through attractive displays, the smell and touch of the real thing, and, of course, tastings. As a result, the very same people who value the speed and convenience of online shopping for standard commodities during the week may allocate some of their precious weekend leisure time to visiting specialty cheese stores or seafood markets.

With certain types of manufactured goods, yet another pattern is developing – one that changes the relationships of manufacturing, warehousing, and retailing. If you want to buy a personal computer, you no longer have to look for a computer store that has what you want in stock. You can, instead, surf into a Web page that allows you to configure the system you want online, immediately get a price, and submit an order. The order is electronically transmitted directly to the factory, where your machine is then produced and shipped directly to you. Analogous systems have obvious advantages for shoes, clothing, and other things that need to be personalized. Where the industrial revolution promoted production of standardized products before purchase, the digital revolution shifts the emphasis to personalized products produced after purchase.

Once again, then, digital systems do not have the effect of virtualizing everything and completely eliminating effects of place and distance. But they do allow interesting and potentially valuable new spatial patterns to crystallize out.

HOMES AND WORKPLACES

It is possible to take building type after building type and subject them to this sort of analysis. What of hospitals? Schools? University campuses? Libraries? Banks, financial services providers, and stock exchanges? Space limitations prevent us from exploring these systems and their transformations here; too many other things have to be packed between the covers of this traditional, physical book. (It would be different, of course, on the Web.) But it is worth taking a quick look at one of the most crucial processes of urban recombination – the relocation and reorganization of homes and workplaces to create new types of neighborhoods.

In pre-industrial settlements, it was common for homes and workplaces to be located closely together. Peasants lived among their fields, craftsmen by their workshops, merchants above their stores, and scholars in their cloistered colleges. This yielded live/work building types such as the shop-houses of (old) Singapore, the machiya townhouses of Kyoto – where textile workers both lived and plied their trade – and the quadrangles of Cambridge with their private rooms, communal dining halls, libraries, and spaces for meeting and discussion. And it also encouraged the formation of professional neighborhoods in which living space and work space were intertwined to produce complex, fine-grained patterns of land use.

In the industrial era, cities grew larger and their grain tended to coarsen. Industrial workplaces generated noise, pollution, and traffic, and so needed to be separated from residential areas. Suburbs grew. Eventually, we got the modern commuter-city in which homes and workplaces were often far apart. Transportation arteries linked them, and morning and evening rush-hours developed as commuters flowed to and from work.

Now, in the digital information age, many workers spend their time with files, documents, and computers that do not produce pollution and noise. Furthermore, these workers can potentially telecommute – for some of the time, at least. Thus it becomes possible to reintegrate living space and work space, and to create new, electronically-mediated forms of live/work dwellings. Where these dwellings cluster together, we get a 24-hour population (by contrast with the bedroom suburb, which loses its commuter population during the day). And this population can potentially support local services like children's daycare, elderly care, health clubs, business centers, cafés, and the like.

In many ways, then, post-industrial conditions open up the possibility of returning to very attractive pre-industrial settlement patterns. We may find that we can create intense, pedestrian-scaled neighborhoods that simultaneously cluster around local services and depend upon their global electronic connections.

THE USES OF DISCONTINUITY

This all adds up to a sharp discontinuity in our modes of creating and sustaining our towns and cities. We are at a moment of change that presents us with some stark social choices, and some very challenging policy and design tasks.

It would be naïve to doubt that the rich and powerful of the world are far better positioned than the poor and marginalized to seize the new opportunities created by digital technology and turn it to their advantage. This technology could well become an effective instrument to heighten inequities and polarize cities into walled, electronically-serviced privileged domains surrounded by zones of disinvestment and despair. But it is also true that major discontinuities provide particular opportunities – if they are cleverly pursued – to multiply and extend opportunities and effect positive social and political change.

It is not hard to imagine, as well, that new commercial and industrial arrangements enabled by digital technology could simply drive up consumption, further fuel urban growth, and even more rapidly gobble up our natural resources. But by partially substituting telecommunication for transportation, and software systems for bricks-and-mortar facilities, they could also yield less resource-hungry, more sustainable settlement patterns.

How will it all pan out? What will the cities of the twenty-first century be like? The answer is not, I suggest, determined by the affordances of the new technology. It is a matter of invention, design, critical discussion, social policy, and political will. It is mostly up to us.

Chapter 19

Planets, comets, and dinosaurs: digital identity in virtual space[1]
Anthony Vidler

The relation between space and identity has been, to some extent, always linked to representation. The humanistic subject in perspectival space, the modern subject in montage space: these tropes of interpretation have, with many variations, come to stand for historically-defined identities if not experiences – the "point of view" representing the viewer, the image of a space representing its apparent effect. The effects of digital representation, however, despite claims of its revolutionary impact, have been less clearly joined to a new construction of subjectivity. Cyber-punk has given us the image of the hacker, but the hacker seems to differ little from the modernist/humanist subject: screens, after all, are readily construed as windows, and the now commonplace images of virtual space seem closer to wire frame emulations of traditional perspective than to any more radical or explosive forms. And yet, the infinite mutability, the seemingly endless permutations and rotations of digital constructions, the speed of virtual travel within the image, not to mention the complexity of the networks of communication themselves, all lead to the suspicion that some transformation in subjecthood is under way. Even if we are not yet at the point where the interpenetration of mind, matter, and matrix is as complete as imaged by the author William Gibson, the relations between image and experience have nevertheless been changed beyond recognition within the processes, if not the outer forms, of spatial design. In the following essay, I want to explore some possible models of what might have become of the modernist subject within these processes, and more especially, what might be the effect of these processes on the architectural projects for which they are increasingly used.

I

I'm not quite sure why, when asked to think about digital identity, I immediately think of dinosaurs; perhaps it's because their identity, like that of the human subject, is perforce entirely "constructed" with all the methodological "rigor" of a Cuvier (or a Spielberg). Perhaps it's because, unlike at the turn of the century, I cannot entirely rid my mind of galactic and planetary apocalypse; perhaps it's just because I'm the father of a five-year-old dino-fetishist. But I rather think, as it will become clear in this essay, that it is something about the newly-discovered digital identity of dinosaurs, the manner in which that identity has changed in the last few years, and most especially the ways in which their new found "liveliness" in movies places them precisely somewhere between architecture and culture. Here Darwin meets late-twentieth-century visuality in a way that, I would hold, has profoundly transformed our own subject position with regard to architecture, or rather which has transformed the subject for which architecture itself is constructed, whether or not our specific identities are taken into account.

There is no lack of evidence for a contemporary fascination, if not obsession, with galactic, apocalyptic, prehistoric and posthistoric life – to the extent that one might descry the emergence of a kind of "new galacticism" over the last few years. Movies like the "Star Wars" trilogy, "Jurassic Park," "The Lost World," and "The Land Before Time," Parts I through IV; scientific works debating the reasons for dinosaur extinction, most recently exemplified by Berkeley professor Walter Ivarez *T.Rex and the Crater of Doom*; the fashion for cuddly purple dinos singing earnest moralizing songs to hypnotized children; the mania for mutant turtles engaged in bloody battles to the delight of the same, less moralized, younger set; the recent appearance of the Hale-Bopp comet dangerously close to our horizon, and the resulting tragic and hysterical reaction of World-Wide Web surfing cults; not to mention the emergence of Dinosaur-like RVs consuming enormous amounts of fossil fuels; and finally, the auction a few weeks ago at Sotheby's of Sue, the most completely preserved T-Rex specimen yet found (with 99 per cent of her bones in place) with a starting price of £1 million and a final sale price of more than £8 million, should indicate to us that dinos have not just arrived, they are true works of art – modern totems, as W.J.T. Mitchell argues in his recent cultural history of the modern dinosaur, *The Last Dinosaur Book*. [2] These phenomena and many more are enough to signal that interest in paleontology and astronomy is in full swing.

This current interest in dinos and galaxies is, of course, not new; nor is it a simple function of our post-millennium decade. Its history goes back to Cuvier's time, or at least to the 1820s, when dinosaurs first began to haunt the romantic imaginary. But our own mania seems to bear special relationship to the dino-fever of the more recent past – that of the 1950s and 60s – of which it appears in many respects to be a survival, and in other respects a revival. One might point not only to the survival of Star Trek and NASA in their various incarnations (recently the subject of an elegant essay by Constance Penley), but also to the re-runs of *The Jetsons* and *The Flintstones* (back-to-back on the Time-Warner Cartoon Channel and now about to be morphed into a new series, *The Jetstones*). Many of the dinosaur exhibits now being reinstalled to reflect current scientific wisdom and to capitalize on film-rights linkage and consumer franchising, were those originally refurbished from their nineteenth- and early-twentieth-century incarnations in the 1960s.

Between the 1960s and us, however, there has emerged the great divide of the digital, which, I would argue, has had results that go far beyond a radical change in representational techniques, and that imply a profound change in the nature of our subjectivity with regard to architectural space. In other words, I am not simply speaking of the way in which digital software has allowed us to re-re-represent things in the way we used to represent them before the enormous efforts of CAD, for example to replicate perspective, or that of so-called "virtual reality" simulators to throw this perspective into a "felt" three-dimensions – the well-known wire frame that with great effort manages to caricature what the Renaissance painter took for granted as "reality". Rather I am concerned to characterize, if not interpret, the peculiar kind of subject, the "I" as Lacan would have it, that has been unconsciously constructed by its confrontation with a "mirror" entirely different to that which faced the 1930s psychoanalysts and his child-subjects. This new mirror, which is more of a screen than a reflective surface, is, I believe, in the process of creating an imago that was hardly imaginable in 1936. In extending the mirror-stage analogy a little further, I should make it clear that I make no claims of psycho-analytic validity or professional competence in psychoanalytical understanding for what follows; rather I want to delineate a kind of "parable" that might be called "The Three Subjects of Modern Architecture" in order to throw into "perspective," as Lois Riegl would have put it, our thoughts on the new digital world.

II

For a long time I have wanted to make a movie of "The Mirror Stage."[3] But just as Walter Benjamin's dream of making a movie of "Paris" foundered on the multiple reefs of his complex spatial and temporal imagination of the city, so my imaginary "Mirror Stage II" has always been blocked by the apparent contradiction between Lacan's pseudo-realist plot of the little dear one propped up before the glass (and surely it does make some difference whether it's supported by a prosthesis – the celebrated "trotte-bébé" – or by a parent or friend?) and the surrealist-style imagery of the dream sequences in the essay, that image everything from exoscopy (Hieronymous Bosch as fragmented subject) to "legendary psychasthenia" (Roger Caillois confronts the leaf insect). And my own imaginary film has been doubly com-plicated because I have always wanted to use it to investigate directly the subject's relationship to architecture as a development of the empathetic, bodily, a projection that scholars like Heinrich Wölfflin posited as the way in which we measure and interpret buildings; as an enquiry into the consistent search for transparency common to modernist and late modernist culture alike; as a way of questioning the sense of "camouflage" inherent in contextualist and some postmodernist fantasies of "blending in" to an existing milieu; or, finally, as a working through of the problematics of spatial as opposed to visual experience, à la Minkowski, and, later, the early Foucault. These questions, difficult to represent in visual form, combined with the obvious difficulties of the "real" versus the "imaginary", excellently but somewhat tragically exhibited in the different historical attempts to "film" Freud, have caused me several times to put my own movie scenario on hold. In this I was supported by the film-maker and critic Peter Wollen who was immediately scornful of the idea, asking caustically, "What would there be to film?"

Recently however, when re-reading Lacan's brief essay for an interdisciplinary class in visual theory, following a conference of digital animators, I began to think about the implications of digital "enhancement" in contemporary movies. I then thought up a quite different version of my old movie project. This version would contain not one, but at least three mirror stages, in the multiple senses implied by Lacan's "le stade": "stages" of development, theatrical "stages," "stadia," and so on, each staged in a different moment of the historical development of modernism.

My first modern mirror stage would thus be set in late-nineteenth-century Vienna: the infant would be surely held in a prosthesis designed by Schreber the elder, father of Freud's Schreber, inventor of mechanical aids for child deportment, as terrifying as the writing machine in Kafka's "Penal Colony." The mirror would be large, perhaps full-length, spotted, and framed ornately in gilt wood carved in the writhing shapes of pre-art-nouveau soft-porn nymphs and satyrs. The combination of the iron frame enclosing our baby, the shadow of nanny hovering in background, the animated eroticism of the mirror frame (definitely not a Kantian parergon), would surely produce a subject ripe for Freud's couch, but it would also construct a specific type of alienating imago, one filled with vague neurasthenia, riven with the mutual anxieties of agoraphobia and claustrophobia, and doomed to live in *jugenstijl* interiors, themselves, to use Benjamin's terms, as sterile as the electric wiring twining around their coldly sexual decoration. The form of this subject's socialization would be perhaps that of Adolf Loos, living, like Kafka, in a Chinese-puzzle-land of little boxes, connected within other little boxes in endless series, each one for a specific purpose, each one of a different scale, each one orthopedic, as Lacan would say, of a totality differentiated by social function; each one incorporated into the next in a totalizing game of what Loos himself called three-dimensional chess: the game of the *raumplan*. Outside the puzzle, however, in the new public realm, our subject would be dressed, Weber-style, without charisma, grey overcoat, black tie, and homburg hat, ready for the office.

My second scene would be that of the original Lacanian subject in the 1930s: surrealist and modernist at the same time, a space of struggle that, as Benjamin put it, might somehow embrace both André Breton and Le Corbusier in a single glance, it order to epitomize an essential "modernity." The child would be held up in its very French trotte-bébé, but a modern mother would be at hand, her face perhaps merging with the outlines of the baby's own reflection, while the room would be white, of ambiguous spatial dimensions, and sparsely furnished. The mirror would hold the transparency of glass, both the glass house in which Breton dreamed, and that which Le Corbusier, or better, Mies van der Rohe, built. Its frame would be chrome, perhaps designed in a circular form by Eileen Gray, with a little enlarging glass extended from its center so that the "relief du stature" of the reflection would be distorted and reversed twice over, as if depicted by Braque, or maybe worse, Picasso. The search for transparency, unity, and what Le Corbusier called happily "l'espace indicible," or "ineffable space" (something akin, one imagines, to the space of de-realization experienced by Freud and Le Corbusier himself on the Acropolis) common to many architectural dreams of modernism, would here be related to the attempt of the alienated "I" to pass through, like Alice, the mirror itself, rather than assuming its armored reflectivity. The socialized subject that developed from this baby might itself be divided. On the one hand, it would have the desires of a surrealist, of a Matta, with his dreams of a soft, womb-like house, or a Tzara, with nostalgic homesickness for the uncanny space of the womb-like cave. On the other hand, it would embody the modernist drive towards spatial power – those epitomized by Ayn Rand, who we might imagine crossed-dressed as Cary Grant in the role of Howard Roark, supremely confident of overcoming the insufferable alienation of tactile-phobic, anti-city, anti-crowd, anti-woman, by a gesture towards the "Aüber-architektur" of the skyscraper. The result would be a subject in which the "I" captates itself within the isolated and fortified "castle" of a glass tower at the center of a landscape that, in Lacan's vivid description, bears an unnerving relationship to the modernist "radiant city" in all its varied incarnations:

> The formation of the "I" is symbolized in dreams by a fortress [un camp retranché], or a stadium, its inner area and enclosure, surrounded by marshes and rubbish-tips [son pourtour de gravats et de marécages], dividing it into two opposed fields of contest where the subject flounders in quest of the lofty, remote inner castle whose form (sometimes juxtaposed in the same scenario) symbolizes the id in a quite startling way.[4]

The inhabitant of this city, as Lacan also notes, might also find its subjectivity, its "I", in an existentialist alibi for the self, a kind of self-imprisonment in which psychoanalysis would find the origin of a socialization in a "concentrationnaire" form.[5] Here, there would be no differentiation between inside and outside; as the novelist Leslie Dick has it, echoing Richard Neutra, "nature is near."[6]

The critique of the high modernist vision, together with that of its corollary, the supposed oppositional model of heimat based on an illusory freedom of the self, has never, I think, been so well framed as in Lacan's essay, and this, it should be emphasized, between 1936 and 1949, long before the evidence for the worst results of either posture in front of the mirror was finally in.

My third mirror stage is more tentative in its construction, and perhaps this is a natural result of our contemporary immersion in its processes and effects. It is a stage at once of refusal, a refusal of reflection, of transparency, of extension, and of resignation; resignation that the grand narratives of introjection and projection that characterized historicist and modernist space/time models no longer hold. It is a space of absolute self-consciousness of pre-history and post-history, as if the baby, now held firmly by a dedicated care-giver of any age and gender, knows all the tricks; is aware somehow, as the psychoanalyst Sami-Ali has proposed, that in looking at itself, and denied its desire to capture the face of the Mother, is committed to a split identity, not only as between imago and I, but as between two imagos, so to speak, blurred and morphed into a distorted physiognomy that is far from transparent or clear, but rather opaque and translucent. It would be as if this subject was truly "lost in space", wandering vaguely in a state of continuous psychasthenia, disguising itself as space in space, ready to be devoured by the very object of its fear. It would be, finally, that we were dealing with a subject whose imago was screened and projected back to it, not as reflection, but as scanned image. In an initial, historical, moment of digitilization, one would imagine this image to be in black a white, a surveillance camera image; now we are more likely to be asked to assume a hyper-real, 3D image, or even a holographic laser gram. I imagine that the socialized version of this subject is caught somewhere between the Lobby of Fredric Jameson's Hotel Bonaventure and William Gibson's greyed-out, neuromantic, computer screen; in a matrix that is, where introjection and projection are merged in a timeless state of warped and intersecting planes: what Gibson calls "a 3D chessboard extending to infinity".[7] Leading to the discomforting conclusion that this, the subject of our third stage, would be something between a postmodern theorist and a hacker, which in architectural terms would situate it somewhere in the space between, say, Peter Eisenman and Frank Gehry.

Perhaps the critical difference between this "third" subject and the earlier two lies in this sense of being caught in a matrix, a web, a space of no time and no place, with a corresponding intimation of historical impasse, of the blockage of modernist progress. For it is clear that the space of which I speak – translucent, screened, scanned – has no history properly speaking, it implies no way forward and no way back, and is thus suspended out of time, or rather at the place where pre-history and post-history meet. This would not be easily construed as postmodern, at least in the way that either Jameson or more literal revivalists of historical motifs have used the term. Indeed it bears closer comparison with an earlier notion, that of "posthistoire" or posthistory advanced in the 1940s and 1950s, a concept whose history has recently been studied by Lutz Niethammer has demonstrated in his recent study, *Posthistoire: Has History Come to an End*?[8] Posthistory was espoused by those who, like the German anthropologist Arnold Gehlen, sought to characterize post-World War II disillusion in the failure of the great nineteenth-century narratives of historical progress – the moment as Gehlen says, "when progress becomes routine." Following Gehlen, and returning the concept of posthistoire to the thought of a nineteenth-century mathematician and historian Cournot, the Belgian social thinker and former labor activist Hendrick de Man, in his posthumously published, and portentously entitled "The Age of Doom", wrote in 1950:

> The term posthistorical seems adequate to describe what happens when an institution or a cultural achievement ceases to be historically active and productive of new qualities, and becomes purely receptive or eclectically imitative. Thus understood Cournot's notion of the posthistorical would [...] fit the cultural phase that, following a "fulfillment of sense," has become "devoid of sense." The alternative then is, in biological terms, either death or mutation.

A contemporary philosopher, Gianni Vattimo, has extended "posthistoire" to coincide with what he sees as an all-embracing technological "Apostmodernism" of the present. Taking his cue from Gehlen, Vattimo characterizes what he calls "the experience of the end of history" as exemplified in the routinization of production, and in the developments of technology and consumerism that, while continuously renewed, nevertheless stay the same:

> There is a profound "immobility" in the technological world which science fiction writers have often portrayed as the reduction of every experience of reality to an experience of images (no one ever really meets anyone else; instead, everyone watches everything on a television screen while alone at home). This same phenomenon can already be sensed in the air-conditioned, muffled silence in which computers work. (EOM 7)

Flattened out, simultaneous, the world appears de-historicized. What made us "modern" – that is, the experience of living every day in a narrative history of progress and development reinforced by the daily newspaper – now comes to a halt. The "master" narrative, once a secularization of religious salvation, now fails, and multiple other possible narratives rise up. In this argument, Vattimo extends Gehlen in order to "prove" post-modernism: "What legitimates post-modernist theories and makes them worthy of discussion is the fact that their claim of a radical 'break' with modernity does not seem unfounded as long as these observations on the post-historical character of contemporary existence are valid." (EOM 11)

But the space of our third mirror-stage does not seem to be entirely "posthistorical" either; its future-orientation, or rather its vision of the future-in-the-present implied by the galactic sensibility, and its search for the past-in-the-present characteristic of its need to unearth prehistoric precedent, precisely delineates it as staged at the intersection of the pre- and the post-historical and belonging to neither. This intersection is, in visual and spatial terms, closely tied to that parallel and complementary intersection between the galactic and the prehistoric that, as I noted, has been a continuing preoccupation since the 1960s, and which perhaps received its most innovative and radical treatment in the work of the artist Robert Smithson between 1966 and 1973.

In the context of our enquiry into the "digital-effect," Smithson's works are interesting precisely because of his prescient recognition of a galactic, dinosaurian, space that potentially displayed the characteristics of our own. For Smithson, it was all to be found, literally on display, in microcosm, in the American Museum of Natural History to which he had paid many visits as a child and the adjacent Hayden Planetarium. In a piece co-authored with Mel Bochner, and suggestively entitled "The Domain of the Great Bear" (*Art Voices*, Fall 1966) Smithson imagined the Planetarium as a model of infinite space: "For some, infinity is the planetarium, a frozen whirlpool at the end of the world, a vast structure of concentric circles ..."[9] In the murals and panoramas for the Planetarium and the Museum, Smithson was fascinated by the recurrent images of "catastrophe and remote times," which seemed to him to portray a world where the normal boundaries between space and time had been dissolved into a "bad boy's dream of obliteration, where galaxies are smashed like toys." (F 32) But rather than producing a repetition of modernist fantasies of space/time merging, or time warp in the present, the cumulative effect was one of "dimensions beyond the walls of time", a coming-together of the two dimensions to produce the effect of stasis. As he wrote, a "sense of extreme past and future" was engendered by the fact that "there the 'cave-man' and the 'space-man' may be seen under one roof," (F 15) or, as he put it in a reminiscence of Charles Knight's panoramas, "Space Age and Stone Age attitudes overlap to form the Zero-Zone, wherein the spaceman meets the brontosaurus in a Jurassic swamp on Mars".[10] In this environment, Smithson found the realization of childhood interest in dinosaurs and reptiles, and his later fascination with the space fictions of writers like Peter Hutchinson (*Creation of the Humanoids*; *The Planet of the Vampires*; *The Thing*), and William Burroughs (*Nova Express*).

In these and many other similar formulations from Smithson's writings and projects in the late 1960s we find all the ingredients of a conception of space/time that recognizes the end of progressive modernist space and its dissolution, fading, Smithson would call it – into a kind of entropic stasis. History, the conventional vehicle of progress, has come to a full and empty stop; indeed it has returned on itself to join its origins, "pre-history" had finally joined "post-history."

The architectural effect of this entropic fatalism was sketched in Smithson's celebrated essay on "Entropy and the New Monuments" from 1966. Here the works of Robert Morris, Donald Judd, Sol Le Witt, and Dan Flavin were seen as so many forms of "inactive history", of "entropy" and of an "Ice Age" rather than a "Golden Age". As if suspended in some prehistoric landscape, "they stop time, decay and evolution" in a way that joins "past and future . . . [in] an objective present." Presciently enough, Smithson finds the architectural parallel to this work in what he calls an "architecture of entropy", that which lines the new Park Avenue and pervades the work of Philip Johnson, which is characteristic of the "bland and empty" objects of contemporary commercial life (F 13). This is the side of modernism that puts the idealist and dynamic abstraction of the 1920s to work on behalf of commerce, bringing the avant-garde explosion of movement and speed to a full stop. Here the "City of the Future" (an evident reference of Le Corbusier's "Ville Contemporaine" of the mid-1920s) is realized in the present, transforming, as Smithson notes, the promise of Malevich's "non-objective world" into a real – as opposed to an imaginary – desert.

> . . . for many of today's artists this "desert" is a "City of the Future" made of null structures and surfaces. This "City" performs no natural function, it simply exists between mind and matter, detached from both representing neither. It is in fact devoid of all classical ideals of space and process. It is brought into focus by a strict condition of perception . . . as a deprivation of action and reaction. (F 14)

For Smithson, the entropic universe tends increasingly towards the crystalline, but again not in the sense evoked by the Expressionist devotees of the crystal after Scheerbart. Smithson's crystals are static and all-enclosing, like the lattices described in Damon Knight's "Beyond the Barrier": "Part of the scene before them seemed to expand. Where one of the flotation machines had been, there was a dim lattice of crystals, growing more shadowy and insubstantial as it swelled; then darkness; then a dazzle of faint prismatic light, tiny complexes in a vast three-dimensional array, growing steadily bigger." (F 14)

In these kinds of science fiction environments, Smithson finds that the traditional evolutionary and progressive thrust of future worlds has been forced into reverse, so to speak, paralleled in art by works such as what he calls Sol Le Witt's monumental "obstructions," Robert Morris' imaging of "a backward-looking future" with lead cast erections and vaginas, or, more directly, Claus Oldenburg's prehistoric "ray-guns."

But it is precisely here, where artist's attempts to overcome history through an appeal to pre-and post-history intersect with philosophic proclamations, that we encounter an obvious problem. For, while Smithson and his colleagues were proposing posthistory as a radical break with tradition and as an avant-garde strategy for destabilizing contemporary art practice, Gehlen, de Man and even, to a limited extent, Vattimo are profoundly conservative thinkers: the former two sympathizers with fascism and fellow travellers with the Nazis. Such connections have, as we know, dogged Heidegger, and significantly enough Paul de Man, Hendrick's nephew, whose early reviews for journals sympathetic to Nazi doctrines bear the stamp of posthistoire fatalism and stasis. In such a context, it is all the more necessary to look at specific practices, artistic and philosophical, in order to construe both intention and effect.

Thus, for Gehlen and de Man, posthistoire represented a kind of end game toward which everything they looked at seemed to be tending; a relentless stasis, an endless return of the same, an impossibility of breaking out of the iron frame of bureaucracy and politics, and a corresponding search for charisma, the leader, the event that would break open the possibility of a different and more active future; thence their fascination with both mass worker-movements on the one hand, and Hitler's program on the other.

But Smithson's purpose was, with the limited means available to him as an artist, to break into and shatter the pervasive and all-dominating rule of the spectacle, to reflect or deflect vision (mirror play) to reassert the power of space in the epoch of the "fading of space". Hence his various photo and mapping projects, conducted with instamatic and graph paper; hence also his varied installations of mirror planes from the salt mines of Cornell to the Yucatan, reflecting and deflecting the sites in which they are installed, preventing framing, picturesque fixing, or even subjective, narcissistic identification. In this sense, his "mirror stages" set deep in the earth, scattered across its surface, reflecting its entropic, geological, and industrially wasted landscapes, threw the subject definitively out of the stadium once and for all, condemned to wander in the marsh lands and rubbish tips of the "outside" perhaps catching glimpses of its pre-orthopedic body in the shards of mirror thrown down like so much jetsam, but only if crawling close to the ground. For Smithson, one might say, the interest of the dinosaur/space man, of the geological galactic, was that it precisely opened up where history had closed; post-history was in this sense simply a blockage erected by history, that to be cleared, had to be joined to prehistory. Here Smithson's tactical and disruptive introduction of "extreme past and future" potentially destabilizes both historicism and its complement, posthistoricism.

These themes were brought together most effectively in the earth-work and movie of "Spiral Jetty" (1972) (F 143–53), where he draws the by-now obvious comparisons between the spiral of the sculpture and outer space galactic nebulae and magma, and, to the inner space of the "spiral ear." The ensuing movie self-consciously tried to map this space/time interpenetration, both in its techniques of fabrication (Smithson likened the movie editor to a paleontologist "sorting out glimpses of a world not yet together, a land that has yet to come to completion, a span of time unfinished, a spaceless limbo on some spiral reels" (F 150)) and its medium – itself seen as "archaic", with the movieola envisaged as "time machine" that transforms "trucks into dinosaurs." In a string of carefully-juxtaposed images, Smithson crafted a map of the prehistoric world seen "as coextensive with the world [he] lived in" (F 151) where the continents of the Jurassic period were merged with the continents of today. Perhaps the most graphic evidence of Smithson's consciousness of the end of history and the space of time, are the blank spaces between the images, absent and lurking with uncanny potential for the return of the past in the future or vice versa: "One must be careful of the hypothetical monsters that lurk between the map's latitudes. . . . In the emptiness one sees no Stegosaurus . . . not a trace of the Brontosaurus." The final end point of the long pan from left to right that comprises the movie is, inevitably, the desert of Utah and Spiral Jetty itself, drawing all time and space together into the vortex of its virtual funnel.

III

In order to bring these considerations back to architecture, where after all they began, and where, it is my implication, they have been transformed, first under the influence of conceptual art, and then under the more extreme impact of digitalization, I want to take a couple of examples of recent projects and buildings that have tried in their own way to exorcize the demons of space and time by reference to wider spatial and temporal spheres, deploying what we might now call the "galactic analogy" as justification, authorization, and even form-giver to the works in question. Most striking was the eruption of this analogy in the recent preliminary competition for an architect to develop the expanding site of the Museum of Modern Art in New York, and especially in two projects for that competition by Rem Koolhaas and Bernard Tschumi respectively; Rem Koolhaas, with his elegantly carved and gem-like model of the site, with MOMA at its center preserved like a fly in amber, and the set-backs cut like diamonds in Hugh Ferris style, and Bernard Tschumi, with notes reminiscent of the *Manhattan Transcripts*, here developed science-fiction style as if a Manhattan Project, complete with the MOMA site described as a giant magma.

Koolhaas, with his precise deployment of biological and geological metaphors, cast in precious materials, and evoking the cities of kryptonite and interstellar luminosity that have held sway in the popular imagination since the birth of Superman, has found a medium that transcends the now equally-popular revival of fifties style, and intersects with current technological and computer-generated images of contemporary fantasies of lost worlds. At the same time, his commitment to the translucent over the transparent endows his especially ironic kind of functionalism with a poetic materialism, one also evident in his contribution to the competition for the French National Library.

Tschumi, on the other hand, with equal elegance, but with a firm avoidance of the physical object, picked his way through the labyrinth of MOMA's site with Situationist aplomb, tracing the expansion of the Museum as if retracing the moments of an asteroid impact, dissolving the existing buildings in a magma of light and matter, and recombining their atoms in the process. It was perhaps no accident that during the last week of the first phase of the limited competition, at the very moment of the first "charette" (homely word for these stirring visions of galactic mutation!) the portentous Hale-Bopp comet was hovering over the clear skies of New York, provoking hysteria and suicide among the cultists of the World Wide Web, but evidently evoking an image of the MOMA site as a potential "crater of doom."

In each of these examples we can detect, not only a desire to go beyond the present limits of a historicism kept warm by postmodernism, but also a return to, if not the style (although Rem Koolhaas has his moments) certainly the substance of debates that emerged in the early 1960s. It would perhaps be easy enough to conclude that these intersecting concerns are simple extensions of the sci-fi and hi-tech interests of the twentieth century as a whole, or that these more recent examples represent a kind of millennial thinking, one that seeks reassurance in the apocalyptic where history and progress have failed. Obviously both of these explanations are in some way correct, certainly the chain of galactic associations in Post-War culture, high and low, has never really been broken; and the late twentieth century has a special place in this cultural mood.

But, as I have indicated, I want to go further, and point to what I think has been a shift in emphasis in this mood in the last decade, that marks our own galacticism, in architecture at least, as fundamentally different from that of Smithson in the 1960s. A shift that has not simply changed the way in which the galactic analogy looks and feels – its style, so to speak, but also the very way in which we conceive of space and structure. Here we touch a subject that has had little attention to date: what I would like to call the "digital effect" in architecture and the arts. By digital effect I do not mean simply the assessment of how computers have changed our lives, nor how they have introduced new ways of doing old things in architecture; nor do I mean simply the examination of the digital arts in order to claim for them the status of a new frontier, let alone a new avant-garde. Rather I mean the quite complicated effects of digitalisation in the arts and architecture with respect both to the aesthetics of digitally-produced objects as well as to their status as objects, in relation to our relatively new-found status as subjects, subjects with equally complicated relationships to our psyches, our bodies, and technology.

Which returns us, not only to architecture and galacticism, but also to dinosaurs, whence we began, and specifically to *Jurassic Park*, released in May 1993, and its belated, if not deflated, sequel, *The Lost World*, issued on Memorial Day, 1997. These dinos were not those of the 1960s. In *King Kong*, the dinosaurs were fierce and stupid, Brontosauri with teeth and man-eating instincts. Spielberg's, by contrast, are "smart" dinosaurs, keeping up with the zeitgeist that sponsors smart missiles, phones and cars; no longer lumbering around on their hind legs, they are balanced according to the laws of physics, fast, and quick learning. Equally, and still keeping up with the spirit of the age, they are blessed with a full compliment of family values, protecting and seeking their lost young (indeed the only trace of plot in *The Lost World*). But that is not the only difference.

The full technical story of the "cg" (computer generated) dinosaurs for these two movies has yet to be written, but suffice it to say that with major improvements for the second film, Industrial Light and Magic, with visual effects supervisor Dennis Mauren (from George Lucas' *Star Wars* trilogy) created both *Jurassic Park* and *The Lost World* dinosaurs. All the cg dinosaurs were developed in concept, then story board drawings, then drawn to scale and modeled in miniature before being computerized. The other dinos, including the T-Rex, were built as animatronic full-size, electronically-operated models, and then shot in action, often with so-called "practical" (i.e. live actors – the movie industry has, it seems abandoned any pretense of virtual reality versus reality). Following the construction of the scale models for the cg animals, the first step to animation was to build a computer model of the nine species featured, a process which was begun by scanning

maquettes provided by Stan Winston. IM animation was executed while model was still in its "wire-frame" form; then lighting was added, together with skin textures. Then each cg shot was match-moved and tracked to the plate, duplicating live-action camera moves; whence each shot was then blue-masked back into the film. The sequence was fast tracked, in that all the computer models had been built by the time principal photography had begun, allowing animations to be segued in immediately on receipt of the plates for specific scenes. In certain cases, as in the stampedes for example, a whole library of running and walking cycles were developed early in the filming process, to be plugged in as needed. Special software was further developed that could draw a path through a live-action scene for a specific cg character and allow for its insertion. One is also not surprised to find that computer animation intruded not only into the dinosaur realm, but also every other realm, a fact of most films shot now is that up to 40 per cent of celluloid shot live is "invisibly" detourned. Thus the T-Rex victims, the trailer, and even the celebrated Mercedes Benz RVs were cg.

I summarize this process as a way of introducing my final architectural example, Frank Gehry's Guggenheim Museum in Bilbao. Now, this structure is not "galactic" in the way in which I have been using the word, as far as I know, it does not rely on any dinosaurian or space metaphor for its form; rather, it is galactic in a new way, and one that is becoming entirely ubiquitous in architectural conception and production, in the sense that it is almost entirely, and necessarily, the product of software, much of it similar if not the same as that employed by Spielberg and his collaborators; to generate the complex and shifting forms of the museum, forms that could not have been even envisaged in plan, section, or static model. To this end, as is well known, Frank Gehry used a combination of software, drawn from aerospace, auto, and medical usage, to digitally map his sketch models in three dimensions, transform the digital model, and return them back to quick 3D mapping models, in preparation for the final stages of design. The production of the building was equally dependent on these programs, allowing the entirely non-standard sections of titanium, steel, and glass to be cut directly "from disk to product" so to speak. Here, of course, the very notion of modern standardization begins to break down. But, more importantly, from our point of view, so does any formal reliance on traditional perspectival space, or for that matter on the traditional subject. This subject is now embedded within the "gaze", not of a hypothetical viewer, but of a scanning system; it is as if by some means, it might be able to "see" through the 3D lens of the cat-scan machine as it maps the observing brain and measures its responses. From this, admittedly problematic point of view, whether or not we can enter the building and walk around inside it; or whether or not we can snatch traces of the old perspectivism in the new folded spaces; or whether or not we can trace its outer forms to early Expressionist precedent, Bilbao remains in the process of its conception profoundly indifferent to our presence. I mean this in the sense that while of course it is possible to construct perspectival and humanistically traditional space through the use of software – virtual reality engines are doing this all the time – the way in which this software is used, and the increasing reliance on its subtle internal and programmatically-defined determinants, gradually moves towards a state where the building begins to construct its own identity like some revived dinosaur, finding solace in its own self-absorption. In a similar fashion, successive introductions of the perspectival and axonometric systems, transformed their own objects of projection in parallel with complementary and new systems of production. With one decisive difference. If, as W.J.T. Mitchell notes, "the early dinosaur ... was primarily an architectural construction" utilizing the newest technology of iron and reinforced concrete construction (as in the case of Benjamin Waterhouse Hawkins' reconstructions for the Crystal Palace exhibition of 1854), now the tables have been turned.[11] It is now the advanced technology of dinosaur reconstruction that serves as a model and process for architecture.

Notes

1   This essay was first delivered as a talk to the Department of Architecture, Berkeley, in the Fall of 1997, and in revised form to the "Architecture and Identity" symposium organized by the students in the History of Architecture and Urban Studies program in the Spring of 1998.

2   W.J.T. Mitchell, *The Last Dinosaur Book* (Chicago: University of Chicago Press 1998), a study that usefully summarizes the place of dinosaurs in western cultural history from the late eighteenth century to the present.

3   Jacques Lacan, Le stade du miroir comme formateur de la fonction du Je telle qu'elle nous est révélée dans l'expérience psychanalytique. Communication faite au XVIe congrès international de psychanalyse, à Zürich, le 17 juillet 1949, *Écrits I* (Paris: Éditions du Seuil 1966) 89–97. Translated in *Écrits. A Selection*, translated Alan Sheridan (New York: W.W. Norton 1977) 1–7. As Sheridan notes, the first version of this essay Le stade du miroir, was delivered at the International Psychoanalytical Congress in Marienbad, August 1936. The revised version of 1949 was first published in the *Revue française de psychanalyse*, no. 4, October–December, 1949, 449–55.

4   Jacques Lacan, *Ecrits: A Selection*, trans. Alan Sheridan (New York: W.W. Norton, 1977) 5.

5   Lacan uses the neologism *concentrationnaire*, a word clearly connected to the life of the concentration-camp, as Sheridan notes, to speak of the anxiety of the individual confronting the concentrational form of the social bond. *Écrits: A Selection*, 6.

6   Leslie Dick, "Nature Near", *ANY* 18 (1997) 18–21.

7   William Gibson, *Neuromancer* (New York: The Berkeley Publishing Group 1984) 52.

8   Lutz Niethammer, *Posthistoire: Has History Come to an End*? translated by Patrick Camiller (London and New York: Verso 1992).

9   Robert Smithson and Mel Bochner, "The Domain of the Great Bear" (*Art Voices*, Fall 1966), in Jack Flam, *Robert Smithson. Selected Writings*, 26–7. Further citations from this text will be noted in the form (F . . .).

10   "Interstellar Flit", undated typescript (*c.* 1961–3) Smithson Papers, reel 3834, frame 645, quoted in Robert A Sobieszek, *Robert Smithson Photo Works*, exhibition catalog, Los Angeles County Museum of Art, University of New Mexico Press, 1993, 19.

11   W.T.J. Mitchell, *The Last Dinosaur Book*, 208.

Returning

Chapter 20

Spaced out
Alan Read

While this volume's structure and purpose is distinct from the shape of the *Spaced Out* series of talks that gave rise to it, it is worth returning for a moment to this original context in order to examine the implicit prejudices, problems and possibilities it carried forward which, in turn, have inevitably inflected on the texts included here.

There has, for some time, been a tacit assumption that the benefits of the interdisciplinary are to be witnessed in the drawing closer or together of previously discreet fields of theoretical speculation and practice. The more recent, somewhat uncritical adoption of terms such as "joined up thinking", to describe a vague but evocative world of connected activity, does little serious work on the specificity of practices and their relations through difference. The ambition of the *Spaced Out* talks, and this book, was to address these possible relations between fields without concealing the value of their discreet identities. The "inter", in interdisciplinary, has often come to stand for an impoverished version of the disciplinary in the interests of alliance. This cannot serve disciplines, such as my own of performance, where the arranged marriage is jeopardised by scant knowledge of the family from which the partner arrives. This blind date of disciplinarity has serious consequences for the claims being made on behalf of the relations between cultural forms and the understanding of their contexts.

The site for the *Spaced Out* series of discussions was the Institute of Contemporary Arts in London. All but two of the discussions which made up the four series of talks occurred there. The two exceptions were a session undertaken in and around the Camden Arts Centre London, to mark the opening of an exhibition by the painter and installation artist Antoni Malinowski, with architect Katherine Heron, whose practice Feary and Heron Architects were responsible for the gallery's imminent development, and a Thames river cruise to explore and discuss the proposed site for a new ICA to be built with Millennium lottery funds on disused Victorian bridge supports at Blackfriars.

Both excursions were significant as they most obviously marked the underlying agenda for the inception and conduct of the series. Lottery fever had struck Britain and its arts establishments soon after the early announcements were made that the Tate Gallery would be provided with close to £50m to refashion the disused power station at Bankside and the Royal Court Theatre was provided with £17m to transform its Sloane Square premises. The city-centric bias of these initial grants and the nature of other early awards: to Sadlers Wells, to the Royal Opera House, to the Serpentine Gallery, prompted those responsible within the ICA for its future to turn their mind towards potential visions of liberation from the Mall, an address at the heart of the establishment close to Buckingham Palace it had cherished since its architectural transformation by Jane Drew in 1968.

Into this milieu the *Spaced Out* talks were intended to shed some broader perspectives, to think the unthinkable about what might constitute built form in the first place, to shift the obsession with a monumental building and all its good works to the nexus of relations an organisation with a title like the ICA might have with its potential audiences and constituencies of practitioners.

Spaced Out was a perhaps esoteric but nevertheless lively chamber in which part of this debate about the future of the shape of arts organisations at the turn of the Millennium in Britain developed, a chamber which on almost all the occasions it took place was so full as to necessitate a returns queue for tickets snaking from the ICA foyer out onto the Mall.

This level of interest was testament to the high regard in which many of the speakers in the series were held. But also it was an indicator of the unusually forceful attraction architectural and urban debate had on audiences at this moment at the end of a century. For some years it had become apparent that the architectural speaker was, among cultural commentators, beginning to be treated in a somewhat messianic like way by audiences of a significant scale. Architectural debates in Barcelona, Rotterdam and New York, the *Any-body/thing/how* series of conferences caravanning the globe, the high profile guest lectures at the Architecture Centre at the Royal Institute of British Architects were early indicators that the zeitgeist was being fashioned with a keen eye to the shapes we were in.

The street had become the privileged site of social discourse and what could be better than to overlay that pedestrian nous with a charismatic approach to town planning or radical building construction? Journals such as *Blueprint* in Britain, *Archis* in Europe and the annual publications of the "Any" conferences in North America were much faster to this trend than academe could manage and more precisely judged the tenor of the debate as being deeply informed, and utterly sceptical, of the fashionable distrust in which theory was said to be held by a wider audience. The audience for *Spaced Out was* that wider audience and there seemed to me a great appetite for thinking seriously about cities with recourse to theoretical strategies where needed and to other, more anecdotal and practice-based perceptions when not.

Theory was important to this field but it seemed rarely to eclipse the social ties of what was being said. Where other discourses were finding themselves further and further removed from any immediate relevance, partly due to the abstruseness of the languages imported from psychoanalysis, the persistent claims of site-specificity within discussion of this kind tethered each talk on the right side of the abstract without sacrificing the imaginative.

The first series of *Spaced Out* was launched by William Mitchell whose book *Bit City* had just been published. It was characteristic of the series that it should begin with a discussion that effectively undermined the very notion of "built space" in its traditional architectural sense and reconvened the possibilities for the city at an electronic crossroads somewhere to the left of future. A version of this talk is included in this volume (pp. 297–304). From this point of radical destabilisation, what could be considered on and off site had to be reappraised, an invitation to rethink starting points that appeared welcome to all the contributors who followed.

Among those were Richard Sennett and Doreen Massey (the latter included in this volume on pp. 49–62) who along with Roy Porter, Professor of the History of Medicine at the Wellcome Institute, debated the relations between bodies and cities; Beatriz Colomina deconstructed the extraordinary history of an Eileen Gray house that had been occupied and defaced by Le Courbusier (included in this volume pp. 141–154), Charles Jencks reflected on the cosmology of millennial architecture; Dolores Hayden analysed the power of place and the politics of race inscribed therein and Bernard Tschumi teased out the nature of the event city and the movement potential of all architectural form (included in this volume pp. 155–176). The series was concluded with an international conference to discuss lottery-related projects for the arts and brought together representatives of art galleries such as Sandy Nairne of the Tate Gallery London, performance companies, writers and artists such as Tim Etchells of Forced Entertainment Theatre Cooperative, Sheffield, architects such as Will Alsopp of Alsopp and Stormer, who at the time were working on the feasibility study for a new ICA at Blackfriars Bridge, as well as theoreticians, politicians and arts producers.

This first sequence of events shaped much of what followed, setting in motion the significance of accessibility for a previously hermitic and specialist field and foregrounding the role of dialogue both between participant speakers but, importantly, between speakers and audience. That this volume does not carry those later dialogues forward in print is something of a loss as it was here that the interface of idea, ideology and identity opened up, sometimes, most effectively. On other occasions these, it must also be admitted, were also the parts of each event where it seemed the concentrated concerns of the speaker became diffused towards the multiple agendas present in the room and, while representative of pressing concerns, these were not sufficiently persuasive to warrant inclusion. Suffice to say that these passages within each event were always equally weighted with presentations from speakers and that all can be heard on the original transcript recordings which are held in the ICA archive at the Tate Gallery, London.

The question of dialogue is something that inflects on many passages within this collection, but here I just want to reflect on the qualities of dialogue that were important to these occasions. Here dialogue, as the critic Richard Kearney, a regular speaker at the ICA once noted, implied both a sense of subjects in conversation with each other about shared concerns and also importantly in dialogue with a historical community of speakers whose work had been discussed within this chamber of speaking (many of the audience for these talks were also present to a wide variety of other discourses we were organising simultaneously which ranged across disciplines from fashion to philosophy). Here meanings could never be said simply to arise from what was said in the moment, but beyond the intuitive immediacies of the subjectivities present and the intersubjectivity of these participants there was a context of thought and practice that informed and galvanised each of the proceedings. Returning speech to text invites this wider context back in to the apparently topical and site-specific, resituating the dialogue in another sphere of texts and contexts. In this sense, it is made to make more sense.

Spaced Out II explored the margins of the city, the threshold sites that anthropologists might once have described as "liminal" spaces. Much talk had already been given to these states of bordering, particularly by already marginal enterprises such as the ICA and academic institutions, on the understanding, most vociferously articulated by cultural studies of the 1970s, that there may be something inherently political in shifting perspectives of enquiry from the centre to the periphery.

Finding ways out from the supervised impasse of Michel Foucault's panopticon, or Louis Althusser's risk of identification in interpellation, theoretical enquiry had shifted attention to writers such as Michel de Certeau who, in *The Practice of Everyday Life*, had lionised the pedestrian poetic, the tactics of those who escaped surveillance at the foot of the observation tower.

In one of the key theoretical expositions of the series, Edward Soja, the author of the groundbreaking study *Postmodern Geographies*, had indeed appealed for a return to aerial perspectives to begin to flesh out the minutae of local views with more panoramic scenes of understanding, to begin, in his words, to distinguish once again the wood from the trees. His ideas about a "thirdspace" had been developed from very precise "above" and "below" observations of border territories in Los Angeles and Amsterdam, and had provoked a reassessment of the assumptions that had begun to be drawn from the rigorous spatial critique of Henri Lefebvre, the "hybrid" politics of identity of Homi Bhabha (in *The Location of Culture*) and the race/feminist nexus of bell hooks (see pp. 13–30 in this volume).

Again, this second series of talks was opened by a conceptually destabilising influence. Marc Augé had recently framed his interests as an anthropologist under the alluring title *Non Places* which was no less than an introduction to the features of what he called super-modernity. The waiting room and the supermarket, the car, train and plane, the spaces of cable, wire and media communications are all non-places. They involve no sense of identity and have no ability to establish relations with others. These are the sites that Augé critiques in his work, believing that the more time we spend in transit from one place to the next the more a new form of solitude provokes questions of new identities. (see pp. 7–12)

Within this series were new takes on established and apparently well-known cities. Charles Rutheiser took a penetrating and perceptive look at Atlanta just prior to the 1996 Olympic Games, memorably evoking the Centennial Park as a cacophony of competing images which was liable to "blow" at any moment. Three months later it did. Two habitués of Manhattan and its under-narratives and street classes, Professor Christine Boyer of Princeton University, author of *City of Collective Memory*, and William Menking of the Pratt Institute, New York, constructed a dialogue that teased out radical re-readings of the crossroads between Times Square, Central Station and 14th Street.

Architects such as Future Systems (who were later to create one of the few dedicated architectural exhibitions in the ICA's history) Zaha Hadid (whose audience for a discussion of the plans for the Cardiff Opera House that had been rejected by the Lottery funders was an indication of the critical esteem held for the project by the architectural and arts professions, see p. 213) and Lebbeus Woods (whose revolutionary rewriting of architectural practice for war-torn cultures can be found on pp. 199–210) spoke in depth about their visionary work, while James Hubbell came from San Diego to discuss his Mexican kindergarten project *Jardin de Ninos la Esperanza*. Here pre-school children, often subject to sentimentalised ideas of appropriate form and taste, were rediscovered, responded to and placed centrally within the planning of a school between Tijuana and the Mexican/US border. While it was not possible to recover this transcript for inclusion here, in the spirit of play and the evocation of the child, Franco la Cecla, the Paris-based anthropologist, has contributed a translation of his work on "getting lost" in the urban landscape (see pp. 31–48).

New kinds of theory-making were espoused by Kenneth Frampton, whose ideas of tectonics and construction can be found on pp. 177–198 while Mark Wigley, whose reflections on architecture and deconstruction were already very well known pulled back his focus to take account of the ubiquitous white wall as a boundary within architecture and design.

One of the most telling events in this series, and one which due to the complexity of its interlaced dialogues and inflections was impossible to pay proper tribute to in this collection, was a discussion chaired by Andrea Phillips exploring the role of the artist as walker. Here pedestrian poetics and the mutability of site was taken apart and put back together by artists, writers and event makers who literally rewrote the conception of artistic practice and its ground, here the expanded field took on an infinite horizon. One of the participants on this occasion, the musician and performance maker Graeme Miller, has contributed a newly-written piece for this collection on pp. 109–118.

The third series was co-curated with architectural/design consultant Lucy Bullivant and concentrated on the "inter" in interdisciplinary relations between architecture and the arts and, importantly, technologies of representation. Again the series was shaped to question a common presumption: that the arts and architecture had a history of alliance and mutual co-operation that somehow reflected well, if unquestioningly, on both parties. From evidence, and against all the creditable efforts of brokering agencies such as the Royal Society of Arts "Art for Architecture" schemes, this old alliance seemed fragile at best and wholly opportunistic at worst. The aspirations of Colin St John Wilson at the new British Library at St Pancras, where a modest proportion of the planned artistic contributions found their way into the foyer, was just the most obvious example of a singular loss of faith between built form and artistic invention. Perhaps this tension was symptomatic of a necessary schizophrenia that had, by the eighteenth century, separated the maker of buildings from the builder of aesthetic expressions. The irony of this split cannot be overestimated when one architect after another in the *Spaced Out* series was left presenting paper projections of visions yet to be realised. For some of these architects, most obviously Zaha Hadid (in her plans included here for the Cincinatti Art Gallery, see pp. 211–232) but also Lebbeus Woods and François Roche, the split between artist and architect seemed a wholly facile one. To adorn their work was to accept the need for a dualistic professionalism which seemed completely at odds with the integrative creativity of their work and an insult to their virtuoso use of materials.

Following the impetus of the first two series, *Spaced Out III* opened with a radical deconstruction of the limits to architectural thought. Ann Pendleton-Jullian spoke about the Open City in Ritoque, Chile, a poetically-inspired laboratory on the Pacific Coast where architects, poets, artists and engineers have for 30 years been involved in one of architectural education's most radical experiments. The city (discussed on pp. 253–286) has evolved without masterplan or hierarchical infrastructure and in its magnificent mutability throws a harsh light on claims made elsewhere for the engagement of architecture and the arts. Here was a project where the two seemed wholly present and yet indistinguishable.

Picking up strands of thought about architecture and its relations with more conventional spaces of artistic exhibition, four sessions focused on the developing identity of building for showing. The new Walsall Museum and Art Gallery, in Great Britain, a major recipient of Lottery funds, was discussed by the architects for the project Caruso and St John who entered into a dialogue with an artist whose work was integral to the development of the project, Richard Wentworth. Wentworth's subsequent dialogue with the Director of the Gallery and its transformation into a photo-text installation entitled "Dear Peter" is included here (see pp. 245–252). London-based *muf* architects spoke about their work in Southwark streets to the rear side of Bankside Power station and therefore in the shadow of the new Tate Modern. This intervention has been developed here with a more up to date review of recent projects ranging from the back of Bankside through to their work for the Millennium Dome project in Greenwich. Oliver Kruse, a sculptor and member of the board of the Museum Insel at Hombroich, spoke with the architect Claudio Silvestrin about the visionary philosophy of the Hombroich initiative, the housing of historic and modern art from different cultures and periods displayed without classification of style or era (see pp. 232–244). The painter Antoni Malinowski spoke about his perception of space in the midst of the installation of his work at the Camden Arts Centre and was joined in discussion by the architect for the development of the Centre, Katherine Heron, and the architect and theoretician Jean-Michel Crettaz. Paul Robbrecht and Hilde Daem completed this sequence of discussions. They are concerned with the emotional impact of architectural definition. As well as linking discussions concerning exhibition space (they had recently worked on installations for major exhibitions at the Whitechapel Art Gallery in London) they extended debate into the museological field with reflections on their recent extension for the Boijmans van Beuningen Museum in Rotterdam.

Rotterdam became an iconic city for this series with the architectural practice Van Berkel and Bos discussing their work on the magisterial Erasmus Bridge for that city. Working with flexible evolutionary design and exploring changing organisational structures, relations and practices, their work raised issues of tactility which were also in the forefront of one of the most innovative contributors to the series François Roche. Based in Paris and on the island of La Reunion in the West Indies, the practice of François Roche and Stephanie Lavaux, Roche DSV, are concerned with the bonds between building, context and human relations. Roche discusses his concept of "chameleon architecture" here, linking the human body to the body of architecture by drawing on the rules of nature, an unstable concept where architectural identity is defined through temporary forms in which the vegetal and biological become dynamic elements (see pp. 287–296).

The centrepiece of *Spaced Out III* was an international conference curated by Lucy Bullivant titled *Smart Practices in a Complex World*. From these sessions which addressed the relations between technological innovation and built form the work of Krzysztof Wodiczko, acclaimed Polish artist and Head of Research with the Interrogative Design Group, Massachusetts Institute of Technology, is represented here (see pp. 87–108).

Despite the appeal to the technological in the title, the engaging focus of much of the debate was on what constitutes new possibilities for human inter-action, new ways of speaking and telling. Marco Susani's work with students and faculty at the Domus Academy in Milan detailed a penetrating and concerted approach to the interactive space of electronic and digital media with an unusually perceptive critique of its social purpose and possibility in the realm of communica-tion: between children working on flexible digital desktops on international collabo-rative projects through to mobile phone users in search of a shelter to speak. In Wodiczko's "Open Transmission", the simplest issues of sharing narratives of auto-biographical destiny are transmuted through low-tech props galvanised by high-tech implants. In this way, the crucial question was not the machinery itself but the possibilities for sharing witness to injustice, the opportunity to speak out. Indeed much of Wodiczko's wider artistic work, from the homeless vehicle projects to the projected images across and onto public spaces have provided an arena for fur-thering what it might mean to be "given a hearing" through city sites.

The fourth series of talks *Spaced Out IV* picked up this provocation to speak, occurred in a single day, and was conducted under the title "Speech Sites". By way of an act of self reflection, *Spaced Out* here moved into questioning the space and shaping of its own conduct, the way in which architecture and its articu-lation in speech was itself shaped by unwritten conventions and formalities. The purpose of the day's various forums was to analyse the way site and speech inter-related, how the meanings of speech were in part configured by the architectural contexts in which they occurred.

The initial impulse for the occasion was an interest I had been developing for a study on the contingency of conventions of address and how these historically had been governed by the auditoria in which they occurred. It struck me that this history, in my own field of performance, was but one genealogy of rhetorical expression and was likely to be inter-relatable to a complex cultural web of equival-ent structural and design developments in adjacent fields: the analyst's couch, the confessional, the summit round table, the political platform and soap-box. Further-more one might trace in a city such as London a landscape of speech-sites, buildings whose architectural and biographical histories might reveal particular genealogies of speech that had given rise to social change yet whose significance for the present had become overlaid by the accretions of historical indifference (see pp. 119–140).

Because of its more specialist nature, this work on speech has already found, and will find, outlets elsewhere, but here it should be noted that work by Allen Weiss on Artaudian speech, Derek Sugden on the historical development of the acoustician's art, Steven Connor on the ubiquity of speech and its history, David Wittenberg on museology and civic experience, Barbara Engh's work on the development of the phonograph and the relationship this had to the emergence of "His Master's Voice", and performance work by Aaron Williamson a profoundly deaf artist working at the threshold of sonic experimentation, were memorable and moving events towards an understanding of what "saying" in space might entail.

While listening to these concerns being presented it occurred to me, at the end of a four-year period of directing talks at the ICA, a period in which more than 500 speech-based events occurred, that the question of address raised earlier had taken on a renewed meaning. In order to make the proceedings as accessible as possible, to as wide an audience as possible, a stenographer was engaged throughout the day in instantaneous typing and projection of the proceedings onto the wall behind each of the speakers. Ironically in an event dedicated to the power of the human voice the spectral re-established itself with audiences gazing above and beyond the speaker to the surreally inaccurate script unfolding on the wall. Here, as script and architecture dissolved into each other, there was a telling reminder to leave these live proceedings and to return to the written forms which most coherently and concertedly reflect their authors' ambitions.

Index